r Talking Taboo

"A diverse range of voices rise together in a song of solidarity and sisterhood in *Talking Taboo*. Bold and beautifully written, these essays will make you giggle, weep, roll your eyes, cheer, balk, gasp, and whisper prayers of thanks. Each story gives the reader permission--permission to speak, permission to ask questions, permission to follow Jesus and serve the church without cramming into a mold. This book is a gift. I hope many will cherish it."

–Rachel Held Evans, author of *A Year of Biblical Womanhood*

"How did Christianity—a faith founded on the reality of "the Word become flesh"—get tied in knots and torn asunder over gender, sexuality, sexual orientation, and other features of the God-given fact we live embodied lives? Scholars argue over that question, but this much is clear: women have been the main victims of this heresy, to the immense loss of both church and world. In the clear and honest words of the women who "talk taboo" in this book, we hear voices of truth that can help Christians reclaim respect for flesh and come to feel more at home in their own skins. *Talking Taboo* is an important book, one that should be read and discussed in every church in the land."

–Parker J. Palmer, author of *Healing the Heart of Democracy*, *A Hidden Wholeness*, and *Let Your Life Speak*

"We in North America today are not in the business of trying to re-define gender equality as a legal or civil matter so much as we are attempting to re-define it as a psychological and religious matter. More than any other collection of essays that I have seen to date, *Talking Taboo* provides us lucid, articulate…and at times even poignant…first-hand accounts of what it means to live within that struggle and as a player in its eventual resolution. Like a multi-faceted and multi-paned window, *Talking Taboo* looks out upon a shifting terrain and grants all of us, at least briefly, the impunity to consider it well."

at Emergence

"When I look over my books and see how few women theologians/ leaders are named in the footnotes compared to the men, I'm sad and determined to do what I can to turn the tide toward balance. That's one reason I'm thrilled to read *Talking Taboo*. It introduces me—and I hope you too—to many new leaders who deserve our attention and respect. I'm grateful to Enuma Okoro, Erin Lane, and all the contributors. By presenting women leaders/theologians/writers/thinkers who are as smart as they are brave, *Talking Taboo* will help us redress an imbalance that has been in place for far too long (as my footnotes evidence) ... which is just one of many taboos that it's time to talk about."

–Brian McLaren, author of *A New Kind of Christianity*

"This array of more than forty stories of Christian women in America is about sexism in church and society, sexism that takes a great variety of forms and has shaped and distorted women's lives in endless ways. Yet these women are all emerging from these distortions and discovering a God who loves them and a good self that loves oneself. The insightful stories in *Talking Taboo* bring us in many ways to that hopeful place."

–Rosemary Radford Ruether, author of *Sexism and God Talk*

"The word taboo in our time connotes dirt and sin. But in its original meaning, taboo also means sacred. That's exactly what this wonderfully diverse collection points to: a sacred God, who knows and loves women regardless of whether they fit the longstanding molds of 'Christian womanhood.' For any woman who seeks to follow Jesus, yet who finds herself beyond the confines of that mold, these stories are a breath of fresh air."

–Katelyn Beaty, managing editor, *Christianity Today* magazine

"*Talking Taboo* weaves spiritual hunger into the power of the female body. Here is a kinship of those questioning the old scripts. Prepare to discover enough courageous questions to help you unhook (unlace, or even rip) the corsets holding you back."

–Jonalyn Fincher, vice-president of Soulation, author of *Ruby Slippers: How the Soul of a Woman Brings Her Home*

"*Talking Taboo* is a groundbreaking book. This chorus of bold female voices is presenting the church with an opportunity to engage real but all too frequently avoided or unseen issues impacting countless Christian women today. Their candid essays cover a wide spectrum of perspectives. Readers will resonate with some and be shocked by others. *Talking Taboo* took courage to write. Reading taboo takes courage too. So buckle up and brace yourself for an eye-opening but vitally important read!"

–Carolyn Custis James, author of *Half the Church: Recapturing God's Global Vision for Women*, www.whitbyforum.com

"The women in *Talking Taboo* break rules that never should have existed in the first place and claim places in traditions that belonged to them all along. Silence—a refusal to talk about bodies and sex and oppression and violence—has driven too many people out of churches. The raised voices in *Talking Taboo* break this silence, speaking up and speaking out for a more just world. This book will remind all faithful boundary breakers that they are not alone."

–Sarah Sentilles, author of *Breaking Up with God* and *A Church of Her Own*

"In *Talking Taboo*, a cohort of bright and passionate women share deeply personal stories about life, God, and religion. I can't help but wonder how their insights would have inspired and altered the course of many women I've worked with in churches over the past 45 years. I will be encouraging many young women and a few older men (like me) to read these stories."

–Jim Henderson, co-author of *The Resignation of Eve*

"For far too long the voices of women have been marginalized in the church and larger society. As a result we've been missing out on the wisdom of the sacred feminine as a guide to helping us live into the wholeness of the kingdom of God. *Talking Taboo* is a confident and constructive conversation led by courageous women about the messy details of navigating life with God in the 21st century. This book is important, refreshing, sassy, and sincere and I look forward to sharing its honest and hopeful message with my own daughter."

–Mark Scandrette, author of *Free, Soul Graffiti*, and *Practicing the Way of Jesus*

"Spiritual wisdom comes in many forms. This diverse collection of fresh voices includes smart reflections on masturbation (Kate Ott), tattoos (Robyn Henderson-Espinoza), contraception (Katey Zeh), community (Alena Amato Ruggerio), and ordination (Gina Messina-Dysert) to mention just a few of my favorites. Christianity, indeed religion at large, will never be the same. Blessed be!"

–Mary E. Hunt, co-founder and co-director of Women's Alliance for Theology, Ethics, and Ritual (WATER) and co-editor of *New Feminist Christianity: Many Voices, Many Views*

"These pages record the voices of women who speak for themselves. Their words don't need my endorsement. But they deserve my thanks, for the good news they proclaim isn't just for women who've been silenced but also for men like me who have too often gotten the story twisted because we've only heard one side."

–Jonathan Wilson-Hartgrove, author of *Strangers at My Door*

"This anthology breaks through the cacophony of 24/7 news pundits and self-help gurus all using "faith" for their own rhetorical purposes and rings so, utterly true. Real women. Real stories. Real relationships with God and faith and all the complexity therein. What a gift."

–Courtney E. Martin, author of *Do it Anyway: The New Generation of Activists*

Talking Taboo

A Note about the *I Speak for Myself* series:

I Speak for Myself ® is an inclusive platform through which people can make themselves heard and where everyone's voice has a place. ISFM®'s mission focuses on delivering one core product, a "narrative collection," that is mindset-altering, inspiring, relatable, and teachable. We aim to deliver interfaith, intercultural titles that are narrow in scope but rich in diversity.

Please be sure to check out our website, www.ISpeakfor-Myself.com, to learn more about the series, join the conversation, and even create an *I Speak for Myself* ® book of your own!

Sincerely,

Zahra T. Suratwala and Maria M. Ebrahimji

Co-Founders, *I Speak for Myself* ®

Books in the Series

Volume 1: *I Speak for Myself*: *American Women on Being Muslim*

Volume 2: *American Men on Being Muslim: 45 American Men on Being Muslim*

Volume 3: *Demanding Dignity: Young Voices from the Front Lines of the Arab Revolutions*

Volume 4: *Talking Taboo: American Christian Women Get Frank About Faith*

Talking Taboo

American Christian Women Get Frank About Faith

edited by Erin S. Lane and Enuma C. Okoro
Foreword by Andrew Marin

WHITE CLOUD PRESS
ASHLAND, OREGON

The views and opinions expressed by each contributing writer in this book are theirs alone and do not necessarily represent those of the series' editors or I Speak for Myself, Inc.

White Cloud Press books may be purchased for educational, business, or sales promotional use. For information, please write:

Special Market Department
White Cloud Press
PO Box 3400
Ashland, OR 97520
Website: www.whitecloudpress.com

Cover and Interior Design by C Book Services

Printed in the United States of America

13 14 15 16 17 18   10 9 8 7 6 5 4 3 2 1

Library of Congress Cataloging-in-Publication Data

Talking taboo : American Christian women get frank about faith / edited by Erin Lane, Enuma Okoro.
    pages cm. -- (I speak for myself)
ISBN 978-1-935952-86-2 (pbk.)
1. Christian women--Religious life--United States. I. Lane, Erin, 1984- II. Okoro, Enuma, 1973-
 BR517.T355 2013
 277.3'083082--dc23

2013030475

Dedication

To our great cloud of witnesses: You taught us to risk boldly and love humbly; to write with purpose and to speak with patience; to rise up each day and do it again. And again. Thank you, again.

Acknowledgements

We wish to thank the tireless champions of the I Speak for Myself platform, Zahra Suratwala and Maria Ebrahimji, who supported our vision, shared our load, and propped us up when our energy lagged. You are human sparklers. And to our publisher, Steven Scholl, who titled his first email to us "Let's Get this Party Started" and endured upwards of one thousand emails as the only man alongside four opinionated women. You are one of the good ones.

We also need to thank all of our contributors who recognized what an opportunity this was to speak up and who worked hard to present the best from their quills.

And of course, thanks be to our vibrant, untamed and ever self-revealing God.

Contents

Foreword | Andrew Marin xv

Introduction | Erin Lane xvii

Going in Disguise | Amy Frykholm 1

The Gatherer-God: On Motherhood and Prayer | Micha Boyett 7

Naughty by Nature, Hopeful by Grace | Enuma Okoro 13

Becoming One Flesh: Thoughts on Male Headship in Marriage
Amy Julia Becker 19

No One Teaches Us How to Be Daughters | aja monet 24

Married without Children | Erin Lane 29

Living (Together) without a Blueprint | Bristol Huffman 35

**High Stakes Whack-a-Mole: Noticing and Naming
Sexism in the Church** | Lara Blackwood Pickrel 41

On Being a Strong Woman | Julie Clawson 48

Crafting Bonds of Blood | Patience Perry 55

Leaving a Marriage, Finding Jesus | Sarah McGiverin 63

The God of Shit Times | Rachel Marie Stone 70

Broken in the Body, Slain in the Spirit | Tara Woodard-Lehman 74

Naming God for Ourselves amidst Pain and Patriarchy
Rahiel Tesfamariam 80

The Silence Behind the Din: Domestic Violence and Homosexuality
Rev. Sarah C. Jobe 85

No Women Need Apply | Gina Messina-Dysert 93

A Woman of Many Questions | K. D. Byers 98

Hinges and Doors | Andrea Palpant Dilley 104

Gender Confusion: Navigating Evangelical Discussions of Gender Roles | Sharon Hodde Miller 112

Being a Voice for the Stranger | Jenny Hwang Yang 117

The Pastor Has Breasts | Rebecca Clark 123

Joiner | Alena Amato Ruggerio 128

Free to Believe: Breaking with Biblical Authority
Jennifer D. Crumpton 134

God in the Bedroom: Does Jesus Care How You Make Love?
Anna Broadway 141

Created for Pleasure | Kate Ott 146

A Thing of Beauty | Katie Anderson 152

Tattooing My Faith | Robyn Henderson-Espinoza 158

Recovery from the Porch | Pilar Timpane 163

Sex, Shame, and Scarred Knees | elizabeth mcmanus 170

Flesh and Blood | Ashley-Anne Masters 176

Finding My Voice | Sarah Thebarge 182

A Pregnant Silence | Katey Zeh 186

A Woman Undone | Grace Biskie 191

What do Cinderella, Lilies, and the Cross Have in Common?
Carol Howard Merritt 197

Running into Glass Doors | Atinuke O. Diver 203

Swing and the Single Girl | Meghan Florian 208

The Beauty in Brokenness | Nikole Lim 213

Celebration of Strength | Christy Sim 220

My Secret Buddhist Life | Mary Allison Cates 226

A Pastor in Hiding | Marlena Graves 232

Foreword

One of my good friends lives in New York City. By day she works at our country's first lesbian, gay, bisexual, and transgender homeless youth center. By night she competes around the city as a highly respected and recognized slam poet.

I'll never forget the first time I watched her compete. Over the years my friend had performed her new material to me, an audience of one, over Skype. Her poems were so raw. So heavy. So real. Yet at the same time they were a powerful assessment of how her story fits in the world's larger narrative (or if you're a New Yorker, you feel New York is the world's largest narrative.) I could see why she was gaining so much respect in a city, and a subculture, that doesn't dish out praise very often.

What I didn't realize that evening I walked into an upstairs bar in the West Village is that my friend's passion for the art of crafting her inner journey into stanzas timed out to three minutes is not unique to her; there was a roomful of others who shared her passion. I stood, packed tightly with a hundred other strangers in the audience, each preparing him or herself to enter into this intensely honest space, a space that deeply fed their souls. This is what I had always been taught the Church was supposed to be like.

For most of America's history, women have been forced to hold it together with a simple, seamless grace. The proper fulfillment of this role must be achieved with an ethereal beauty; a woman must be everything to everyone. And all too often the source of these unrealistic expectations has been the Church.

Church. The same institution that represents Jesus, who intentionally recognized the reality of women's sacrifice, role, and leadership in his countercultural movement. Church. The same institution that, at times, demands women's unique voices remain silent, always overlaid with a smile.

Too many women have had to grind their teeth and clamp their lips, even as many of the most important cultural responsibilities of American life fall on them. Their voice has been muted because too many men at the top of the religious power structure aren't ready to release their privilege.

I think about the women in my own life: comforting and cutting, righteous and insecure, soft and strong, powerful and gentle; filled with areas of deep pain, yet fully alive. Women are *the* survivors of dual expectations.

Erin and Enuma have done a masterful job bringing together the diverse realities of these stories from young Christian women in America as each directly, and accessibly, addresses the taboos facing her gender in contemporary culture. With every page turn, this collection gives you permission to enter into some very raw parts of their lives, parts which can't remain hidden. As you read this book, I pray that you, like I, will bear witness to these new voices.

As a young American man committed to shifting church culture toward a more open, peaceful, and productive engagement between opposing worldviews, I believe not only in the importance of this book, but also in the contributors who carry its message. All too often I have been asked to take the stage at churches, institutions of higher education, and government agencies across the globe based on the fact that I am man. I know that this book will move the Church toward further dignifying the equality and individuality of all humanity. This collection of essays is another reminder that everyone has a voice and journey to be known.

Much love,

Andrew Marin

Andrew Marin is the author of the award winning book Love Is an Orientation, *and president of The Marin Foundation (www. themarinfoundation.org), a public charity working to build bridges between the LGBT community and conservatives through biblical and social education, scientific research and diverse community gatherings.*

Introduction

Iwas a graduate student of theology when word of her actions reached me. During a seminary class on preaching, her professor had warned students not to wear open-toed shoes in the pulpit lest they be a distraction to wandering minds (and libidos). Better yet, he advised, men's black dress socks were recommended for all—women included. She showed up the following day in dress socks as instructed. Except they were pulled taut. Over bare legs. Beneath a miniskirt. Her transgression was small but potent. By literally following her instructor's words, she unmasked their unspoken message that to exercise authority in the church she would have to become like a man. The anecdote stuck with me as I began collaborating on this book with my co-editor, author Enuma Okoro. It revealed how even the bodies of young women in the church, never mind their voices, remain taboo for some, and in twenty-first-century America, no less.

Taboo. It is a word we seldom use in the United States, where freedom of speech is a cornerstone of our foundation and the boundaries of what is socially acceptable have stretched wide. The notion that there are still experiences that remain off-limits for expression sounds antiquated, or even prudish. And yet we still bite our lips. Hold our tongues. Swallow our words in fear of being stigmatized, ostracized, or vilified. The power of taboo is still palpable.

Young American Christian women have more freedom than ever before to speak for ourselves; we are being theologically trained in unprecedented numbers, accessing leadership in our communities through both orthodox and unorthodox avenues, and playing the roles of professional, wife, mother, daughter, girl-friend, and friend, among others. As the first line of an evangelical magazine article titled "50 Women You Should Know" affirms, "Christian women who want to pursue influential roles in politics, the church, and other sectors of public life in the United States and Canada have never before had more opportunities to do so." But with all of the perceived progress, why does it feel like our voices still aren't fully being heard? And if we could speak honestly, what would we want to say? This is a collection of essays that aims to address what happens when we speak the unspeakable about our sacred experiences of faith, gender, and identity.

Our book is part of a series of anthologies on young American men and women from three Abrahamic faiths: Islam, Judaism, and Christianity. While the first volumes on Muslim American men and women explored the relationship between faith and country, Enuma and I knew a volume on the experiences of Christian Americans would need to be positioned differently. Christians continue to make up three-quarters of the population in the United States, a majority that is reflected in the number of Christian memoirs and narratives on the shelves of bookstores across America. Put simply, we wondered what hadn't already been said and who hadn't said it. The pages that follow are our attempt to flesh out this silence.

We began work on the book with an email to potential contributors asking, "What taboos remain in the church at the intersection of faith and gender? What expectations have you noticed from yourself, your partner, your community, or your God to conform to a Christian identity not your own? And how do you draw courage to step out of the silence and encourage others to do the same?" (We also had to ask the awkward question, "Are you under 40?" in order to hear from a younger generation of women, many of whom were writing about these taboos for the first time). What emerged were responses from young women with different affiliations—Presbyterian, Methodist, Catholic, Evangelical, Mennonite, Baptist, Unitarian Universalist and Christian Agnostic; young women with different ethnicities—Mexican, Korean, Italian, Chinese, African, and Anglo; and young women with different perspectives on their gender—both egalitarian and complimentarian, both "straight" and "queer." We heard from writers, educators, advocates, artists, pastors, professors, and students, all with a story to share.

Some of the women and their essays surprised us. Like outdoor educator Patience Perry, who writes about the practice of using menstrual blood to fertilize the earth, despite its pagan association among her Christian friends. Or writer Amy Frykholm who confesses at one point to wanting to hide her body behind a monk's cloak despite her feminist commitment to embodiment. We were also surprised by the similarities among some of the essay themes, even as contributors wrote with their own nuance. Young women still experience sexism in church leadership (although they are not supposed to mention it), as evidenced by the essays of Lara Blackwood Pickrel and Marlena Graves. Singleness can still be a stigma or a puzzle, as Meghan Florian and Anna Broadway write. And many of us still have little room in communities of faith to publicly express our doubts and desires.

Wherever the essays might converge and diverge, we all had to agree to "speak for ourselves." This was an underlying principle of the anthology (and the editing process). However, personal narrative has often been considered the only kind of writing women are qualified to do with any authority, and even then we are lumped together and dismissed as uninformed or untrustworthy—even whiny. Our character, rather than our ideas, becomes the source of the critique, with some even using the words of our sacred texts to silence us. As writer and theologian Sarah Sentilles has noted, women who write in such a confessional style are often called "brave" rather than "smart." We believe that speaking for ourselves has the ability to be both.

While we don't all agree with one another, we believe in the power of personal stories to build bridges of understanding where there were none, to give faces and names to what were previously only "issues," and to bind people together in their common humanity.

The theme of the anthology is taboo, not hot topics. From masturbation, miscarriage, and menstruation to ordination, cohabitation, and immigration, this collection of essays explores provocative experiences of faith, gender, and identity left largely unspoken in twenty-first-century American Christianity. Enuma and I hope readers will both find themselves and stretch themselves as a result of exploring these essays. The tensions within Christianity cannot easily be silenced; it is our belief that bringing them to light can only strengthen our faith as we learn to speak the unspeakable.

Do not be afraid.

Erin Lane

Going in Disguise
by Amy Frykholm

AMY FRYKHOLM is the author of three books of nonfiction: *Rapture Culture: Left Behind in Evangelical America*; *Julian of Norwich: A Contemplative Biography*; and *See Me Naked: Stories of Sexual Exile in American Christianity*. She works as an editor for *The Christian Century* and lives in Leadville, Colorado.

True confession: All my life I have wanted to wear a cassock like a monk. In my mind, I am dressed like a Franciscan in a brown, coarse robe with a rope belt, the female body underneath it concealed. None of my serious feminist training, my hard work on embodiment, my attempts to experience the goodness of the sensual world and my own body have done much to shift this desire.

In sixth-century Lebanon, legend has it, the only daughter of a wealthy man was distressed when her father arranged for her marriage so that he could enter a monastery and become a monk. She decided to join him. She donned a monk's habit and lived her entire life in and around the monastery, with no one knowing that she was actually a woman until her body was laid out at her death. This woman, St. Pelegia, is one of many women in the Christian tradition whose sainthood is directly connected to cross-dressing: St. Anna, otherwise known as Euphemianos of Constantinople, St. Eugenia/Eugenios of Alexandria, St. Theodora, St. Thekla of Iconium, St. Pelegia the prostitute, St. Hildegund, and St. Athanasia. Throughout ancient and medieval

Christianity, the monk-who-was-actually-a-woman became a regular trope. For these Christians, there was something so compelling about the secret woman dressed in a monk's habit, it was frequently called "sainthood."

For women, perhaps, it is fairly easy to see where the fantasy lies. In the monastery, dressed like a man, a woman would have access to all that men had—the books, the learning, the labor, the community of equals. She would be taken seriously, unencumbered by the weight of a female gender identity, no asterisk behind her name, no question of the capacities of a woman's mind or soul. She could pursue study and prayer based on her abilities only. Perhaps these stories persisted because women could share in the fantasy of checking their femaleness at the door of the monastery. They could drop femaleness like a garment to the floor, becoming male ABG—All But Genitals.

For men, the fantasy may also have suggested a kind of freedom: a way to be in a relationship with women without being threatened by them. Women's bodies indicated sexual desire, lust, forces beyond control of the disciplined life, among the things that men sought relief from by entering monasteries. But these stories suggested a way to overcome the brokenness that resulted from exiting the world. At the same time, the stories also suggested that completely hiding a woman's body is itself a form of saintliness. That is troubling, and yet somehow, for me, true. These women concealed as monks did in fact attain something that I still seem to long for. I have always wanted to go in disguise.

At the age of seventeen, at a weedy, mosquito-y Christian camp in North Dakota, I encountered directly the detrimental relationship between womanhood and Christianity. I had been going to this camp for several years, as a camper and then as a counselor. It was an evangelical camp, with plenty of late-night campfire confessions and conversions. This particular summer, the "area minister" of the North American Baptists was traveling through. He had been invited by the camp to teach several sessions, and he had decided to focus on the question of gender and the proper ordering of the family. He seemed fairly obsessed with the subject. At one session, he drew a ladder of God's intent for creation. Men, of course, were at the top of the ladder. At another session, he said, "Someday, you will be pastors. Someday you will be the wives of pastors. Someday, you will be spiritual leaders. Someday, you will be the wives of spiritual leaders." A wave of fury overcame me at that moment, a distinct light-headedness that made me feel like my mind was being ripped out from my body. I got up and stumbled into the hot, bright North Dakota sunshine.

The words seared my brain, as if I had been branded by them. It wasn't that I imagined myself as a pastor. Other young women, sitting in that same room, would later struggle with that question mightily. They did feel a call, and having that call denied in such stark terms created lifelong pain. For me, it did not. But that other, more vague category, "spiritual leader," I thought had something for me. I was already a "leader"—president of my youth group, president of the association of North American Baptist Youth, president of the student council. But "spiritual leader" suggested other qualities to me—wisdom, insight, compassion—that I wasn't ready to surrender to men.

As I write about that long-ago moment in a place I no longer call home, I can't really believe that it had such a strong effect. I can't imagine that it could cause me to crave the denial of something as essential to my womanliness as my body. The preacher was not someone I loved. I had barely met the man, and when I later approached him to raise my objections, he looked through me so completely I might have indeed been wearing an invisibility cloak. Yet these words were spoken into the soft clay of my life, and even as I rejected them—passionately, furiously—they still somehow entered me. Perhaps the silence of the women around me—women who had encouraged me, who had given me whatever leadership I had to that point possessed—perhaps their complicity and their fatigue caused the pain. Perhaps then, it was their version of womanhood that I wanted to walk away from into my monk's hood.

Years later, I caught another glimpse of a woman who had decided not to go in disguise. The room where I saw her was a bland hotel conference room, packed, stuffy, and moist. People filled every chair, lined the back and sides and poured out the doorways. The room smelled of cheap hotel shampoo and aftershave. I had arrived too late for a seat, so I stood against the back wall, my shoulders pressed against the suit coats of men on either side of me. I longed to take off my high-heeled boots that had already begun to make my feet ache. But I was afraid they might add to the smell of the sweaty room. And I rely on those boots to make me—a very small person—closer to average size, something irrationally important at the very back of a crowded room.

We were gathered to hear an eminent theologian speak about her new book, and as I glanced around, I estimated that the room was at least 80 percent male—a mix of old and young in tweed, shiny loafers, and dress shirts. When the theologian rose from a chair in the front row and moved to the podium, I almost audibly gasped. She was wearing a tight black dress and a short red jacket. The dress was cut so low that the tops of her breasts appeared. I quickly looked around to see if anyone else had registered the strangeness of this. Was anyone else surprised that a woman who had been called upon to display her theological eminence would appear in a low-cut, tight dress? Or to put it more crudely: Was I the only person in this room of more than 300 scholars staring at the theologian's cleavage?

"Theologian's cleavage"—can those two words actually be placed together? The woman in question was not young, maybe twenty years older than I am. She was attractive, but not conventionally beautiful. She had spent most of her life in libraries doing close readings of church fathers. Her works were weighty and sometimes luminous. She'd angered the feminist establishment and the theological establishment all at the same time, charting a course marked by both independence and faithfulness to ancient texts. Here she was in front of me, arguing earnestly, sifting through her readings of Augustine, skillfully maneuvering the objections raised to her work, deftly answering questions. I continued to stare, mesmerized. Did she know what she was doing? A ridiculous question: she seemed to know not only her own mind, but also to be reading the minds of everyone else in the room. I couldn't help but think that she had calculated how much of her breasts to show as carefully as she had chosen which passages of Thomas Aquinas to quote. She was offering this dress in this moment as a challenge, as yet another dare: She was risking a fully female theological incarnation. And using her breasts to do it.

Her cleavage *was* calculated—that I know almost for certain. She showed just enough that no one could mistake it. It was not a shadow. But not so much that it could be called distasteful. No bounce. There was nothing flirtatious in it. That is perhaps what made the gesture still more remarkable. Her cleavage, I decided, was a subtle mark, a distinct challenge to Christianity's usual ways of speaking, a gesture in the direction of the unsayable. She rejected the bargain that the rest of us seemed to have struck: that we would leave our bodies outside the room. That we would be sexless in order to be taken seriously. Maybe the women would add a dash of the "feminine" in the form, usually, of a scarf, a pair of glittery earrings, a shade of lipstick, so that femininity could act as an accessory to the endless parade of gray suits, a flare, a touch, but never the thing itself, the female body. We were willing, subtly, to perform gender, but only if bodies were somehow excluded. Here we'd agreed, for the time being, not to be the bodies that bore and nursed children, that undressed for lovers, partners, husbands. Here we made a bid for pure mind. Later, after dark, a little drunk, maybe, or extremely tired, we might cede something to the body; we might let that underlying erotic charge step forward.

But this display of breasts was not flirtation. Perhaps it was that rarer prize: Embodiment. I heard this theologian saying, but not in so many words, "You will not separate my work from my body; my body and my work are one with my being and with my soul. I offer them to you together." That's an earnest version. The less earnest would be, "I will not show up here bodiless so that you can feel safe in your Empire of the Tweed-Suited Mind."

But I remain uneasy. The androgyny of academia—that bodiless suit—has been my friend as much as my enemy. It is as close to the monk's hood as I have dared come. It has allowed me to sneak, invisible, through walls without ever challenging the wall itself. It has allowed me to "become male," as an ancient Gnostic writer in the Gospel of Mary put it. Even as I reject the very concept of becoming male, I still would choose, like the irresistible wrong answer on a multiple choice quiz, the monk's hood. The alternative—to put my female body on display, to challenge the separation between mind and body on which women's inclusion in the system seems to be based—feels very dangerous indeed. Either the walls will fall down on my very own head or they will close in around me, locking me in—or out—for good.

I stand poised on this threshold. On one side, the safe, old, comfortable cloak. On the other, the terrible risk of exposure and perhaps a fuller incarnation. The saints of old chose to face exposure only after death. And me? What will I choose?

The Gatherer-God:
On Motherhood and Prayer
by Micha Boyett

MICHA (pronounced MY-cah) BOYETT is a youth minister turned stay-at-home mom trying to make sense of vocation and season and place in the midst of her third cross-country move in three years. On a slow journey of learning prayer with eyes open and arms deep in sticky dishes, she blogs at Patheos about motherhood, monasticism, and the sacred in the everyday. Her forthcoming memoir *The Mama Monk* will be released in 2014 from Worthy Publishing. She lives in San Francisco, California with her husband and two sons.

A friend introduces me at a cocktail party: "Micha writes a blog about motherhood and prayer."

My new acquaintance, a mother of four, wants to know what I say about prayer. I take a sip of wine and launch into my usual story. How the emotional and physical demands of becoming a mom were more than I could have imagined those mornings I walked and prayed along the leafy trail by our home, eight months pregnant and filling out my husband's old college T-shirt. I had been full of hope for the sort of spiritual renewal that would come with motherhood. Instead, what arrived was a deep, consistent guilt for my failed attempts at making space for prayer. I spent that first year fearful that all the diapering and rocking and waking early with a baby (in the place of time I'd always reserved for my spiritual life) had somehow distanced me from God in a way I couldn't undo. I feared I was replacing my love for God with love for my son.

Her eyes soften, something releases in them for a moment. She understands about guilt, about exhaustion, about the longing for connection with God.

"I've been thinking about that lately," she says. "A new mom shared the same sort of struggle with me: how she wasn't finding time to study scripture or pray. I told her this season of life is really difficult for everyone. I gave her a way out."

She continues, "And then I went home and felt sick to my stomach because I realized I'd given her the same excuse I'd given myself. I realized my kids were my idols. I was prioritizing them above the Lord."

I take a deep breath and raise my eyebrows.

I don't believe a mother of four is idolatrous because she's caring for her little ones instead of praying in the quiet. In the evangelical subculture in which I am immersed we offer clichés like these to one another with soft smiles and concerned expressions. We hold them out as if they are prettily wrapped packages and then are surprised when they shatter in our hands.

I know there are mothers who make idols of their kids. Mothers crippled by anxiety for their children, mothers who live for nothing else in this world and suffocate their kids by hovering, mothers who demand success from their children out of fear for their lack of it.

But, more often, we are the moms who lie in bed sodden with guilt that our day of demanding child care—diaper changing, block building, park chasing, book reading, feeding and washing and storytelling—has meant we haven't pleased God, that somehow we have worshipped our children instead of our Savior. All the while we are forgetting the power of God's mercy. If we believe God doesn't hold grace out over our tired, aching bodies but instead see only God's disgust at our idolatry, we have not understood the Beatitudes; if we assume God doesn't dance over us as we lie in bed and offer us rest, his gentle hand set warm on our heads; if we imagine God looks unhappily at our prayer-less (tired) day spent loving the weak, the tenderhearted, the little ones to whom the Kingdom of God belongs; if we feel that grace is not held out for us, we have missed the cross.. The same Jesus who shocked the religious by declaring blessings on the "poor in spirit" is the one who forgives and restores out of the deep riches of unmerited love. Who are mothers to question our place in the gospel of grace?

I stand in the middle of the party, before this woman in whom I see myself so clearly. Wine swirling in my glass, I explain the deep-settled change in my spirit these last four years spent raising two boys. I speak of God's refreshing mercy, the hope I've found in embracing the work of thanksgiving, the sweetness of discovering that the time I'd always thought was missing was there all along. It's just that prayer looks different now.

In the dark rocking, in the late night quiet, sometimes shivering in the open winter air of my baby's room when I awake to his cries, too frantic or distracted or confused to find my robe, this is where I pray best.

I pray best when my mind is fuzzy and I have no book before me. No ancient monastic prayers. No evangelical "Mother's Prayers for her Baby Boy." I pray best when the words are jumbled and all I have is my body. The milk I've made without trying. My baby's mouth fastened to my breast. I rock in the haze. Sometimes I sleep, my chin hanging low to my chest. Sometimes I touch his hair with my fingers and whisper, "Look at this one, Jesus." And Jesus and I meet together in that room and both of us sigh at the beauty of moonlight on a new face in the darkness. Sometimes I whisper scripture my mouth has formed a million times. "Give him a heart of flesh instead of a heart of stone," I pray. Sometimes I pray my boy will love the secret things God loves. But mostly, I ponder, taking my cue from Christ's own mother, who twice is described as "pondering" at the work of God in her son. Why else would such a prayer be mentioned in the Gospels unless to call us to such deep work?

When I consider how busy I feel with these little ones, with a grocery store nearby and a washing machine in the house, I try to imagine my great-grandmother's life. Did she feel her time was a gift from God? Did she worry about "idolatry"?

Mama Mac was born at the end of the nineteenth century. A true pioneer lady who grew up in a dugout with a crop-sharing cowboy for a father, she raised seven kids on a farm in West Texas at a time when it was one of the last places in the United States to be settled. Dust storms, rainless fields, zero shade. (It's the plains; trees don't show up naturally.) I imagine her in the kitchen of her farmhouse, her children in from the cotton fields, begging for lunch. She spent the morning hand-scrubbing the worn clothes of her farm kids, hanging them out in the sun to dry, baking bread from scratch, working the garden, begging vegetables to sprout.

I wonder what she thought about motherhood and God. Her husband was the strictest kind of religion-keeper: no card games, no dancing, no drink. She was taught to grow her hair long, clear her face of makeup (as if they could have afforded such a thing), and cover her legs in long skirts. Their denomination required the fiercest kind of obedience. Grace rarely factored in. Instead, salvation might be lost at any moment. Every sin might undo the work of the cross. How could she have trusted the God she was taught to fear? Did God approve of her life and its simplicities: her unending manual work, her third-grade reading level? For her, was motherhood a spiritual weakness? Who can pray with babies at her feet? Who can ever live up to holiness when children are hungry, when the garden must be nurtured, the diapers wrung and hung?

Mama Mac lived till I was eight and she was ninety-seven. I sat in her bony lap every Saturday morning in her upholstered rocking chair. Sometimes I wonder, did she pray for me then, her hands on my hair rocking and rocking, her ancient ears hanging low, long white hair wrapped around itself, pinned tight?

What if, all along, mothers have always known the most about prayer?

What if, all along, nobody told them they were experts because their prayer was not loud enough to be heard, because their prayer was not cultivated in the quiet? Their prayer was (has always been) formed in the chaos, in the bright light of playtime and work time and feeding time.

What if, all along, mothers have been the experts in the laying on of hands? It's just that their hands were doing all the earthy things at once: re-pinning the fresh diaper, rocking the teething baby, kissing the scraped knee, tilling the dirt in order to feed those mouths. Their hands were praying all along, blessing and blessing the bodies around them.

Perhaps no one but God knows the secret of prayer and faithfulness. Perhaps the voiceless have always prayed the loudest.

Guilt comes easy for me. This life I lead is small. And, oh, how I've wished for a bigger life, "changing the world" like I promised God when I was fourteen and my heart was swelling under the music of the youth missions conference. I would have run to the edges of the earth in earnest, shouted prayers on the corners of dirt roads, preached loudest until the God of my childhood heard me above the rest, until that God said, "Yes, you *are* special, you *do* deserve my favor."

Instead, I was rescued from the anxiety of spiritual success. Instead, I was given a small calling. I was given the picture of the mother hen to which Jesus compares himself in Matthew 23, the God whose wings offer refuge in Psalm 91, the Lord who gathers her chicks into the safe place.

After my first son was born and I was at my most anxious, when I was most afraid that the God I longed for was not proud of me, was disappointed, was sighing over my failure to hold both the Spirit and my children, I read one small sentence about Benedictine monks. Kathleen Norris had written it in her preface to *The Cloister Walk*. Her words were hardly significant to the purpose of the book, her sentence mostly unimportant. "The Benedictines," a friend had told her, "more than any other people I know, insist that there is time in each day for prayer, for work, for study, and for play."

I grasped those words with frantic fingers. I held them in my gut for months, begging God, "Make this true!" I might as well have been praying, "Love me!" And somewhere in the midst of all the mothering, the cutting of grapes in halves, the blowing of bubbles, the quick hands catching the falling toddler, I heard God's answer. *It is true.*

There is enough time. There has always been enough.

My wine glass is near empty. I stare deeply at my cocktail party acquaintance. "Maybe prayer is simpler than I ever thought it was," I say. "Maybe it's just noticing the beauty, the gifts around me. Maybe it's listening to God's Spirit in the moment, paying attention, loving well because I'm experiencing God's love for me in his nearness."

I can tell she does not agree when I say this. It makes her uncomfortable. Of course, prayer demands more than simply noticing, her expression says. She is now *concerned.*

Like her, I am broken. I am fearful. I still long for a life that "changes the world," a life that stretches wider than the bodies of the two boys who sleep in the rooms down the hall. But, what I'm discovering is that sometimes the narrow spiritual work is also the deep work. Sometimes the prayers offered with eyes open and elbows soaked in soapy water are the holiest.

My space and purpose and calling in Time is held by the Gatherer-God, the one who sets me in her ancient lap and rocks with me, hands on my tired head, blessing and blessing and blessing.

Naughty by Nature,
Hopeful by Grace
by Enuma Okoro

ENUMA OKORO is a Nigerian-American writer, speaker, and spiritual director. Her interests intersect religion and spirituality, identity and culture, women's studies, race relations, and the visual and literary arts. Her first book, the spiritual memoir *Reluctant Pilgrim: A Moody Somewhat Self-Indulgent Introvert's Search for Spiritual Community* (Fresh Air Books, 2010), was a winning finalist in the 2010 USA Best Books Award and received the 2011 National Indie Excellent Book Awards Winning Finalist in "Spirituality and African-American Non-Fiction." Enuma is a coauthor with Shane Claiborne and Jonathan Wilson-Hartgrove of *Common Prayer: Liturgy for Ordinary Radicals*, (Zondervan Publishers, 2010). Enuma's third book, Silence (Upper Room Books, 2012) is a meditation on faith in the midst of doubt, unanswered prayer and the seemingly silence of God. In June 2012, Enuma had the honor of being the first woman of African descent to preach at the historic American Church in Paris. (Martin Luther King Jr. was the first man of African descent to preach there in October 1965.) Visit Enuma at www.enumaokoro.com.

I liked Chris from the start. And he liked me. We liked each other. And we thought it was good. Very good. We had so much to talk about: shared interests, similar concerns, and vocational worries. He was disarmingly attractive in a "I rode my bike five miles to your house cause earlier on the phone you said you'd kill for this book" kind of way. We met at the wedding of a mutual friend. We both came alone. But that didn't last very long.

"So, how do you know the couple?" It was an innocent enough question to ask the guy seated next to me at the reception.

"Oh, Sam and I worked together on a writing project a few years back. He's a great guy. I'm really happy for him." He smiled kindly at me. "What about you, bride or groom?"

"I went to seminary with Sam." I smiled back. "Are you a writer?"

"Some people call me that. I mostly work behind the scenes. I'm in design." He turned to face me more fully and caught me off guard with his outdoorsy, boyish good looks and the earnest kindness of his eyes. We relaxed into this new conversation with instant ease and chatted for the rest of the evening. Before we left the reception we had exchanged emails and phone numbers. It would be good to stay connected about one another's writing projects, support each other vocationally.

And that's what we did over the following months. It felt like a gift. It was a gift, this ability to bond so quickly and effortlessly with someone in my mostly solitary professional life. Though I am an introvert, I adore connecting with like-minded men and women, especially as it relates to navigating the vocational challenges of writing and publishing. Cross-gender friendships occur naturally and somewhat frequently in my adult life, so getting to know Chris was not terribly out of the norm. I was just surprised at how quickly and easily it happened.

I would text him Joan Didion and Gail Godwin quotes about the writing life—"The choice is always a killing one....I do little murders in my workroom every day." Sometimes he would text me from conferences I couldn't attend. "Just got done speaking. Wish you were here to meet all these great writing folks!" We shared simple email pleas for professional affirmation and healthy reminders about sticking with the challenges of work. There were longer exchanges too, phone calls that allowed more room to really talk about our writing goals and accomplishments.

But it wasn't simply our shared vocation that drew us together. We really enjoyed each other as people and soon became friends. Eventually it was normal for our conversations to take tangents into other aspects of our lives: the upcoming medical exam that had me worried, his growing involvement at his church. Our slowly growing friendship felt beautiful, fitting, and life-giving at this season of our lives. And it was.

Then it happened. I didn't mean it to. But at some point I started getting flutters at the "dink" of my iPhone. A text or phone message from him could easily redeem the half-heartedness of an otherwise mediocre day. When something lovely or saddening occurred he quietly became one of the first people with whom I wanted to share the experience. I already knew I loved him; I called him my brother from another mother. But at some point I started crushing on him.

Maybe things would have been different if his wife hadn't gone to her twenty-year high school reunion the same weekend as that wedding. Maybe if she had been there he and I never would have met.

I am beginning to realize how little the churches of which I have been a part have taught me about the beauty of boundaries and the reality of fine lines. No one really wants to talk about the normalcy of temptation and how, if unacknowledged, it can lead to behavior that goes against what is life-giving, what is of God.

I get it now in a way I haven't before; how temptation can slip slowly from shiny surfaces into the sin of unfaithfulness and undisciplined desire, from things that look good and usually are good, in the beginning. But no one talks about how to keep your balance on the slippery slope. No one wants to talk about it till everyone has slid right off. Then every pastor, priest, and prophet begins to preach about Eve and Delilah, biblical women culturally synonymous with the evils of temptation and the fall of men. (Why women are often blamed in these two-way streets is another discussion worth having at a different time.) In my friendship with Chris I felt the flutters growing and I wanted to start talking about it. I wanted to steady my stance on the slippery slope.

"So, I really like talking to Chris. Should I be worried about that?" I was at my girlfriend Jules's house working on a project. I had taken a break and was sitting quietly on the plush green sofa, petting her mutt, Chico.

Jules looked up at me from her computer screen trying to gauge the seriousness of my comment. "What do you mean? Like you find him super interesting intellectually or you think he's hot?"

"Um...both? Not hot. But cute. He's cute. But it's more than that. He's just so great. But I'm starting to get butterflies when we talk and that's not good 'cause he's married. Crushing is normal, right? Never mind. Forget I said anything."

When I finally stopped talking, Chico jumped off the couch, Jules closed her computer screen, put it on the coffee table, and sat up straighter in her armchair. "How often do you talk?"

"Like once a week or every ten days or something. I'm probably just overreacting. I just want to be thoughtful and sensitive, Jules."

"No, you're right. I think it's wise to be aware of whatever you're feeling," Jules affirmed. "Like even being able to see where the potential for harm might be in the midst of a really beautiful thing." She looked over at me as I started to chew on my lower lip.

I know the whole cultural conversation around "Can men and women be friends?" is as old as can be. So many evangelical-minded Christians have such firm opinions on the issue, mostly that it's not possible or wise. But no one really talks in a healthy, reflective way about the real point of the issue: how to deal with sexual temptation in platonic relationships between heterosexual men and women. No one gets to avoid dealing with temptation, sexual or otherwise, in life; it's really a matter of how we do or do not discipline our desires. I know that being attracted to someone, regardless of their relationship status, is not in itself wrong, or something of which to be ashamed. But I also know that it matters how aware I permit myself to be of a growing desire to be in a relationship with that person and how I respond once I have acknowledged the desire.

Maybe we'd all be either more self-aware, or more willing to be, if as communities of friends and faith we talked more openly about how to navigate those seemingly innocent areas, those gray areas. But I can't have these conversations with just anyone. I trusted Jules that day and knew she wouldn't judge me. Rather, she would be committed to helping me think through this, holding me accountable, and not letting me delude myself. I know she cares about me, *and* she cares about the health and integrity of Chris and his marriage even though they've never met. And that comes from her faith perspective and worldview about what it means to honor covenant *and* what it means to love one another well, even strangers. That makes all the difference.

"So, what are you going to do about this new revelation?" Jules asked.

I sighed and slumped deeper into the couch. "Well, I'm just going to stay aware of it without blowing it out of proportion or overanalyzing it. There's some naturalness to it. He and I are both healthy, attractive, intelligent, fun people with lots of similar interests. It might be weirder if crushing *wasn't* a factor. But we are also both thoughtful, self-aware individuals trying to live sincere lives of faith that reflect what we believe in as members of the church and as Christians. So, I'm going to keep talking to you and other girlfriends about it. And I'm going to expect you to check in with me every now and then and to not be afraid of being honest with your thoughts or concerns."

"Are you going to maybe think about not talking with each other as much for a while?"

"No, not really. That's not an issue. There already seems to be a natural ebb and flow to how much we communicate. But I am going to be even more intentional about asking about his wife when we do talk."

Jules quietly got up to refill our teacups. I called out to her as she walked toward the kitchen. "It's not like I think anything is going to happen. I guess I just don't like being attracted to a married man, that's all. It sucks remembering you're a sinner, weak in flesh and spirit."

Later that night after leaving Jules's house I lay in bed and did what I told Jules I wouldn't do: I started analyzing my feelings. I began to recognize that my flutters, my crush on Chris, weren't so much about him as it was about feeling seen and heard in a way I hadn't experienced in a long time. Chris is a compassionate listener with a generous heart and deep regard for fostering good relationships. He makes friendship a priority to the extent that I know I can call on him at any time and he'll drop everything if I really needed him to. What I was really crushing on was the experience of being loved well by another one of God's children.

I love talking with Chris and wish I could see him in person more. And yet, there's a part of me that's grateful for the distance of our friendship. It permits for more natural and necessary boundaries given our life circumstances. Maintaining good boundaries in any relationship takes certain energies and requires thoughtful self-awareness. But I think men and women are conditioned both within secular culture and within the church to relate to one another in primarily sexual ways rather than as friends. So even when such platonic relating occurs between a man and a woman it is instinctive to question the lines between what seems healthy and beautiful and what might be tiptoeing in temptation's backyard.

As an imperfect creature, I am always prone to temptation. It's part and parcel of being naughty by nature, or as St. Paul puts it in the New Testament letter to the Romans, "For all have sinned and fall short of the glory of God" (3:23). But I also think that the love and the redemptive power of Christ found in a community of believers can trump my naughty nature. That grace keeps me hopeful.

Becoming One Flesh: Thoughts on Male Headship in Marriage

by Amy Julia Becker

 AMY JULIA BECKER is the author of *A Good and Perfect Gift: Faith, Expectations, and a Little Girl Named Penny* (Bethany House), named one of the Top Books of 2011 by Publisher's Weekly, and *Penelope Ayers: A Memoir*. A graduate of Princeton University and Princeton Theological Seminary, she blogs regularly for Patheos at Thin Places. Her essays have appeared in the Motherlode blog of *The New York Times*, *First Things*, *The Philadelphia Inquirer*, *The Hartford Courant*, *The Christian Century*, *Christianity Today*, The Huffington Post, and Parents.com. Amy Julia lives with her husband, Peter, and three children, Penny, William, and Marilee, in Western Connecticut.

We got married young, at twenty-two, three weeks after my husband graduated from college. It was a beautiful day, with the sun peeking out from behind pale gray clouds. The pews were filled with beautiful people, many of them churchgoers, from every point on the spectrum of Christian belief. There was my mother-in-law and her cohort from New Orleans who had come of age in the 1960s and asserted a woman's right to choose whatever she wanted for her body, who used gender-neutral language to refer to God, who worried that Peter and I were too conservative with our Bible studies and evangelicalism. There were our friends from Christian fellowship groups in college, who volunteered for Young Life and passed along *Passion and Purity* and challenged us when we slept in the same bed during weekends together throughout our long-distance courtship. Many of their faces looked alike, but the theology underneath spanned divides of history and culture and practice.

And then there was the service itself. On the one hand, we were wed by a female pastor in an unspoken but public affirmation of the potential for women to lead within the church. At the same time, we asked one of my roommates from college to read Ephesians 5:21-28, the primary New Testament passage about the relationship between husbands and wives. Although it begins with the conciliatory, "Submit to one another out of reverence to Christ," it also contains the controversial lines, "Wives, submit yourselves to your own husbands as you do to the Lord, for the husband is the head of the wife as Christ is the head of the church."

We weren't thinking about headship that day. We chose the passage for its description of the relationship between husband and wife, a relationship of mutual love and respect, of giving and receiving to and from each other. We chose the passage because it taught us about marriage as both a source of great joy and a hard path to walk. And we chose it because it assumed an indelible link between the covenantal vow of a husband and wife and the covenantal relationship between Christ and his church.

Before our wedding day, I had wrestled with the roles Scripture allowed for women, within both the church and society. I wanted to be able to trumpet the egalitarian ethos of my faith, but I wasn't sure Scripture backed up my ideology. I believe that the Bible is the authoritative Word of God, and my own cultural norms and personal feelings do not, must not, trump Scriptural truth. When I read the Gospels, I saw the ways Jesus's ministry subverted social norms, including those surrounding women. And yet Paul's words that "women should remain silent in the churches" troubled me. As much as I wanted to ignore that directive altogether, I felt compelled to learn more. In time, I learned that scholars disagree about Paul's meaning, and that his admonition may have been directed toward a specific group of women who disrupted church services. Within the same letter to the Corinthians, Paul refers to women praying and prophesying publicly, and he refers to female leaders within the church in other letters. In the midst of my own investigation, the woman who married us offered a gentle defense of her ministry, with stories from Deborah and Esther to Mary Magdalene and Priscilla. I became convinced that a faithful reading of Scripture could affirm women's leadership in every aspect of church life. I memorized Galatians 3:28: "In Christ there is neither Jew nor Gentile, neither slave nor free, nor is there male or female, for you are all one in Christ Jesus."

I came to a firm conclusion about women in the pulpit. And yet I hadn't wrestled with the roles of men and women within marriage itself. Even though we chose Ephesians 5 for our wedding service, I have avoided the question of male headship within marriage since the day we wed. It pops into my mind every so often. When a friend makes a comment about understanding herself as a member of "the weaker sex," I recoil, and yet also wonder if she's right about gender roles. When I see children wander away from the faith as adolescents and notice that their dads didn't participate much in church life, I wonder whether Peter needs to be the spiritual leader in our household in order for our kids to embrace our faith. I even think about it in passing when I wonder if it makes a difference if Peter or I sit, literally, at the head of our dining room table. But it's not something I talk about, and I've started to wonder why.

On the one hand, I'm skittish about bringing up the topic with my "conservative" friends because I don't want them to question my allegiance to Scripture. On the other, I don't broach the topic with my "liberal" friends because I assume my concerns will be dismissed out of hand. I do believe that Scripture is the Word of God, and that the truth contained within it is not limited by cultural context or historical "progress." I also believe that Scripture has been misinterpreted in countless instances over the course of the life of the church, and often those misinterpretations become "truth."

Starting on my wedding day, I took what I wanted from Ephesians 5 and left the befuddling idea of male headship behind. I suppose I had told myself that if women could pastor a church then men weren't really supposed to be the heads of households, but I now realize that leadership within the church and headship within marriage can be very different. When I read Ephesians 5, my first reaction is to equate headship with leadership, to think it means that Peter must always take the lead spiritually. But that isn't how it has worked out for us. Over the years there have been times when I have stepped into the role of spiritual leader. When he first became a teacher and found himself with few colleagues who believed in God, much less Jesus, I decided we needed to become a part of a small group. So I began a group that met in our home, first with one other couple, and then a few more. I'm the one who prays more consistently with our kids at bedtime, the one who introduced the storybook Bibles. But at many other points, Peter has led me toward greater holiness—as he exhorts me through his example by trying to curtail gossip or setting reminders on his phone to read Psalms throughout the day. Sometimes it is as he stops to pray with our daughter before she heads out the door to school, as he seeks out wise counsel when a significant decision is looming, or as he sets time aside to spend a night at a retreat center.

And so I return to Ephesians 5 wondering what this language of headship is all about. Is it really about a hierarchical relationship between man and woman? Or is it more complicated than that? When I take another look, I'm drawn to the analogy itself. Yes, Ephesians 5 offers instruction for believers about marriage and about what self-giving love ought to look like within marriage. But perhaps all the more it is intended to offer a concrete human example of what might otherwise seem an abstract relationship between Christ and the church.

I often take my children into my arms and put my thumb and index finger close together. Then I ask them, "Do I love you this much?" They shake their heads. I put my hands about a foot apart. "This much?" With a trace of a smile, they shake again. And then I stretch my arms out wide. "Do I love you this much?" They grin and nod and then I say, "Nope. Even wider than my arms can reach." My outstretched arms are a meager attempt to give them a picture of my love for them. I wonder whether Ephesians 5 is most fundamentally intended to convey the depth of Christ's love for the church. At its core, perhaps, this is a passage about the nature of God's sacrificial love, God's faithful and enduring and costly love for us. Only secondarily is it a set of instructions for husband and wife.

But what of those instructions? What of the words, "wives should submit to their husbands in everything"? What of "husbands ought to love their wives as their own bodies"? Once again, the language of mutuality comes to mind, and as I think of other meditations on the nature of love, I remember that love always involves reciprocity. Love always involves neediness and giftedness working in tandem. Love always involves sacrifice. And love always, ultimately, leads to joy.

There have certainly been times in our marriage when I have needed someone to be my spiritual eyes and ears, to lead me toward the light when I am shrouded in darkness. There have also been times when I have taken that role. I've been hesitant to talk about it, and yet grateful for the ways in which our marriage has reflected a fundamental truth contained in Ephesians 5, that it is difficult to lay down our lives for one another, and that it changes us for the better when we do so. That love is costly and rewarding. That we sometimes experience love by giving it, like Christ, like the head. That we sometimes experience it by receiving it, like the church, like the body. Perhaps it shouldn't surprise me that in our marriage we both play both roles. We are, after all, one flesh.

No One Teaches Us
How to Be Daughters

by aja monet

In 2007, at the age of nineteen, AJA MONET became the youngest individual to win the legendary Nuyorican Poet's Cafe Grand Slam champion title. She works as an inner-city youth mentor and is staff faculty at Omega Institute, using poetry and prose as a holistic healing tool. With a BA from Sarah Lawrence College and an MFA in Creative Writing from School of the Art Institute of Chicago, aja monet has performed at various venues, colleges, and universities across America. In 2008, she was invited by the United Nations Youth Delegates to perform at the United Nations in New York City. In fall of that same year, she was invited to perform for NAACP's Barack Obama Inaugural event in Washington, DC. aja monet independently published her first book of poetry, *The Black Unicorn Sings* (Penmanship Books), in 2010, and in the fall of 2012 collaborated with poet/musician Saul Williams on the book *Chorus: a literary mixtape* (MTV books/Simon & Schuster). She is currently writing Science-Fiction.

No one teaches us how to be daughters.
There was the born.
The us, with slits and insides,
we shed and shape shift.
We, to blame for the
first despair, the being here.
When our heart melts,
our bodies morph into a vessel,
the genuflect.
The first face we see is a woman.
The first God we know is a mother.
There will always be a man at the pulpit—
the woman who birthed him,
the someone who fed and bathed.
Lest we forget her name,
call her prostitute
call her temptation
the bad apple
of the eye
whisper she as a myth.
Remember whom she loved
and not that she lived.
Say, she's gone mad
she has
and she
will break into
the father,
the son,
she must be,
the Holy Ghost.

My mother is often possessed—sometimes by anger or joy, laughter or love, or all of the above, and most brutally by guilt and fear. Hurt. I have seen how a spirit can storm through a woman's gaze. I am the gaze. A daughter learns of God in a gaze. One day she is to learn the art of creating, the process of bleeding; also, how a name can be mispronounced, how it can be used in vain. A daughter studies a woman as she is always becoming one. She sees how the world treats her. She listens because she is often not heard. There is always a consciousness of power. She withers and weathers through and around it. She swallows it whole, finds it delicious. She learns defense before offense. She is a will-be, a force willing things into existence. She is patient and ill-tempered, fierce and soft, full of scorn and forgiveness. My mother made me of her body, of her flesh and her blood; I ate from her umbilical cord. For nine months, every day was a communion and then I was born.

I first accepted Christ at the altar of an upstate New York sleep-away Christian camp. It was summer. I was no older than thirteen. I remember it was at evening church just after family dinner. We were children singing worship songs, running thoughts of knucklehead crushes, and shouting out to a God who sounded a lot like a schizophrenic Santa Claus; except he was our *father* without the reindeer, the red gear or the carefully calculated elves. And that was okay, to have a father that wasn't my father because I didn't know much about fathers. My mother raised three of us without the men that were said to have been there for the making. Somewhere in a recent past, there were men who once made love with my mother.

Similar to Santa Claus, fathers came once a year. They had a lot to say about upbringing but no presence to make a difference. They often came with presents. When they came empty-handed or didn't come at all, I assumed it was for all the bad deeds we had done. No, I guess God isn't Santa Claus. However, there was something loveable about this *God* in that story the Bible told. We knew about Him in quotes, within the connotation and intonation of phrases and sayings.

I was a quietly bold girl. Having been raised by a stubborn lioness Brooklyn mother, I've always held my head high, a protected cub with a silent roar. In the middle of singing, the pastor called out to the congregation of little people. He invited us to be saved. Some of us giggled; the girls wanted to be liked, the boys wanted to like. My mother was in the hospital. I remember calling her just after the service, how difficult it was to reach her, the cry I had, waiting for the nurse to transfer me to her room.

In the midst of us *opening the eyes to our hearts*, I walked out from the sea of innocence and into the parting, up to the altar so that I could mumble words in a whispering plea toward this saving grace. There is no telling what possesses a young girl to want to be saved. I do not recall a story told where we were not being saved from or saved for or saved with, too.

The altar was a stage assembled in front of rows of folding chairs in a gymnasium turned worship space. We played pickup basketball games and had silly summer camp dances in the center of the savior's headquarters. I wonder whether Christ was ever not there. Had he left after we disassembled the choir, anxious to be home, hoping to catch the Knicks on the television? I wanted him to hurry, to stop everything he was doing, and rush by my mother's bedside. A hand approached and lay gently on my right shoulder. I recall the sobbing and how the eyes became swollen wounds. Children less shy to be seen carrying the weight of their mothers and fathers–the empathic creatures and the disappointed/ing adults we would later become–we all gathered at the altar. Some of us just for show.

I was not yet taught how to make a man my life, not before being born again. It was the first time I turned from a mother toward a father.

I never understood why God would've chosen to be a man, why he allowed my mother to be sick, or even cared about my virginity. But I know this—he has the uncanny ability to birth beings, again, without the grueling high-endorphin labor of maternity. What does it mean to be born? *Again*? Was there some sort of complication with the *first* birth? Had my mom's mom not *birthed* her right?

God must be in my mother's belly. I was completely surrounded by the universe floating inside her. My brother was the last person in her womb before I came along and I suppose I spent an awful lot of time reading what he left inside there. It must have been interesting to see oneself inside a woman's body as a boy. I suppose it is scary. It was also scary for me; something so close to magic.

I came into the world in a Long Island College Hospital room in Brooklyn, New York. It was the week of the Harmonic Convergence.

August 21, 1987. There are many Queens walking amidst the county of Kings. Their name is mother.

In 2002, my mother was diagnosed with Lupus. It's an autoimmune disorder. It's a disease where essentially the immune system attacks the body. As her daughter, I saw the strongest woman I know begin to fight the greatest battle–one with self. She is a self-taught genius. She overcame great obstacles in Corporate America and struggled to raise three children in a society that uses morality and faith as weapons. If anything is to be credited for her perseverance and strength, I'd call it a God. Anything to be grateful to for her deciding to have me when her life afforded her no means to do so, I'd call it a God. I call it this because I pray to it as such. I pray to it because I was told it was something worth praying to. Truth is, she is God.

We are often taught to identify with being sons, the son of man, the Son of God, of a king, of a father–mankind. Where are our daughters?

Our daughters are in the bathroom of an apartment in a city of a country, learning how to love the faces in their mirrors. They are holding babies in their arms while cooking dinner, doing taxes, and educating our future leaders. *They* are whispering the art of nurture all around us. We are not tools. We are discovering our bodies as vessels. We are somewhere being women, creating societies. If God is a presence, is an entity, a being—let us love one another.

Married without Children
by Erin Lane

ERIN LANE, MTS is a communication strategist for faith-based authors and organizations. Her latest work with author Parker J. Palmer and the non-profit Center for Courage & Renewal combines her background as a book publicist with broader marketing consultation and program development for clergy and congregational leaders. She is also an active board member of the Resource Center for Women and Ministry in the South and is writing her next book about the hard work of belonging to communities of faith. Confirmed Catholic, raised Charismatic, and married to a Methodist, she blogs about the intersection of her faith and feminism at www.holyhellions.com.

I've never been gaga for babies, their newborn bodies pinked and puffed. It's too soon to know who they really look like, what sort of personality is buried beneath their chub, and when they'll start saying the darndest things.

This admonition is a shock to many and a relief to some. Church folks in particular have a hard time believing a virile young woman like me could feign anything other than adoration during a baptism. One Sunday in college, a chorus of throat squeals and arm squeezes broke out amongst my friends at the sight of babies on stage preparing to be dedicated.

"Erin, are you seriously not loving this?" Jacki asked.

I shrugged. "If they were puppies, I'd be right there with you."

When my husband and I became engaged seven years ago, we sternly told our marrying pastor, "No talk of children. No talk of being fruitful. No multiplication." We agreed to be married a few years before really posing the question of if and when we were ready to be sleepless, selfless, and salty parents. It's been posed, and we're still happily obsessing over our dog, showing off her picture on the smartphone with the rest of the proud moms and pops.

I'm not alone in a new generation of men and women who have chosen to remain childless. We've been called the No-Baby Boom by *Details* magazine. There are many practical considerations for not having a baby—such as the $350,000 it's estimated to cost to raise an American child from birth through public university—but there are few articulated theological reasons for why the common good might be served by some couples remaining without a nuclear family of their own.

Christian theology can be quite radical in the possibilities it affords childless individuals. Some scholars argue that the current focus on the heterosexual nuclear family is a development only of the last century.[1] By contrast, Jesus encouraged the development of the spiritual family. He refused to identify as Joseph's son (Luke 4:14-30) and instead pointed to sonship in God alone, admonishing his disciples that "whoever does the will of God is my brother and sister and mother" (Mark 3:33-35). While these words would have been startling to his early followers, it wasn't until the sixteenth century that such teaching would be reversed by Christian reformers seeking to separate themselves from the Catholic Church in their elevation of celibacy over matrimony.[2] Today Jesus's words reflect what some would call anti-family values because of their de-emphasis on the necessity of marriage for the common good.

In the Roman Catholic tradition in which I was formed, marriage is largely defined on the basis of a couple's willingness to bear and raise children. In an official statement in 2003 from Cardinal Joseph Ratzinger (who would later become Pope Benedict XVI),

---

1. In his book *Sex and the Single Savior: Gender and Sexuality in Biblical Interpretation* (Louisville, KY: John Knox Press, 2006), Dale Martin presents Jesus as a figure who creates and lives apart from the traditional household. However, in ancient Jewish culture, this household would have been much more extensive than the modern nuclear family, likely including extended relatives, concubines, slaves, day-laborers, and house guests, among others (104).

2. Martin, 119.

sexual relations were deemed *human* in so far as they occurred in marriage and were "open to the transmission of new life." Implicit in this definition is an argument that what is *inhuman* is any sex act that does not allow for the possibilility of biologically bearing children. Masturbation and homosexual unions are two such examples of disordered behavior according to the Catholic Church. Birth control, too, is likewise condemned. According to Catholic doctrine, these deviations subvert God's intention for male and female relationships and threaten the "survival of the human race."

I have often wondered if the survival of the human race would be better served by my *not* becoming a mother. I was a terrible babysitter growing up. In high school I let a newborn baby roll off its changing table as I tried to keep its bratty brother and sister out of the room. When they finally broke down the door, they looked at their baby brother on the floor and screamed. "Samuel! What have you done to Samuel? You are a bad, bad lady." They were right. I was too embarrassed over my gaffe to share it with the parents when they returned home. It wasn't until I was sort of chuckling at the whole fiasco that my own mother, a labor and delivery nurse, looked at me sternly. "Erin, that baby could have a concussion. You had better get on the phone and tell his parents." I can't think of a worse phone call to have to make than one that starts: "Hi. It's your babysitter. I dropped your baby on its head earlier, failed to confess on the scene, and now my mother tells me it's important you know because he might have brain failure later today."

It felt normal to admit my anti-mothering tendencies as a fourteen-year-old. My Jewish friend Jen and I would commiserate over a bag of jelly beans about the endless exhaustion little ones brought me as a babysitter and Jen as the eldest of four siblings. We imagined a life different from that of our mothers, where we would be free to run marathons unencumbered (Jen) and watch *Days of Our Lives* marathons uninterrupted (me).

I saw Jen recently. We met for brunch at a dive bar in Seattle that played Lady Gaga a few decibels too loud. I asked her about her boyfriend. She asked me about my husband. "We're still not talking kids," I laughed. "Dogs are just fine for now. You can lock 'em up when they get whiny and not have to pay a dime for someone to watch them on date night." She looked at me with pursed lips. "I'm actually really excited for kids. I even want four, like my brothers and sisters." Jen wasn't one for sarcasm, so I stopped grinning and tightened my own lips in embarrassment. "Oh, that's lovely for you. Really."

What was once a childish aversion to the responsibility and commitment that having my own kids would require now feels like a moral deficiency as an adult, like everyone has stopped their Zima-crazed partying ways and I am still that overgrown girl sleeping off a hangover in her mascara. My indifference to babies not only seems to undercut my maturity but also challenges my virtue as a Christian woman. I've been reassured by well-meaning parents, "It will be different when you have one of your own. Your mothering instinct will kick in," to which I wonder, "But what if it doesn't? Haven't I then sort of screwed the pooch for the next eighteen years?" Besides, in many ways my husband and I don't fit the stereotypes assigned to our biological sex. He is the one that plops down on the floor with a toddler and begins making funny faces. I am the one that waves at said toddler from a distance and says, "Hello...you."

Just as we find ourselves not quite fitting the expected two-sex model of gender, so too do we find ourselves outside of the two-choice model between celibacy and family life. An old adage about the latter distinction is summed up as follows. "If you want to know Christ, be married. If you want to serve Christ, be single." The assumption is, of course, that a married person has a hard time serving Christ when pressed by the demands of a spouse and children clamoring for your attention (and breasts). A single person, who is presumably remaining chaste, likewise has a hard time understanding the deep desire of Christ without it being imaged through a partner. Could being married without children be the coveted middle ground whereby one knows Christ through the intimacy of marriage but is freed to serve Christ through hospitality toward neighbors?

The very idea that married couples can have sex and not get pregnant is a recent phenomenon, made possible in large part by advancements in contraception. I recently heard a Protestant pastor lament "the sexual looseness this technology engendered" without also considering the social good it might produce. For instance, how could deciding to remain childless make better use of the earth's resources? By the fourth century AD, theologian John Chrysostom had asserted that the command to "be fruitful and multiply" from the Old Testament had already been fulfilled as evidenced by the swelling population growth in his own time. Perhaps deciding to remain childless could be seen as taking seriously the New Testament command to care for widows and orphans, especially in the wake of war, genocide, and the worldwide AIDS epidemic. If my husband and I ever do change our minds and decide to have children, we plan to adopt, an option that would likely not be possible financially or emotionally if we already had seven biological children by now. How is the common good served when, in the words of Catholic teaching, we are "open to the transmission of new life" through not just our loins but our time, energy, and resources given freely to all God's children?

Christians like me who choose not to have children are not anti-family. Regardless of our own biological decisions, I believe we are all called to mother and father the kin of Christ in a communal project of parenthood. C. S. Lewis, who never fathered biological children of his own (his wife already had children when they married), nevertheless recognized the need for all persons to care for these tiny, fragile bodies. In her book *A Sword Between the Sexes?: C.S. Lewis and the Gender Debates*, Mary Stewart Van Leeuwen explains his position: "Certain virtues (like delighting in children) are demanded of us just because of 'the kind of things we are,' as creatures made by God. And while we may not all have equal success in living up to these virtues, we need to recognize that they are the kinds of standards we should aspire to and grieve when we fail to reach them." Although I do not plan to "have children" in the conventional sense, I am beginning to recognize the need to "have children" in my life, to know the discipline of hospitality they require, to heed the call to care for them in service of the common good.

Close friends of ours welcomed their first child during Holy Week. My husband and I drove to the hospital with high anticipation.

We held this baby, this admittedly beautiful baby. We brought his parents a DVD of the comedy-duo Flight of the Conchords to get them through the next couple of nights with a sense of humor. And we started a food schedule to ensure they had meals through their first week home.

As we walked back to the car, high off the smell of baby powder, I turned to my husband and said, "So, you want one of those yet?" He looked at me with a grin and said, "Nope. I'm good for now."

And it is true. We are good, oh so good with the idea of raising this baby, although not our baby, as a little red-blooded member of Christ's body. Sure, I wonder about the intimacy we will miss by not rocking this baby to sleep in the silence of night, or about the connection we will lose if his parents move away from the neighborhood. But I also trust that the "survival of the human race" depends on sacrifices of many sorts, made for the good of all and the love of God.

Living (Together) without a Blueprint
by Bristol Huffman

BRISTOL has spent much of her life in the "in-between" places. She grew up in the middle of the country but has spent the last few years moving between the West and East Coasts. She has been a wilderness guide, an outdoor educator, and an academic tutor. Recently, she completed an Americorps term of service teaching kids in Oakland public schools how to play. Bristol studied religion at Loyola University Chicago, where she was deeply inspired by the activist theology of Roman Catholic Social Thought. She later studied Christian social ethics at the Graduate Theological Union, a progressive interfaith seminary. Her theology bears the fingerprints of all the people and places she has loved—from the conservative evangelicals of her hometown, to her feminist Catholic professors, to her queer seminary classmates. She has learned something important about Jesus from all of them and looks forward to what her next adventure will teach her about the deep, wide love of God. Bristol currently lives in Cambridge, Massachusetts with her wonderful Unitarian Universalist boyfriend, her engineer brother, and her artist sister-in-law, where she directs children and family ministries for a Lutheran church.

I told my family I was moving to Berkeley, California over dinner at an Italian restaurant in my hometown. I'd lived in the Midwest my whole life, and the journey west was prompted by my enrollment in a master's program at a progressive interfaith seminary. For my moderately Protestant, moderately conservative family, this was a bit of a stretch. Tersely expressing the views of the group, my great aunt said, "I'll pray for you."

I made the move to California with Jason, my on-again-off-again boyfriend of six years. This was our last go at on-again. I started graduate school completely convinced that we'd be engaged by the time I finished. We'd met in high school, both of us well-behaved over-achievers, leaders in our youth group, and musicians in our church worship band. We followed the blueprint we'd been given for a successful relationship: We never lived together and we never had sex.

We never got married either.

Like most of my female friends in high school and college, I was concerned with reconciling my love life with my personal faith and achieving that elusive ideal of Christian courtship. Some of the rules were straightforward—physical touch, we all knew, was a slippery slope of danger—but other rules were more confusing. Women were meant to wait faithfully for the right man to pursue them. But what exactly should your dating life look like *before* you got married?

The Christian communities I was part of didn't seem particularly comfortable talking about the more thorny ethical questions of sex and relationships. Instead of sex education, my Lutheran high school offered a required class called "Commitment and Marriage." For our final project, we were split into boy-girl pairs and given a budget with which to plan a wedding ceremony. My partner Paul and I diligently researched options for embossed invitations and reception venues. While we finished with a greater respect for the financial commitment of a wedding, I don't know that we gained any understanding of the life commitment of a marriage.

In college, I was part of a Christian community that often spent time in gender-separated discussions about appropriate values and behavior. Tension developed between the leaders and me when I disclosed that I believed it was acceptable for women to romantically pursue men. Unable to speak openly and honestly about my relationships or to find answers to my questions, I was bumbling my way through young adulthood as best I could—lonely, confused, and ashamed—like so many of the other Christian women I knew.

The end of my long-term relationship with Jason was a breaking point for me. Dating according to the Christian blueprint was supposed to come with a marriage guarantee. It worked for so many of my peers who had married right out of college. When I found myself single in my mid-twenties, halfway through seminary, I didn't understand what I'd done wrong. I felt like a failure—as a Christian, as a woman, and as a future wife. The model for relationships that I'd grown up with had let me down, and I needed a new one.

That's when Tom walked into my life.

Tom was also in seminary, studying to be a Unitarian Universalist minister. He lived fiercely, with an intensity that instantly drew me in. Despite my tattered emotional state, *he* pursued *me*. This pulled the first of many threads out of the tapestry I'd woven of what the perfect, lovable woman looked like: stable and unwounded. Tom's decisiveness, freedom from social expectations, and willingness to voice his attraction to me were shocking and appealing. He came from a place refreshingly different from where I'd been. Raised in New England by a single mother, he'd found a home in the progressive, sex-positive atmosphere of his UU youth group. He was six years older than I, and he wasn't particularly chaste.

Dating Tom would require a whole new blueprint, and I was ready to explore the process of creating one.

However, the process was neither easy nor simple. Before my wounded heart had come close to healing, I dove into this new, radically different relationship. My church friends, unsure how to categorize his politics or his religion, didn't hesitate to share their concern about my controversial new boyfriend. Jason and I had been part of a close-knit small group for two years, and we all struggled with how to navigate the breakup as a community of Christians, a community of friends. Eventually, our group disintegrated and disbanded.

I also struggled with the transition. Once I called Tom in tears after listening to a sermon about faithful womanhood. Ashamed and confused, I apologized to him for not being more submissive to him. Despite years of effort and discernment, I felt as though I'd somehow been disqualified from Christian womanhood because of my dissension from the traditional religious culture in which I'd grown up. Tom's tone was gentle as he assured me that he did not want me to be more submissive. "You're a wonderful partner," he told me, "and I want you to bring your whole self to the relationship, not hold parts of yourself back."

I realized then how much I needed to quiet the outside voices so I could tune into the voice that mattered—God's voice.

Over the course of our relationship, Tom's loving acceptance of me as a Christian woman, with my complicated dating history and baggage, helped me open space in my own heart to accept myself. Our relationship was a safe context in which to untangle my confused ideas about dating and marriage, to separate what I *really* believed from what I *thought* I should believe. Our relationship was healthy and alive in a way my previous relationships hadn't been; I was more focused on fostering a loving partnership than I was on obeying a set of unclear rules.

When Tom and I decided to move in together after a year-and-a-half, everything about the home we made together was intentional. Long before we signed a lease, we talked about our timelines for the future, our lifestyle preferences, and our expectations around cohabitation. We went to counseling together, not because our relationship was in jeopardy, but because we wanted to build a strong, lasting foundation. The choice to live together was complicated and scary, but it was a positive one, a step toward greater commitment. It wasn't a test-run for marriage or a convenient way to save money.

We could only afford a small place, and the move-in process required all kinds of cooperation, from figuring out storage dilemmas, to combining our kitchen utensils, to hand-building our bed to fit in the space. It's not possible to avoid mundane decisions when sharing the same roof, particularly when sharing the same bed. We weren't on some kind of shortcut to "easy street." We were slogging through the tough stuff together, one day at a time.

Our home became the way home should be: sacred and safe. We wanted a space that was quiet and peaceful, so we minimized the technology that came into our home: no Internet or TV, no dishwasher or microwave, and no landline phone. We developed a habit of praying together each morning before we left the house. We set up an altar with crosses, prayer beads, stones, and a chalice—the symbol for Unitarian Universalism. We listened to sermons and sang worship songs together. None of this happened in a way that felt showy or pious; it happened in the way that spirituality breathes in and out of our everyday lives. Our home became a melding of all aspects of our lives.

That we weren't married didn't diminish the importance or the delight of those early days of living together. We did crosswords in bed, cooked meals together, danced to 80s music, and played late-night board games. We also argued about financial decisions, struggled to maintain our self-care, doubted our future, and disagreed about how to organize the dish rack. It was awesome and it was terrifying and it was fun and it was challenging. Our relationship deepened and expanded in new ways.

When it came to living with my boyfriend, I spent surprisingly little time and energy worrying about how much God was judging me and more time and energy worrying about how other Christians were judging me. I don't know whether this was because other people actually were judging me or because I was projecting my own fears and insecurities onto them. Either way, it was hard to be "out" about my new status.

It took me nine months to get up the courage to tell my parents. My parents weren't openly critical of my decision, but they weren't unconcerned either. Within the first few minutes of every visit with them, my dad would say, as if on cue, "So, when's this engagement happening? You're running out of time." And he wasn't the only one. Even complete strangers, who knew nothing more of me than what five minutes of small talk had revealed, would ask if I was getting married soon. The complex reality of my relationship with Tom seemed somehow less relevant than my marital status.

I quickly became aware of the double standard involved: Aside from me, no one was pressuring Tom to get married. This was a message for young women. *Why should he buy the cow when he can get the milk for free?*

Living with my boyfriend, it seemed, was like a public announcement that I was giving away my milk for free. The problem with premarital cohabitation wasn't so much the issue of sexual sin or financial risk; it was a direct challenge to traditional gender roles. In the Christian culture I'm part of, there's something unfulfilled about a single woman, something dangerously incomplete. I kept getting the feeling that once I settled down and got engaged, everyone would breathe a big sigh of relief.

I do want to get married. I've spent plenty of nights fretting about my future, fearing that I've thrown away my chance for lifelong partnership and worrying that if things don't work out with Tom, no man will want me because I've wandered too far from that model of Christian womanhood I abandoned in college. Letting go of one's childhood romantic fantasies is painful. I've had to let go of the idea that being a woman who loves God necessarily translates into being a wife who marries her first serious boyfriend. In reality, Tom and I are partners who are committed to building a life together, and marriage has always been part of our plan.

I'm not a cow, I'm not for sale, and I'm not giving anything away for free. When Tom and I decide to get married, it will be a choice we make together. It will be a choice we pray about, a choice we talk about with our friends and family, and a choice we have grown into. It will be a choice we make because we love each other, not because our religious culture expects it of us.

Sometimes I wish I had a different story to tell, but this is the story that's mine. This is the life that I live. I want to live that life with integrity, acting in front of people the same way I would act in front of God, to follow the path dictated by a faithful spirit, even when that path leads out of places that are familiar and into places of fear. There are no blueprints for that kind of living. You just have to discover as you go.

High Stakes Whack-a-Mole: Noticing and Naming Sexism in the Church

by Lara Blackwood Pickrel

LARA BLACKWOOD PICKREL is an ordained minister in the Christian Church (Disciples of Christ) and serves Hillside Christian Church in Kansas City, Missouri as their associate minister for youth and young adults. She is passionate about finding ways to weave together ancient Christian stories and practices, contemporary needs, and many generations of God's people. Writing and other creative practices are an essential part of her ministry, along with summer camps, social media, women's issues, sexuality education, and deep conversation over coffee. Lara co-edited and co-authored *Oh God! Oh God! Oh God: Young Adults Speak Out About Sexuality and Christian Spirituality* (Chalice Press, 2010). You can find more of her written work at Chalice Press, The Thoughtful Christian Blog, and her personal blog: http://serendipitysoiree.wordpress.com. You can also check out how she and her youth ministry colleagues are taking risks for the sake of the Church by visiting www.nPartnership.org.

I stand at the back of the aisle, near the main entrance to the sanctuary. The benediction hangs in the air above us as congregants converge into a line, waiting to shake my hand. I accept the "good mornings," sermon comments, and updates on prayer concerns with a smile on my face in spite of the drained feeling that always accompanies preaching. Exhausting though it may be, I love preaching the Gospel.

Then it happens. A woman shakes my hand and with downcast eyes says, "That was a lovely talk."

My mind jerks to attention, reeling a bit. It's amazing how much one seemingly innocuous sentence can sting. *That was a lovely talk.* You see, this isn't an isolated incident—it has happened before. Every time our head of staff preaches, this woman compliments him on his *sermon*—but when I preach, it's a *talk.*

I notice this difference every time it happens. Am I being too sensitive? The words are nice enough, after all. What could possibly be wrong with something so simple and sweet?

In my church tradition, the Christian Church (Disciples of Christ), many of the battles fought over women's leadership took place several generations before I was born. We began ordaining women in the late 1800s. In the 1970s, women began to enter theological schools and pursue ordination in greater numbers, and those numbers steadily increased in the years that followed. By the time I entered seminary in the fall of 2000, close to half of the students were women, and it had become far more common for people in our congregations to consider hiring a female pastor. Some congregations still held out, refusing to have women as elders or pastors, but these churches became the minority. To many, it seemed the battles had not only already been fought—they had been won.

In seminary, when I carried around textbooks for a course in feminist theology, some of my classmates scoffed. Sure, feminist theology had value, but it was purely historical. Feminism was anachronistic, a movement from a different age: a time when sexism was real. What was the point of taking a class that focused on women's issues when those issues were a thing of the past, no longer alive or relevant in church life? Our congregations were losing members, young people were viewing the church with greater ambivalence, and no one could figure out how to compete with the megachurches. With so many other "real issues" facing pastors, what was the point of resurrecting problems that no longer existed?

When I pointed out the ways that women still struggled to find work, still dealt with prejudice and gender stereotypes, and still fought to have their prophetic voices taken seriously in the Church,

I was told that I had a chip on my shoulder. I was supposed to focus on what I *could* have, the churches that *would* hire me, and the improvements that *had* been made, rather than the places where sexism had moved underground. In other words, when something sexist was done or said, I wasn't supposed to notice.

A decade later, I still notice sexism all around us—especially in the Church. My sisters in ministry are many now, and most of us are employed, yet we still are paid less money than our male colleagues. We are more likely to lead small congregations or to serve as associate pastors in larger multi-staff churches. Though our denomination's general minister and president is a woman, our "big steeple" churches still hire mostly men to serve as senior or executive pastors. When things go wrong and a congregation fires a clergywoman, the immediate response is often to say "Well, we'll never hire one of *those* again." Systemically, there is still a problem, and though many of us notice and speak out, more often than not we are treated like a nuisance when we do so. To notice is a "distraction" or a betrayal because we should be focusing on other things, like saving the church from the steady decline in membership that has taken place throughout the United States over the past few decades.

At the local level, things are much the same but even trickier to deal with. If I stand up and point out the sexism present in the denominational system, it is less personal. I'm confronting the system, a thing, an object. But in a congregation in which I serve, work, and live, if I stand up and point out sexism when I see it, it is very personal. I'm confronting individuals, and individuals rarely enjoy being confronted.

Consequently, in day-to-day congregational life, dealing with sexism has become an activity somewhat akin to the old arcade game Whack-a-Mole. Things may seem normal for a while, but then, seemingly out of nowhere, a sexist attitude or prejudice pops up. I turn, mallet in hand, to confront the offending statement or behavior, but my surprise at its arrival gives the offender just enough time to drop underground, insisting that offense was not meant. Disoriented, I stare at the empty hole a bit too long, wondering, "Did that just happen?" And, in that delay, another attitude or comment pops up across the board.

As I look back over twelve years of ministry, the game board stretches out long and wide. Though the moles pop up in ways that seem unpredictable, I'm beginning to see that there are patterns at work—patterned types of attack, patterned timing, and patterned excuses. These patterns include the following:

Your Work is Less Than . . .

For those of us who work in very specific types of ministries such as youth ministry or children's ministry, this pattern is often more easily observable than others. Men who feel called to youth ministry or children's ministry experience dismissive attitudes from church members and have likely heard this sentence: "When you become a *real minister*, you will . . ." Women who work in these areas of ministry often receive a double dose of disdain because they are women *and* they work in specialized ministries that are less valued by the Church at large.

As a youth minister, I've been told that I'm less capable of leading a whole church, because I have no pastoral care experience, no experience with budgets or fundraising, and no experience with people of other generations. But that's hogwash. Youth ministers provide pastoral care nonstop because teens are constantly in a state of crisis, both large and small. Beyond that, youth ministry is usually the one programmatic piece of a congregation that is not fully funded in the church budget, so youth ministers spend a disproportionate amount of time raising money, spending personal funds, crunching numbers, and observing line items in order to make ends meet for their ministries. And, in the midst of this, people who minister to young people end up ministering to entire families: parents, stepparents, foster parents, grandparents and other extended family. So why are these specialized ministries "less than"? It is because of the underlying assumption that working with children and young people is *women's work*.

You're Unprofessional . . .

Often, women clergy are subject to all manner of criticisms and accusations that are couched in terms of "professionalism." For example, my hair is a common topic of conversation among some church members. Because I keep it long instead of in a shorter style, I have been informed on numerous occasions that my hairstyle is unprofessional. If I pull it back in a ponytail, my hair is childish; if I keep it in a braid or bun, it is matronly; if I wear it loose, it is distracting.

Similarly, female pastors meet constant criticism about the clothing we wear. Wear something shapeless and you are frumpy; wear something tailored and you risk being ogled; wear that amazing pair of zebra-print pumps and you are too flashy. Though there are certainly outfits that would be inappropriate to wear to the office or to Sunday morning worship, this doesn't explain the dynamic that is at play here. What is really going on is that some people don't know what to do with our hairstyles or clothing (and the bodies they cover), because we are women. Breasts and curves are so closely associated with sex and desire that some church members are uncomfortable no matter what women wear.

Hey, Good-Lookin'. . .

In a similar vein, sexist jabs often arise disguised as compliments. Operating under the assumption that "women need to be told that they look good," church members already focus too much on our outward appearance, greeting us over post-worship handshakes with remarks about our earrings or our choice of blouse. In the midst of this environment, it is easy to lob a velvet-covered brick at the pastor. For example, after pinch-hitting for my head of staff one Sunday morning, a church member who bristles at women in leadership shared the following appraisal of my sermon, "Well—you're better-looking than the other preacher." Other folks in line could take this as an innocent compliment, rather than seeing it for what it was: a jab meant to dismiss me and my work.

I'm Just Old-Fashioned . . .

Sometimes I manage to actually whack a mole as it pops up from underground. In the course of a conversation, someone makes a blanket statement about what women are like and I am able to call her on it, naming the proclamation for what it really is: a stereotype. Or in a meeting, someone goes on about which jobs and ministries women would be good at, and I am able to point out the gender bias that is woven throughout the speech.

When the proverbial mallet makes contact, there is generally a brief moment of shocked silence. Then the excuses come. "I guess I'm just old-fashioned." Citing cultural and generational differences, the offender wipes her hands of the matter and assumes a posture of innocence. Sometimes the Bible is pulled out and a snippet of Paul is read aloud to bolster that position: "I permit no woman to teach or to have authority over a man; she is to keep silent" (1 Timothy 2:12, NRSV). With a proof-text and a smile, the mole slips back underground before I have a chance to counter the jab with the historical context of Paul's saying or the places throughout his letters in which he celebrates the ministry of individual women who were his colleagues and supporters.

You're Too Sensitive . . .

And sometimes when a mole is caught, the person goes straight into offensive mode. "You're just too sensitive! You see things that aren't even there!" With these words and a shrug, the burden of proof gets thrown back onto my shoulders. I must either prove that someone really does have a bias against women, or I must let it go, allowing the mole to escape so that he can attack again another day.

Most church folk I encounter really do support women in ministry. Most of the people I serve have a genuine appreciation for the ways that I serve alongside them, and many of them have truly come to love me for who I am. A majority of our congregation encourages and empowers women to serve at all levels of leadership, and they have demonstrated a commitment to educating and nurturing the youngest girls and women in our church family so that they can make their own place in the church. Even those who continue to carry traces of sexism in their beliefs show their support for the women on our staff. On the whole, they are good people most of the time.

This is a good thing, of course. But it also makes noticing sexism all the more troublesome. Because most do support women in ministry, there is more cover for the few who don't. Like someone who says, "I'm not racist—I have a (insert ethnicity here) friend," they can hide behind the fact that their congregation has a woman pastor, using her presence as proof that they don't have a problem. And because some people fervently believe that they have moved beyond sexism in their church, they are less willing or able to see the traces and pockets of prejudice that remain in their midst.

When I notice the bias that remains, I force my people to look at a reality they do not want to see. When I notice the comments, the assumptions, the unequal value placed on different kinds of work, I confront my people with a reflection of themselves that they don't like. When I notice sexism, people become uncomfortable.

Consequently, in the very act of noticing and naming the sexism that still lingers in the Church, I do the unspeakable.

On Being a Strong Woman

by Julie Clawson

 JULIE CLAWSON is a mother, writer, and former pastor who lives in Austin, Texas with her family. She graduated from Wheaton College in Wheaton, Illinois, where she also earned a graduate degree in intercultural studies. She then spent over a decade serving in churches in the Chicago suburbs and is currently back in graduate school studying theology. Julie's passions include working for social justice and gender equality. She is also a bit of a theology nerd, a huge sci-fi/fantasy geek, wannabe foodie, and board game fan. Julie is the author of *Everyday Justice: The Global Impact of Our Daily Choices* and *The Hunger Games and the Gospel: Bread, Circuses, and the Kingdom of God*. She can be found at julieclawson.com.

As the superheroes rode in on their motorcycles, my daughter clamored to get a glimpse of her favorite characters. For a seven-year-old recently obsessed with comic books, our family vacation to Universal Studios allowed her a chance to see a few of her heroes in action. After the characters acted out a swift defeat of a villain for the cheering crowds, they announced they would be available to sign autographs and take pictures. As the crowds parted, we were able to easily spot the long lines that were forming around Captain America, Spiderman, and Wolverine, but Storm and Rogue (the only two female characters) were nowhere to be seen. My daughter, having wanted to meet these two most of all, commented with disappointment, "No one wants to see them because no one thinks girls can be superheroes too."

We finally found Storm and Rogue stationed together seemingly out of the way beside a building with no one in line for pictures, and my daughter was able to meet her heroes. But the entire incident troubled me.

Like any good feminist mother, I try to encourage my children to challenge the constrictions of gender stereotypes. Naturally, I want my daughter to believe that girls cannot only like comic books and be superheroes, but that there is nothing strange about it, either. This is becoming increasingly difficult though as she gets told repeatedly by other kids and adults that it isn't normal for girls to read comic books, or like Star Wars, or play with LEGOS— some of her other passions. I can hardly count the number of times she's come up to me at the playground crying after a group of boys told her she can't play superheroes with them because she is a girl. I even had to recently defend her to her counselor regarding a Mother's Day card she was making for me. My daughter had been instructed to create a card that reflected my interests and she, knowing that I read comics with her and that my husband had already bought a Batgirl t-shirt as my present, decided to draw pictures of Batgirl on the card. Her counselor insisted that my daughter was doing the assignment wrong since there was no way that a mother would want Batgirl on a card. My daughter was hurt and even more confused when the counselor accused her of making things up when she tried to explain that her mommy really does like superheroes. That she immediately assumed no one wanted to meet the female superheroes that day at Universal Studios demonstrates how deeply those messages are affecting her.

In this highly gender-segregated world of children's games and toys I want to help her overcome these messages. I know for that to happen she needs to be surrounded by strong women, both real and pretend, who demonstrate that girls can do anything. I want her books to be filled with girls who go on adventures and her movies to show confident girls who seek to make the world a better place. I want her to think it is just as normal for a woman to be a brilliant and humane doctor, scientist, politician, or pastor as it is for women to be mothers and schoolteachers. And while I know there are numerous books and movies that depict strong and healthy female characters, the ones that seem to gain the most popularity, and therefore attract my daughter's attention, often limit this definition of strength to simply the physical ability to defeat one's opponents. I find myself cringing frequently as my daughter defines heroes as characters whose strengths directly contradict the Christian faith that I am trying to model for her.

As a follower of Christ who believes in loving my neighbor and choosing the path of peacemaking, I am uneasy with labeling the ability to hurt and destroy others as a strength. Sadly, popular culture (especially superhero stories) often defines strong women primarily according to their ability to be just as violent, if not more so, as their male counterparts. I can understand the basic rationale behind this depiction. Male superheroes have always been out there physically fighting for their cause—just picture Captain America fighting Nazis in the Second World War or Superman defeating bad guys for the sake of "truth, justice, and the American Way." Thus when comic book writers and movie producers include strong women in their stories they simply give those women the same characteristics already seen in men, but with the addition of a skin-tight costume and high-heels. So we get to see Black Widow taking out a group of thugs and firing away at invading aliens all while looking sexy with perfect hair. What we don't get is any nuanced understanding of strength beyond the ability to fight.

The problem is that while these modern superhero stories appear to include strong, self-sufficient women rather than mere love interests, they do so by reinforcing harmful gender stereotypes even as they seemingly try to subvert them. In the modern Western world there is a pervasive assumption that physical strength and the ability to fight are masculine attributes that constitute strength. Attributes typically seen as feminine, such as being nurturing, creative, and merciful, are seen as weaknesses. Thus if a woman is to appear as strong in this cultural context she must accept these stereotypes by rejecting the supposedly feminine attributes and adopting the masculine ones. For this reason, female lead characters in our films and video games generally tend to be ultra-violent, unforgiving, and often incapable of relationships. We get Wonder Woman, the Amazon warrior, with her deep-seated suspicion of men, and Lara Croft, the sexier and far more violent version of Indiana Jones. There's the self-centered and suspicious Cat Woman and the cold, friendless, zombie-killing machines of Resident Evil. Even in the shows targeted for younger audiences, like *Teen Titans*, it is the female character who struggles with relationships and social contexts outside of fighting the bad guys. Everything typically associated with so-called feminine weakness—mercy, compassion, humility, vulnerability, and self-sacrifice—is discarded as these women become exactly like, if not better than, the male heroes the world already accepts.

This message is disturbing enough insofar as it reaffirms gender stereotypes that assume that women are weak and inferior, yet as a Christian what I have a harder time accepting is the definition of strength itself. I do my best to follow the teachings of Jesus as guidelines for my life, and his words are as countercultural today as they were in the first-century Roman world. Instead of supporting cultural habits like admiring the privileged, powerful, and wealth, Jesus proclaimed that the meek, the merciful, and the poor are those blessed by God. He taught against taking revenge by encouraging his followers suffering under Roman occupation not to take an eye for an eye but to love their enemies instead. His message encouraged people to work for freedom for the oppressed and to stand against systems of injustice. He offered an alternative to patterns of revenge and retribution. Strength, as Jesus defined it, had nothing to do with violence and power, but with one's ability to choose the harder path of forgiveness, subversive living, and sacrificial love. His followers still resisted the dehumanizing ways of their culture, but they did so through creative, nonviolent acts of strength.

The way of life Jesus taught has never been popular with the dominant culture. His habit of welcoming women, children, and the poor did not appeal to those whose privilege and power rested on the presumed inferiority of others. As the church became more culturally accepted, it often left behind the teachings of Jesus for the very ways of the culture it initially had been called to resist. It came to accept the power of the sword instead of the call to love and care for both neighbor and enemy, reaffirming the false idea that violence is a strength while love is a weakness. As these traits were commonly associated with the masculine and the feminine respectively, men continued to be valued as strong and superior while women were seen as weak and inferior. Inasmuch as these attitudes persist in our own culture today, those of us who try to follow the way of Jesus often find just as much opposition from within the church as we do from the culture. So despite the call of Jesus to feed the hungry, lift up the weak, and bring freedom to the oppressed, I've heard some Christians reject such endeavors as socialist propaganda antithetical to Christianity. In some churches I have even heard that my Christian faith is suspect if I do not support the preemptive wars of the United States. Those with power to control or defeat others are praised, while the way of loving one's neighbor is rejected as weak and inferior—it's the comic book narrative that associates strength with power and violence, just with religious packaging.

As I see my daughter claiming female heroes who take on this cultural definition of male strength and who fight and kill their enemies as proof of their liberation as women, it disturbs me. And the trend is not just confined to popular culture. As women find liberation from reductive definitions that restrict them to the roles of wife and mother, the traits typically associated with such roles, such as nurturance, forgiveness, and sacrifice, are rejected as well. While the message that women must nurture and sacrifice themselves for a family has been used to silence and restrict women, it is not those traits that are themselves oppressive to women. On the contrary, forgiveness and sacrificial love are the very things Jesus affirmed as strengths blessed by God. These aren't traits that imply weaknesses, but strengths that are needed to build up and heal others instead of seeking to destroy them. Loving others sacrificially does not mean giving up one's personality or freedom, but choosing to honor the image of God in others by treating them with love in all things. Women shouldn't have to choose between giving themselves up as a means to forgive and nurture and abandoning such traits in order to appear strong. But all too often the message I hear from both popular culture and the church is that those are the only two options.

Caught between the cultural assumption—which the church seems to echo—that such traits connote weakness, and the feminist urge to resist reductive definitions of women, I find it increasingly taboo to affirm the way of being that Jesus proposed. As a feminist, a Christ-follower, and a mother, I think it is more important than ever for both the imaginary and the real world to be populated with women who demonstrate such strengths in all aspects of life.

Instead of seeing women squeezed into leather cat suits and ridiculously high heels so they can round-kick the bad guys and blow up things to prove their strength, I wish I was seeing women and men upheld as heroes for building a better world in the ways Jesus proposed. Instead of perpetuating gender stereotypes that associate strength with power, violence, and men, which then lead women to reject positive traits like care, forgiveness, and self-giving love, I want to challenge the taboos and redefine what true strength is.

I don't want either my daughter or my son assuming that, like their heroes, the only way they can be strong is by defining forgiveness and sacrificial love as feminine and therefore weak and inferior. I want them both to see such things as strengths. Period. Strength isn't hurting others or giving in to fear by seeking revenge; strength is resisting injustice and oppression by living in the countercultural ways of mercy. One builds a better world not by destroying one's enemies, but by nurturing relationships and caring for those in need wherever they might be found. Such acts are neither masculine nor feminine, but simply what Jesus defined as the best way to be human. Sadly, this way of living challenges the ways of a world that would rather cling to domineering power and privilege (and use gender stereotypes in order to do so).

My daughter still reads comic books and pretends to fight for the rebellion in a galaxy far, far away. There is much to be valued in such stories despite their flawed portrayals of strength, and, unlike women of generations past, at least she is surrounded by a popular culture increasingly populated by assertive, strong, and capable women. From Princess Leia and Hermione to Wonder Woman and Spidergirl, her movies and books depict women as more than just pretty objects for men to rescue. Despite the boys on the playground telling her that girls can't play superheroes, she is also exposed to messages that let her know there is nothing she can't do simply because she is a girl. I just wish I did not constantly have to deconstruct for her the negative messages tied to those depictions of strength. I hope that together we can smash the cultural taboos feeding the insidious lie that strength involves destroying and harming others and instead live in the way of Christ—a way in which strength means that we, women and men together, creatively and lovingly work to build a better world.

Crafting Bonds of Blood
by Patience Perry

PATIENCE HARRISON PERRY is an educator, dancer, farmer, counselor, artist, and athlete. She enjoys grueling physical activity and dirt under her fingernails. She is mother to three hobbits and married to a giant. A lover of all creatures great and small, she started her career as an inner-city elementary school teacher, then left the city to travel the world, eventually returning to North Carolina to become an outdoor educator. Today, she lives on High Haven Farm and continues to facilitate holistic experiences that explore the intersections of the mind, body, spirit, and nature as the assistant director of Watauga Global Community at Appalachian State University.

My tale is one of creative exploration. Of tinkering and toying with human, spiritual, and environmental elements. Of re-weaving earth-based rituals and Christian traditions into spiritual and sensual female fabric.

Growing up, I spent a lot of time in the woods. My mother held the conviction that kids should spend their free time outdoors. There was no coming inside until she called us at next mealtime. Two things resulted: I developed a love for nature, and I became an extreme tomboy.

Things ran smoothly until puberty. I couldn't seem to reconcile how to be attractive without being a distraction to my guy friends. I didn't want attention for my potential as a make-out partner, but rather wanted to be their partners in throwing rocks, jumping in leaf piles, spitting from bridges, and racing alongside each other. I knew from Mom (both religious teacher and moral guide) that premarital sex was a sin and that Mexicans are "very fertile people." Therefore, my body became something to hide and cover in order to keep on playing with the boys.

I learned later that there is a BIG difference between what is *sensual* versus what is *sexual*. Women are sensual creatures. Sensuality involves what is tactile, visual, auditory, olfactory, and delectable. It involves joy and confidence in our bodies. It involves cooperation rather than competition among one another. It involves peace and beauty as we dance and flow with the Holy Spirit. In other societies past and present, beautiful and elaborate rituals occurred in celebration of women's sensual nature. And plainly, *nature* is an essential component in the alchemy of womanhood. Out in nature is where our senses are best explored.

As a youth exploring the out of doors, I felt alive, big, expansive, curious, connected. On Sunday, when I crossed the church threshold, I felt stifled, subdued, insignificant, and artificial. Instead of the chatter of birds, the sound of the wind, or the smells of foliage, I heard stale silence interrupted by the echoes of high heels on the tile flooring. A chorus of mothers shushed their toddlers in an environment devoid of smells.

At the time, I perceived indoor church activity as superficial, and I assumed everybody was looking at me and making judgments. Meanwhile outdoor activity was rich with meaning and provided a freedom from human criticism. Daily, I was wearing sport bras to flatten my chest and baggy clothes to veil my figure. I wasn't getting any help from my available Christian resources about how to be a beautiful "child of God" without shame. What I needed to ask Mom / *Abuela* / priest / someone / anyone is, "How can the church address my transition into womanhood?"

I'm positive my mother gave me a copy of *Are you there God? It's me, Margaret* to read, but I can't remember having any revelations afterward. A little homily about becoming an adult and expressing our powerful inner animal would have been timely. The church offers sacred ritual through Baptism, Communion, Matrimony, and Ordination to deepen our understanding of self and fortify our relationship with God. But how about something to address Menarche? Pregnancy? Or Childbirth?

Today, a girl seeking information about her anticipated first period generally utilizes two sources—the Internet and her friends. Neither of these brings her closer to God, elevates her status in the family, celebrates her role in the community, or promotes her role in the web of life and the natural world. Yet, these are the precise goals needed for Christians to save their daughters from the perils of our hyper-sexualized culture.

Other cultures embrace girls as they undergo puberty through rites of passage ceremonies signifying physical and spiritual gravity. Contrary to the paradigm in the Judeo-Christian tradition that women are "ritually unclean" during their period, several indigenous cultures recognize menstruation as an auspicious occasion. Among those, the Navajo and Mescalero Apaches of North America, the Aztec and Incas of Latin and South America, Aborigines from Australia, certain Japanese, people from various regions in Asia, and the Zulu and other tribes in Africa utilize menstruation rites of passage.

I would have benefitted from something powerful and complex to resolve my inner turmoil. Something to surmount self-absorption and the fog of an identity crisis. Wisdom imparted by female mentors. Domestic lessons on topics from sensual expression to culinary magic. A challenging physical task to complete. Reflective time in isolation. An opportunity to listen for a message from God. An outward sign, service performed, or handmade offering demonstrating an individual's capacity for mature responsibilities. A feast signifying a coming of age. Something vaguely reminiscent of a *Quinceañera* but without all the *bling*.

Despite being of Mexican-American heritage, I was never introduced to the concept of a *Quinceañera*. Being of an inquisitive disposition, I consulted Mom. No luck. My two aunts. Nothing concrete. They suspected that our families were unable to conduct a *Quinceañera* because they were too poor. Since my grandparents are deceased, I was referred to my eldest maternal great aunt. Maggie, at 84, is the only Alonzo, out of thirteen siblings, still alive. She confirmed it "Honey, I never even heard of it until I was an adult and after I had children," she said. "There never was any money, so I guess they figured, what's the point?" The Villaseñors, Alonzos, Valdivias, and the Gonzales were the families of my four great-grandparents, who were all born in Aguascalientes, Mexico and migrated when it was basically an open border. They took up residence in the newly established state of Kansas and commenced to labor and toil. Devoutly Catholic, but stricken with poverty, they refrained from passing this cultural tradition and rite of passage on to their children.

Yet I crave a version of this rite of passage for my daughter. To be honored for her womanhood. To be confident in her relationships with her body, family, community, and the earth. I want her to be able to talk about having a period in front of others without embarrassment or to dispose of a tampon and not need to wrap it in half a roll of toilet paper to disguise the object in the bathroom trash can. What a glaring waste of resources and an example of the skewed proportions the taboo of menstruation has attained! Why hide our menses?

Imagine if ALL women were validated for their potential to create life as evident in their monthly cycle. Imagine if such rites existed and were available for girls and women in Christian culture. How is it that we bless "beasts" (during rituals honoring and protecting household pets) and bless throats (during rituals to stave off illness on the Feast Day of St. Blaise), but the church does not acknowledge a girl celebrating her first menses or a pregnant woman anticipating birth? Surely these are occasions of initiation, and ones which draw us closer to the divine. They are occasions marked by blood, humility, and faith.

I am seeking ways that we can strengthen and reinvigorate women through the common bonds of blood. Menstrual blood. Monthly blood which all women shed with sacrificial cramps. Fertile blood which when rinsed out of cotton pads or diluted from menstrual cups may be ritually applied to houseplants or outdoor landscaping as a natural fertilizer. Sacred blood which could be included as a nutritious ingredient in foods to be consumed by people. A sacrifice both Jesus-like in physical and metaphorical significance. His words at the Last Supper linked Christians to ancient earth-based practice: "This is my body. Take this and eat it. This is my blood. Take this and drink it." Literally, our menses were intended to nourish a life. When flushed out of my body, it can still serve the same purpose as it did in the time before Christ. Although Christians struggle to navigate this discussion that conjures deep pagan connotations, when I show them glorious Christmas cactus blooms in the middle of July (fertilized with my own blood) they are inclined to view my actions favorably.

Women can hardly talk about their bodies, their urges, or their menstruation comfortably (and most men squirm right out of their chairs, add a humorous remark, and promptly depart the room). Marketing ads encourage us to *"outsmart* Mother Nature" with brand-name disposable "feminine products." Plastic panty liners, pads, and tampons consist of chemically laden cotton, rayon, polyester, polyacrylate, and other petroleum-derived ingredients. In the case of tampons, we directly expose the vaginal tissue to these toxic chemicals, fragrances, and synthetic fibers where they can accumulate, irritate, or enter our blood stream. *Really?* Upon removal, feminine products linger indefinitely in a landfill or oceanic gyre (floating pollution which has accumulated in each of the five oceans) along with their plastic wrappers, strings, and applicators, since they are not biodegradable. Do the math: three products used each day, during a five-day period, twelve months each year. If started at age sixteen and ended with menopause at fifty-one, that's an estimated individual contribution of 6,300 menstrual waste products in one lifetime. *How is any of this smart?*

When describing my menstruation, I refer to it as my Moon Time. That way, I acknowledge the cycles of life and death. I validate my similarities to the oceans and tides. I try to avoid all the negative connotations of weakness surrounding "having a period" and instead summon elemental and divine strength. A woman's body operates in accordance with nature. AWESOME. Women intuitively and hormonally respond to each other. We're like wolves. COOL. I remember taking an extended camping trip with other women and being startled when I started bleeding much earlier than anticipated. That was the day I discovered that menstrual cycles are relational. We are inextricably linked to the women in our closest proximity.

Now, when I lead camping trips or retreats, I forewarn the female participants to prepare for their Moon Time and recognize its arrival as a symbol of our common bond. I suggest journal prompts, eco-art, authentic movement, percussion music with found objects, horticulture projects, and extended wilderness immersion to examine our natural selves. They begin to ask, "Where does the 'me' end and the natural world begin?" The boundaries of the ego start to blur and with it, a wave of creativity and sensual confidence emerges. We establish an opening ritual and class agreements which validate individuals as well as those of the collective whole. One year, students decided that an individual would feed the class on the occasion of her Moon Time. Toward the end of the semester, we were enjoying hormonally synchronized monthly feasts. Working with young women has opened my eyes to the possibilities of the future. As Western society shifts to embrace dynamic visions of what is feminine, act more sustainably, and become more environmentally conscientious, the relevance of women's menstrual practices becomes obvious. And lingering taboos seem, well, archaic. Shouldn't a modern babe be able to discuss her cramps and have her hip boyfriend respond with compassion and maturity?

I'd like to see our society embrace women's rituals and reconcile our disconnection with creation. I choose to make decisions regarding my body, blood, and birthing which align with this end goal in mind. After the birth of my first son, we asked the hospital nurses to save my placenta for us to take home. Incredulous, the nurses complained, but eventually complied. I was astounded at the massive resistance from the medical community. Apparently their version of birthing did not include this lack of sanitation. But I had big plans for it: to plant a tree with the placenta under its roots. Now imagine our family connection to this tree.

Although I have been the recipient and facilitator of many women's rituals, several Christian friends have been shy, fearful, unsupportive, and occasionally unable to participate because these rituals borrow concepts from other indigenous cultural traditions. However, for the most part these rituals have been warmly received. They are intended to unify, not polarize. I have been pleasantly surprised by the enthusiasm of some of my most staunchly conservative Christian friends on a few occasions. One of my neighbors, a homeschooling mom, and devoted wife, took photos throughout my Mother Blessing ritual. Her black-and-white photographs captured the soft textures of my pregnant belly. When reviewing them later, she expounded on the striking similarities to a globe. Something clicked (other than the camera). "Ahhhh," she said. "Mother Earth."

Of the many women's rituals in which I have participated, the most powerful occurred outside on our farm and helped me prepare during pregnancy for the home-birth of my second son. Three female friends coordinated a ceremony for invitees. While the husbands supervised children and slaved over supper, the women hiked up to a secluded place in the sunny pasture.

During this Mother Blessing, each read poems and prayers, shared quotes from scripture, sang songs or hymns, contributed to my foot massage, and added flower embellishments in my hair. I was garlanded with a chain of daisies and sat among a circle of women. Collectively, they created a physical symbol of strength and support for my upcoming labor as each participant added three unique beads to a bracelet simultaneous with a prayer. One prayer was for me. One prayer was for the baby. One prayer was for our family.

The ceremony waned as each female member wrapped a spool of red string around her wrist—bonded together briefly. This visceral symbol remained while a poem was read. Then, shears were passed around. We knotted our individual bracelets. But the sentiment of connectivity lingered. Just as we are part of our mothers until the umbilical cord is cut but remain unified in love. Just as we are part of God's great mystery, yet he resides within us. I was filled with joy and touched by grace. Our ceremony was one elaborate version of prayer.

The women were instructed to wear the bracelet 24-7 until they received a phone call that I had begun labor. Each lit a candle and said a prayer when they received the call. When the baby was born, they cut the string bracelet off of their wrists and blew out their candles with a second prayer of thanks. While my first birth took thirty hours at a hospital, my second birth at home took just six. *Thanks be to God!*

Prayer is, perhaps, the simplest ritual act in which I engage. *Abuela* taught us to work hard, love fervently, and pray often. She could be found many hours of the day, lips silently moving, with her rosary in hand. I know she prayed for me. She told me such. She also asked me to pray for her. When I was young, I couldn't quite understand how little prayers coming from a small me could possibly have the same potency as powerful prayers coming from Domatila Alonzo Gonzales—devout Christian servant. I was quite convinced I was running a deficit. But later in life, I realized that she had many, many people praying for her and praying with her. As she aged, she would sit out on the back porch and say, "These old bones ache." And so I would offer her a massage. It became our ritual. She would pray for the world, and I would simultaneously massage as I added my prayers to hers amongst the beauty of her roses and statue of Our Lady of Guadalupe.

Although she is gone from this world, her grandmother ways permeate my actions today. I seek opportunities to acknowledge my miniscule role in God's great creation through a lifestyle and faith practice that maximizes sensual expression, ecological wisdom, and creative ritual. I am learning. Still learning. Humble as I craft.

Leaving a Marriage, Finding Jesus
by Sarah McGiverin

SARAH MCGIVERIN has always loved to meet new people, to learn their stories, and to get them talking about Jesus. She has brought Jesus into the conversation on her elementary school playground, from behind the wheel of a cab and behind the counter of a coffee shop, at college keggers, while having her hair cut, and in the back office of a convenience store. Through these continuing weekday encounters Sarah encountered the holiness of life beneath the Sunday morning performance of perfection. As a Sunday school teacher, a pastor, and a teaching assistant at Duke Divinity School, Sarah encouraged those in her charge to be wholly authentic and to allow their whole selves to be loved—even and especially the scariest, ugliest, most hidden parts. Now as a writer and a consultant to local church pastors, Sarah continues to believe that learning to accept God's love for our whole selves is the key to loving others wisely and well.

Every night Chris would stomp around the apartment shouting that I was ruining his life: by not agreeing to invite a friend to have sex with us, by not sweeping that day, by allowing him to run out of cigarettes. After throwing a biscuit at me one evening, he blamed me for reacting poorly and thereby ruining dinner. But this night was worse than usual: Chris's angry monologue had gone on for more than an hour. I was trying something new: not shouting back. It wasn't working. My occasional quiet replies seemed to be making him angrier.

"I understand, Chris, but my therapist thinks—"

"Oh your *therapist*! Your *therapist*!" he mocked. "It must be nice to get to be depressed," Chris said bitterly. "It must be nice to just lay there and not do anything."

Yeah, it was a real vacation, feeling like an empty shell of myself. Just getting out of bed and dressing each morning was an effort.

"*I* have too many responsibilities. I have to be *at work*. If I don't work, I don't get paid! And then where would you be? Because you sure as hell don't pay for anything!"

It was true that he made more money than I, but I was no free-loader. My parents paid my college tuition, so my student loans contributed to the rent. I also worked fifteen hours a week as a model for the art school on top of my five classes and my unpaid 15-20 hour/week internship. I was doing the best I could. When I didn't respond immediately, he escalated: "You contribute NOTH-ING to this relationship!"

"What?"

"You heard me! Nothing! What the fuck do you do around here? What are you for, anyway? Nothing!"

Nothing. Cooking dinner, reconciling him with his mother, remembering his brothers' birthdays, all these were apparently nothing. Taking care of the cats, doing the laundry, paying the bills, preparing the taxes . . . more nothing. Sex, companionship, encouragement; it was all nothing, nothing, nothing. He shouted his way into the bedroom, out of his clothes, and under the covers. He turned to face the wall and fell asleep, lightly snoring out a mumbled, "Nothing."

Standing there alone in the kitchen I felt as if I had awakened. My husband believed I contributed nothing to the relationship. I could not stay. I would not come back unless he could convince me that he knew he had been wrong.

When Chris woke in the morning, he was in a terrific mood, as usual after a big fight. We ate breakfast together, and I kissed him goodbye at the door. I was relieved that I had pulled it off. He hadn't noticed anything different about me. Then I went to the phone.

"Mom? I'm leaving Chris. Can Dad pick me up on Monday?"

Mom was quiet for a little bit. Then she did something wonderful:

She didn't ask a lot of questions. She simply trusted me.

"Sweetie, if you are really sure, then you need to leave today. You can't wait until Monday. You won't be able to keep it from him, and something worse might happen."

"Dad can't come today! It's Saturday!" My father was a pastor. Saturdays were for worship preparation. I couldn't ask him to make such a long trip on a Saturday.

"Don't you worry about your father. Wait right there—don't hang up. I am going to talk to him."

I had been waiting less than five minutes when she returned. "Your father is already on his way. Do you want to tell me what happened now, or when you get here?"

Mom and I talked for more than an hour. When I hung up the phone, I walked through the apartment doing a quick inventory of what was mine to take with me and hoping that Dad would bring boxes. He came with boxes, along with my gracious uncle and his pickup truck. I watched numbly while they packed up all my things.

When everything I owned was out of the apartment, I called to tell Chris that I was leaving him, that I would not be there when he got home from work. Suddenly, he recalled that I did in fact contribute something to the relationship. "But—who's going to clean the litter box now?" he asked.

"I don't know, Chris," I answered. "Not me."

I came down the stairs of our apartment building for the last time and fell onto my knees in the parking lot, wailing and beating my knuckles bloody against the gravel. My father stood beside me until my sobs grew quiet and my hands lay motionless beside my crumpled body. Then he bent down and gently lifted me up and supported me to his car to drive me away from the man whom I had chosen as my love, my home, my family.

I was full of questions. Every idea I had had about myself and my future was broken, and I didn't know what was going to happen next. "Dinner," said my father, as if reading my mind. "What would you like for dinner tonight?" Yes. Dinner was next. Dad was a pastor. He had seen crises before. He only had to keep me going until dinner, and then until bedtime, and so on. His job was to keep my future coming at me in two-hour increments. My parents and siblings did a good job of keeping me going with a minimum of questions and recriminations—even though some of my family wondered if I had not made a terrible and impulsive decision to leave.

But it hadn't been impulsive at all. For weeks, I had been hoping that Chris would die suddenly. No one would blame me for the marriage ending, and I would get all of his photography equipment and the car. I was shocked by how matter-of-factly I could imagine which things of his I would sell and which I would keep. I had been a well-meaning, friendly Christian girl when I met Chris, always thinking the best of everybody. But my goodwill to all people was more fragile than I had imagined; as his wife I would be praying for him to drop dead while looking right at him. I had become alien to myself; an opponent of the death penalty, I didn't even wish murderers dead, and I was wishing my own husband would die. But no matter how twisted I had become, I resisted leaving him. I had married him, and Christians did not get divorced.

I had spent a lifetime in the church. I knew that mistakes were not welcome there, that I had to be perfect to have a place in the pew. I suppose that I heard the word "grace" from the pulpit and in hymns—but believing that God's love was equally available to every person without contingency? Nonsense. Little I saw in the way people spoke and acted in church testified to that unconditional love. I could choose to be good through a sheer act of will and so be pleasing to God. When that failed, I had failed God. I contributed nothing to our relationship. I had never absorbed the idea that love was not a quid pro quo transaction.

A few years after leaving Chris, I was living with my boyfriend Brian in San Francisco. I wanted us to try going to church together, but when a kind older lady in the pew behind us asked me, "Tell me your husband's name, dear," I decided that we could never go back. She had assumed we were married! What could I say to her? I felt outed, as in the story in the Gospel of John when Jesus tells the woman at the well, "You are right in saying, 'I have no husband'; for you have had five husbands, and the one you have now is not your husband. What you said is true!"

Every sermon I remembered about this story focused on how Jesus met the woman as she came to the well alone in the middle of the day. The other women would draw water in the cooler morning and evening hours, but the fact that this woman behaved differently clearly indicated that she was a pariah in her town; she didn't want to see the other women, and they didn't want to see her. By extension, I too was a pariah. I felt that I could not return to church again until Brian and I were married. If only I had remembered that Jesus does not condemn this woman, and that the entire town comes to believe in Jesus because of this woman's testimony!

Instead, I continued to wrestle privately with Jesus's teaching that divorce and remarriage constituted adultery. By divorcing Chris and marrying Brian, I was breaking one of the Ten Commandments. How could I reconcile this teaching with the wreckage of my first marriage and the increasing blessing of my marriage with Brian? How could I reconcile it with my growing understanding that I was loved by God no matter what I did—that everyone was—and that nothing I could do could make God love me any less?

I hoped I would find the answers at divinity school, where I was preparing to become a pastor. By the end of my third year of school, I had learned what it meant to forgive Chris for hurting me, and to forgive myself for marrying him. But I could not repent the divorce. I had made mistakes as part of the divorce process, but the divorce itself was the closest I could come to correcting the mistake of marrying Chris in the first place. Being sorry to have left him would mean being sorry I was married to Brian, sorry I had gone to divinity school. I was sorry I had met Chris, not that I had left him.

I had known Christians—even pastors—who had been divorced, but I also knew that the stain of divorce would draw the eyes of some Christians away from anything worthwhile in me. I had married Brian when I was 25, so there was no reason to suspect that I had been married before. Aside from a couple of close friends at graduate school, I allowed everyone to assume that this marriage was my first and only. I was so thoroughly closeted that I was unprepared when a fellow student discovered the truth from a mutual acquaintance, and confronted me at lunchtime in the student lounge.

"I heard you were divorced!" she hissed at me.

I started shaking. I steered her out of the student lounge to a secluded place and began a mixed confession and justification while she gaped at me.

"I just, I don't understand! How can you call yourself a Christian? How can you think that you can be a minister?"

It was my turn to gape. Was it only my tight circle of friends who spoke derisively about "works righteousness," the idea that you could be "good enough" for God, as opposed to the idea that none of us deserved God's grace, that God's love was a free gift? I didn't know where to begin.

"Isn't there anything in your past that you would be embarrassed if people knew?" I asked desperately.

"I guess. I mean, my uncle and aunt are divorced. I guess I would be embarrassed if people knew that."

"I'm not talking about *divorce*! I am asking about anything *you* have done! Is there nothing in your *entire past* that you would be at all uncomfortable for absolutely anyone to know?"

"No," she responded simply, establishing that she wasn't ashamed of her treatment of me, for example. "Don't worry. I won't tell anyone you are divorced. I understand it is embarrassing for you. But I hope you will consider whether God isn't calling you to something else."

In Matthew's gospel, Jesus advises, "Do not throw your pearls before swine, or they will trample them and turn and maul you." To my twenty first-century American ears, this sounded unfeeling. It was not until a couple of months after being ambushed in the student lounge that I realized that a pig is simply an animal that lacks understanding, that cannot recognize the value of a pearl. In the years that followed, I came to understand my hidden story as precious and holy, an encounter with the very depths of what I could endure. For every sister or brother in Christ who has turned and mauled me when my divorce was revealed to them, there have been many others who revealed their own wounds, some fresh and some festering with age. For these wounded ones, my abilities to preach forgiveness, to sing passionately of God's grace, and to tend to the pain of others were signs, a living witness of God's transforming love.

I still bear the scars of my divorce, though they are growing faint with age. But I hope one day I will learn that I need not be wounded by those who fail to understand my story as a precious sign of God's transforming love. After all, I have met Jesus. He knew everything I had ever done, and yet he stayed to talk with me. Some others in the church might not approve, but because of my testimony, there are those who have believed.

The God of Shit Times

by Rachel Marie Stone

RACHEL MARIE STONE is a writer, a mother, a doula, and a mission coworker with the Presbyterian Church (USA). She has contributed to numerous publications and her first book, *Eat With Joy: Redeeming God's Gift of Food*, was published by Inter-Varsity Press in 2013. Her current writing projects include a book on Jesus for children and a book exploring what technologically advanced birth cultures and traditional birth cultures can learn from each other.

When I was very small, words had a magic power. I had been raised with the kind of faith that involved people saying a "sinner's prayer" which, when uttered, supposedly moved them miraculously from the Damned to the Saved. It was the kind of faith in which science began with God speaking words that literally brought the world into being roughly 9,000 years ago. And the kind of faith that put a Bible into every child's hand and urged us to take, to read: because these words would change us, shape us, and make us better. In this kind of faith, words were almost frightening in their power. We couldn't lose our salvation, except, maybe, if we committed something called "blasphemy"— which seemed, again, to involve words—against the Holy Spirit. And we were never, never to "take the name of the Lord in vain," which seemed to mean little more than not saying "Oh, my God" or even "Ohmigosh"—phrases that caused me to physically recoil if I heard my classmates utter them. It was also the kind of faith that taught that words of prayer could possibly heal the deathly ill. I uttered such words feverishly, by the hour, when my cat was dying of leukemia.

But when I was seventeen and recovering from a surgery that had all but separated my top half from my bottom half, rearranged my spine, and put me back together, no magic words could make it better. I had to get up, to move my body, to try and convince my muscles and bones that they would, after all, be all right again. One day I was shuffling around the hospital with my mom, IV pole and morphine drip in hand, all but gasping in pain as I shielded my broken body with stick-thin arms. We decided to take the elevator downstairs. As I shuffled in, the doors began to close, and my spaghetti arms lifted in feeble defense. "Oh, shiiit," I breathed. I thought my mom would be horrified, but she laughed. It was the first time she'd ever heard me say a bad word. It was, in fact, the first time I'd ever said a bad word in front of anyone. The only times I'd ever said bad words were under the covers in my room, mouthing "damn" and "hell" and "bitch" for the quiet, evil thrill of saying those forbidden things. My pain-breathed "shiiit" released something that I'd been storing up for a long time.

As much as my faith has changed since I was a child, I still believe in the power of words. In some ways I wonder if that is why I am a writer. Books have always been more to me than amusement or entertainment; they are like living beings that I turn to for comfort, advice, explanation, and reassurance. I never thought there was anything odd in the fact that I would, even from the age of nine or so, reread key passages in various novels at points in my life when my own circumstances seemed congruent. That, after all, is what the grownups did in church: find passages in the Bible that said something that was related to the point they wanted to make and then read them aloud to back up their point. I might not always have been able to get God to cosign what I was thinking, but I could get Beverly Cleary. And that was good enough. When, in those pre-Amazon days, I could not find a book that went exactly along with my own obsessions, I would find an empty notebook and start writing the book I needed. It always made me feel better somehow.

Saying bad words—like shiiit in the elevator—is not something that a nice Christian lady (least of all, a nice Christian lady writer who should have "better" words at her disposal) should do. Our tongues are burning fires, says the epistle of James, capable of evil; they are the rudders of the ships of our lives and can steer us into ruin. What we say shows everyone who and what we really are, or so the Bible seemed to tell me. Nice Christian women don't say "shit," or, at least, I didn't think they did, and, anyway, nice Christian publishers often won't print words like that. When I lived in Germany for a year, a nice Christian lady offered to sit next to me in church and quietly translate the service into my ear. During one particular service, a woman was offering a testimony to God's faithfulness during a particularly bad year. And my translator-friend kept rendering the German *scheisse*—which has barely the strength of "crap" in English—as "shit": "God loves us in the shit times," she said, "And if we can learn to trust God in the shit times . . ." and "Everyone's life has some shit times." I stifled my laughter, sure that my translator would be horrified if she knew how what she was saying sounded to an American church lady's ears.

When my friend Ellen had cancer, she made a cancer playlist to listen to during her daily radiation treatments. In reflecting on some of the language in the songs that comforted her most, she declared what many people outside the church are comfortable acknowledging: that profanity has a purpose. "In the midst of my frigid and tedious winter," she wrote, "I needed some good profanity to adequately describe how much it all sucked. Sometimes an f-bomb is the exact, right word." That's what I experienced with my shiiit in the elevator: the exact right word to name the fearful pain and absolute absurdity of being squashed in the doors of a hospital elevator when I was there to recover. I was not cursing God, or anyone else, for that matter. I was naming the pain and the absurdity as shit-like: one inglorious aspect of being human. Yes, we write symphonies, paint masterpieces, construct cathedrals, and compose poetry, but we also—all of us!—shit. And there's nothing particularly glorious or lovely about it. In fact, it stinks. Which is why when I hear terrible news, of a friend's untimely death, of a gravely ill child, of a grievously unjust court decision, I think, shiiit.

In most churches I've been in, that kind of talk is still not for nice ladies, which is why the exchange in Germany ("God is with us in our shit times!") was amusing. But it was more than amusing. If it remains verboten for me to name my "shit times" as such in church, how can I also receive assurance that God is with me in those shit times? I do not think God only wants to hear from me in the glorious times, when I am looking and smelling good, when I am behaving myself, when I am doing good work and being a nice Christian lady. God is with me when life is, well, shitty, and there is a certain power in naming it that way. It is the power of acknowledging the depth of one's suffering and, thus, the depth of God's mercy and compassion and love. Those writers who penned psalms of lament—psalms that Christians regard as part of the breathed-out words of God—aren't afraid to complain and cry out to God in their suffering. As a person who loves words, I'll never love mindless cursing where the "f" word is made to stand in for virtually all parts of speech. At the same time, I'm not willing to condemn those words to the outer darkness, or to believe that I will be similarly condemned for using them, because God is a God of glorious wonder.

And of shit.

Broken in the Body,
Slain in the Spirit
by Tara Woodard-Lehman

TARA WOODARD-LEHMAN is an ordained PCUSA minister. Since 1998 she has ministered to and with young adults and university students. Prior to coming to Princeton, Tara served as the William C. Bennett Chaplain and assistant professor of religion at Peace College in Raleigh, North Carolina. Over the past four years Tara has served as the executive director of Westminster Foundation and Presbyterian Chaplain at Princeton University. Tara also serves on the pastoral staff of Nassau Presbyterian Church in Princeton, New Jersey. She enjoys good wine, post-apocalyptic films, salvage art, dark chocolate, fresh ocean air, and gardening. Tara and her husband, Derek, live in Princeton, New Jersey with their two beautiful and hilarious boys, Josiah and Eli.

I'm nineteen years old, rumbling down a highway via Greyhound bus. Next to me sits a petite, wrinkly, Catholic nun. She is wearing a full habit and cradles a stack of religious literature in her lap. The nun raises a knobby, knuckled hand and waves a pamphlet in my direction. On the front, there's a picture of a dove.

"Dear," she asks, "do you know about the Holy Spirit?" Her voice crackles when she talks. She seems fragile but determined.

I flip my hair, shrug my shoulders, and continue to click my minty gum. Sometimes gum helps with motion sickness. "Sure, I know about the Holy Spirit," I reply.

Of course I know about the Holy Spirit.

My family attended a traditional United Methodist church for most of my childhood. Still, it was the 1970s, and the charismatic renewal movement was in full swing. The Holy Spirit was marking territory all over our little Pennsylvania town. Even historic mainline churches began to have "spirit-filled" bible studies, play groups, prayer groups, nursery schools, and dinner clubs.

And then there were some congregations that were all Holy Spirit, all the time.

My first experience at one such church was baptism by fire, so to speak. I wasn't gently eased in with feel-good praise hymns or friendly biblical teaching. Right from the get-go there were ecstatic shouts and Spirit-induced moans. Prophetic words were proclaimed and broken bodies were healed. I was just a young girl, cowering behind my mother's skirt. It was both awesome and awful. But, like many things in life, the strange became familiar over time.

Even during my rebellious teenage years, I had a growing affinity for revival tents and healing services. In these places the boundary between heaven and earth seemed penetrable; the supernatural and the natural blurred. I became a charismatic junky, always on the prowl for another dose of the Holy Ghost.

This sort of faith was incarnational, fleshy. Fingers dipped in oil and anointed the sick. Hands pressed on bodies for healing. Water soaked heads. Bread and juice touched lips. Food was prepared, houses built, and clothing stitched for those in need. Ironically, the more a community *talked* about the Spirit, the more it seemed to *care* for the Body. Even *my* body.

Still, not every "spirit-filled" experience was positive.

Like the time I went to the altar for prayer, but no prayer was offered. Instead, a man with a greasy comb-over and blue polyester suit bent over and told me to pray in tongues. Like those first Christians on the day of Pentecost, he wanted me to speak in a language that was not my own, whether from the nations or of angels. Though I wanted this spiritual gift, nothing happened. "Just start to make noises. It will loosen up your tongue," he instructed.

Instead I prayed aloud, "Lord, if this is from you, I happily receive it." Again, nothing.

Bewildered, the preacher grabbed my jaw and commanded the "spirit of rebellion" to leave my body. When I still failed to utter foreign tongues, the preacher sulked away frustrated. I slinked back to my pew, unprayed for and confused.

This wasn't the only time I felt spiritually shortchanged. It also happened at camp.

By the end of a week at camp, most kids were sleep-deprived. Bodies were tired and emotions ran high, especially as we entered the final evening worship service. It was there we sang our favorite praise songs, hands raised, arms outstretched, the singing punctuated only by an occasional tear-filled testimony.

I found it hard to breathe there, and it's no wonder. The chapel was jammed to the gills with a bunch of spiritually strung-out, perspiring teenagers. The pews were damp. The air was thick. I reached for my inhaler but realized I must have left it in my bunk.

At some point, the outside doors in the front of the building were propped open. The cool night air blew in.

Inhale, exhale. Inhale, exhale. Inhale, exhale.

I could breathe better now.

We were invited to receive prayer. This wasn't your average, run-of-the-mill sort of prayer. This was hard-core holy-ghost prayer, the type of prayer that lands you flat on your back and bowled over in a Holy Ghost stupor.

"This is a special time," a camp counselor explained, "when the Holy Spirit can minister to you in an intimate way." Over the next several hours the bodies of campers were strewn about the floor, "slain in the spirit." Apparently some prefer the term "resting in the spirit." I didn't care what it was called; I just wanted to experience it.

I recalled the prophet Ezekiel's vision of the valley of dry bones. God's mighty Spirit moves over them, reconnecting the dismembered skeletons, sewing together sinew and flesh, recreating them from their dusty decay like Adam and Eve. Even after this, they do not yet live. They remain limp and lifeless corpses until the Spirit breathes into them.

I ached for God's Spirit to breathe into me.

Inhale, exhale. Inhale, exhale. Inhale, exhale.

It would have been nice to have had my very own mystical vision. I'd even have been up for another shot at speaking in tongues. But what I wanted more than anything was an illness-free body, and word had it that healing was part and parcel of the slaying experience.

Despite my lack of slaying or tongue speaking, I remain confident I've witnessed enough Holy Ghost action I don't need a nun's instruction, or her pamphlets. Nor do I have the wherewithal to respond to her questions. The bus is swerving down a twisty road and I'm dizzy. Sometimes the gum doesn't help with motion sickness.

"You know, you can't do *anything* without the Holy Spirit?" the nun continues.

"Yes," I say confidently, trying not to feel offended.

The nun pauses, obviously not convinced. "You can't do one single thing. You can't even *breathe* without God's Spirit." Her emphasis on *breathe* seems oddly exaggerated, but I ignore it and respond *"Yes, I know."*

A foul stench oozes from the bus bathroom. Exhaust fumes trail up my nose. The smell of stale cigarettes wafts from the obese, snoring man across the aisle. The steel tube of the bus closes in on me. Both my motion sickness and claustrophobia kick into high gear. I'm queasy.

But I can tell the sister is persistent. And skeptical. I blurt out, "Trust me. I know I can't do *anything* without God's Spirit. Thank you for reminding me." She eyes me suspiciously, but must notice my wooziness because she ceases her interrogation.

Then a familiar salty, sour taste fills my mouth. *Oh no.* I think. *Not now, not here . . .*

Much of my life I've suffered from regular bouts of acute vomiting, accompanied by vertigo. Sometimes the episodes have an obvious origin, like motion sickness or the flu. Other times, there is no clear cause. Once an episode starts, it doesn't let up for several hours, sometimes days. (During one of my pregnancies, a dreadful case of morning sickness prompted an episode that lasted for nearly five months.) Though most frequent in my early twenties, they continue to this day.

When this happens, my body tightens, contorts, and hunkers over. My heart races and my head spins. Everything's a nauseous blur. I vomit until there's nothing left. Then I dry heave until my body produces green bile. I toss that up until there's blood. Dehydrated and exhausted, I feel like a rag doll squeezed through an old-time laundry press; wrung out of life, hung up to dry.

I press my head against the bathroom floor. I like the cold, hard, reliability of the tile. I eventually go to the hospital and find relief in an IV that ushers in some anti-vomiting drugs and much needed H_2O.

And how does it all start? With a salty, sour taste in my mouth.

Just like now, on this wretched, hot, smelly bus. I may or may not suffer from a rebellious spirit, as suggested by the polyester preacher. I *can* confirm, however, that I suffer from a rebellious body.

I try my best to breathe slow, deep breaths.

Inhale, exhale. Inhale, exhale. Inhale, exhale.

Maybe if I concentrate on my breathing, I can stave off the nausea.

It works. For now, I've won the battle over my belly, and its contents. It seems I've also appeased the nun, as she's now sound asleep. When I finally arrive at my destination, I promptly forget about the nun and my Greyhound catechesis.

Until a few months later, when my lung collapses.

A "spontaneous pneumothorax," it's called. Thin, stretched places in my right lung pop like a balloon. Air gets trapped between my lung and chest wall. I can still breathe, but the pain is intense.

At the hospital they stick a chest tube in my side. My lung reinflates. I'm almost fully recovered when the lung collapses again. The surgeon explains I need a more permanent fix, or it will continue to collapse.

I'm laid out in a surgical prep room. While hunting for a vein, a student nurse accidentally pokes one of my arteries. Dark, warm crimson pulses out and drenches my sheets. My teary-eyed parents bear brave smiles while nurses escort them out to a waiting room. Pairs of hands move my limp body off the blood-soaked bed. That's the last thing I remember before I'm put under.

When I come to, I learn they scraped my lung and chest wall with surgical sandpaper so the two are permanently stuck together. Air can't get trapped there again. "Even if it continues to pop, your lung won't deflate," the surgeon informs me cheerfully. Despite the successful surgery, I'm not quite ready to slap on a smile and play Suzy Sunshine.

In fact, I'm not quite ready for anything. Or anyone. I wish I could just go back to sleep until all the pain goes away, but that's not in the cards. The inflatable pillows squeezing my legs may prevent blood from clotting, but they also prevent me from sleeping. Worse, something strange is happening to my senses.

Beeps sound like bullhorns. Whispers sound like shouts. Someone plops down a tray of hospital food. I gag and push it away. A nurse flaps open window blinds. I curse and tell her to close them. A visitor from church stops by. I bark at her to leave. I'm irritable, doped up, and depressed. I ask that all lights stay off, all blinds stay shut, and all visitors stay away. All I want is stillness, silence, a bed pan, and more morphine.

Time passes. I focus on one breath at a time.

One. *Inhale, exhale.* Breath. *Inhale, exhale.* At. *Inhale, exhale.* A. *Inhale, exhale.* Time. *Inhale, exhale.*

Sometimes, one breath at a time is all you can do.

A few days later, I'm doing a little better. When a friend stops by, he reminds me the Hebrew word for "breath" can also be translated as "wind," or "spirit." I think back to the vision of the valley of dry bones; holy wind whipping through the dead, blowing out resurrection life.

I close my eyes and try to take deep breaths.

Inhale, exhale. Inhale, exhale. Inhale, exhale.

With every inhale, I imagine God's Spirit breathing new life into me. With every exhale, I imagine all manner of sickness leaving my body. No longer a member of the walking dead, I join the ranks of those infused with the Holy Ghost. It seems I've been slain in the spirit, after all. It's just been in a hospital bed, not on a camp meeting floor.

And then it all rushes back: the nun, her pamphlets, her persistent questions. She was right. I can't do anything without the Holy Spirit. I can't even *breathe.*

Naming God for Ourselves amidst Pain and Patriarchy

by Rahiel Tesfamariam

RAHIEL TESFAMARIAM is a writer, social activist, public theologian, and cultural critic. She is the founder and editor-in-chief of UrbanCusp.com, a cutting-edge online lifestyle magazine highlighting progressive urban culture, faith, social change, and global awareness. Rahiel is also a columnist for The Washington Post. Born in war-torn Eritrea a decade prior to independence, Rahiel Tesfamariam's roots can be traced to slum villages off the coast of the Red Sea. As a product of her nation's tenacious struggle for self-determination, she went on to earn a BA in American studies from Stanford University and a master of divinity from Yale University, where she was named the school's inaugural William Sloane Coffin, Jr. Scholar for Peace and Justice.

As a seminarian at Yale Divinity School, it took me some time to adjust to the terminology my professors and classmates used to identify God. We were asked to replace masculine descriptors for God with feminine or gender-neutral ones when writing term papers and speaking publicly in chapel. Using "God's Self" in place of "Himself" was initially an awkward and unnatural shift for me, particularly among friends on my breaks home.

I reduced this language mandate at my seminary to a manifestation of white privilege. I thought it was evidence that well-off white folks had too much time on their hands—enough time to care about things that had never mattered to me before.

My indifference about the naming of God didn't last long. After noticing that my African-American peers were the most resistant to imagining God in new ways, I began to care a great deal. It was as if people feared that renaming God would shake up their faith confidence. That was when I realized that white folks weren't the only ones invested in a particular image of God; black men were pushing back as well. And there were too many women (myself included) who had never thought to challenge them on it.

The charge to be aware of how we name God is grounded in cultural and gender sensitivity. We were told that descendants of slaves may hear "Lord" and "Master" differently than white students. We were also asked to be mindful of women who may have been deeply harmed by men. "A rape survivor will inevitably have a harder time worshipping a deity personified as a man," I remember one of my professors saying.

This was a critical moment in my theological journey. I was being challenged on my faith assumptions. Everything about God was now up for debate, including the image of God as a father. It was at that time that I began to think about how I came to name and describe God in the ways that I did.

Growing up in an Eritrean-American home, Christianity was always prominent. Surrounded by images of white biblical figures, a rosary, and an ever-present supply of holy water, my family's Eastern Orthodox religious customs were shaping my understanding of God daily. And that was often incongruent with what I was learning from my African-American friends outside of the home. I also wasn't cognizant of the barrier that language would place between me and the Christian faith; the worship services we occasionally attended and the Bibles in our homes were all in my native tongue, which I could no longer understand. As an adult, I now recognize how much of my spiritual growth was stunted by these cultural barriers.

In my early twenties, when I sought to know God and, specifically, Jesus Christ for myself, a new set of challenges met me head-on. My feminist ideals were in constant tension with Christianity. I found it difficult to visit church after church without ever finding female pastors serving as the spiritual guides of their communities.

I was always pained after reading story after story in the Bible depicting women as nameless, voiceless sex objects. As a woman of faith, I have never found the Bible's telling of womanhood to be life-giving. Rooted in stories of domination, torture, silence, and invisibility, Scripture complicates my best efforts to understand God's unique message to me as a woman.

Initially, I struggled to comprehend that God loves women when everything suggests that womanhood was an afterthought in God's grand plan of Creation. But I didn't find the safe space to voice that. While Christ redeemed much of this hurtful imagery through the unconditional love he offered the women he encountered, I wanted to talk about how the silencing of women always restrained my worship.

It was only in recent years that I came to realize that the bruises from my past became theological baggage. I carried them into my understanding of God, believing that God's love for me was limited to the flawed love that I had been offered by my closest confidants, family members, and partners.

I constantly fought to not see my Maker as punitive and judgmental as a result of growing up in a rigid African-centered household. I struggled to trust that God loves me and has my best interest at heart despite wounds from past relationships. The fear that God will one day abandon me loomed over my faith walk. God was bearing the burden of everything that this world has done to me.

Today, these theological challenges remain a part of me. But I've come a long way. Much of that progress came from allowing myself room to question the Bible, to be mad at God, and to have periods of spiritual drought. It was only when I could be honest with myself about the times that I had felt let down by God that greater intimacy could be cultivated. Building a healthy, whole relationship with Christ required me to have the courage to face theological uncertainty and to make peace with the darkest moments of my life. Only in finding meaning in those places of deep pain was I able to trust that God was not indifferent to the suffering that I had experienced or witnessed.

This required a lot of solitude, prayer, journaling, deep refection, and even therapy. Amidst that process, I realized that there was a lot more at stake than just naming God; I was trying to internalize once and for all that God loved me—Rahiel—unconditionally. That effort was complicated by the image of a Santa Clause-like figure that was in the heavens checking his list to see if I had been naughty or nice. There was no way to win with that God, to feel loved and cared for by that God. In contrast, the image of my Maker as a "soft, still voice" or "gentle whisper" found in 1 Kings 19 was comforting and reassuring. The more I went toward this image of gentleness, the easier it became to accept that I was smart, beautiful, and valuable in the eyes of God.

In the same way that I decided to read the Bible cover to cover at the start of my faith journey, I determined to read my life story and womanhood through a holistic lens as well. I could perpetually zoom in on those places of pain in the Bible like Egypt and the cross, or I could rejoice in the journey to the Promised Land and the glorious moments of resurrection. I could dwell on the voicelessness of women in the church, or I could create my own platform that allowed me to be heard daily. I decided that, for me, it was time to stop playing victim.

Going through my own process of self-determination freed me up to fall in love with a God that a large segment of the church is not doing justice to—a God whose shoulder I can lean on in moments of vulnerability to absorb my tears, but who also commands that I roll up my sleeves and get back to my place of ministry. This God is both nurturing and convicting, and simultaneously wants the best for me and requires a lot from me.

I have done the hard work of unpacking God for myself. But that responsibility should not fall solely on me as an individual. The church also has a lot of work to do. It must stop its passive approach to cultivating the next generation of disciples and church leaders. Women faith leaders play an integral role in this; we must be sought out, supported, and equipped to fill in the ministerial gaps that exist within today's church.

The unique price that women have had to pay for their faith has historically been too high. The church has sustained its programmatic and financial needs on our backs. We hold so little decision-making power but do so much of the work. We usher the next generation of believers into the sanctuary weekly without receiving the same support in the homes and schools that those children return to. We also are often expected to carry the banner of sexual purity as a mark of our religion while the church upholds that "boys will be boys."

Men cannot continue to be a conduit of theological interpretation between women, their Bibles, and their God. We must make sense of God for ourselves, as single women, wives, mothers, seasoned saints, and religious outcasts. The church must see this mission as an imperative in keeping Christianity relevant. Otherwise, it faces the threat of being generationally unappealing to masses of progressive feminists and womanists who have no interest in gender subjugation disguised as religious tradition.

Will more churches rise to this occasion, commit to being cutting-edge on matters of gender equality, and go where women of faith dare to take them? Is the church ready for a generation of women who are determined to define God on their own terms?

The Silence Behind the Din: Domestic Violence and Homosexuality

by Rev. Sarah C. Jobe

SARAH JOBE is an ordained Baptist pastor, prison chaplain, doula, and mother of two. She lives with her family at the Rutba House in Durham, North Carolina. The Rutba House is an intentional Christian community devoted to hospitality, discipleship, and peacemaking. Sarah also serves as an instructor for Project TURN, a program that offers seminary-style classes inside North Carolina prisons in which incarcerated and non-incarcerated people can learn alongside one another. Sarah is the author of *Creating with God: The Holy, Confusing, Blessedness of Pregnancy*.

Growing up in polite Southern company, I quickly learned that there are some things one doesn't say in church. These taboos were not taught to me explicitly, but by the time I received my first Bible, bound in leatherette and bearing my name, I knew these taboos as deeply as I knew the words of John 3:16.

I knew that one should not say aloud that Ms. Malinda's shaking voice seemed too old to be the soprano soloist. I knew that one should not mention that Ms. Diane's "homemade" snicker doodle pie had been on sale at the grocery store the morning before.

I also knew that no woman would ever say out loud that her husband was beating her, and I knew that if a woman suspected she was gay, she should keep that to herself, too.

I learned these taboos the way Southern Christian girls learn everything—through stern but subtle glances. By about age five,

I could tell if my mother approved of what I was saying simply by how she looked at me. On the rare occasions that I did not correctly interpret her glance, she might escalate to a slight squeeze on my shoulder. I can only remember a handful of times in which she had to interrupt some unknowing foray into taboo territory with a cheerful, "Well now, I think that's enough about that." As a Southern woman, I inherited a veritable arsenal of tactics by which to dismiss even the hint of a taboo conversation. So while I knew not to speak about domestic violence or homosexuality, I never really thought about how these two silences are connected.

Until I met Tina.[1]

Residents loitered around the trailer after worship ended. The prison dorms are cooled by 1950s drum fans, and no one was ready to head back to them in North Carolina's blazing summer heat.

I saw Tina weaving her way toward me from across the trailer. Her usual smile was replaced by a tense mouth and heavy eyes.

"Hey Chap, you think you might have time to talk later?" she asked.

I mustered my most open and inviting look. "Of course, Tina. Could you come by in an hour?"

She nodded, and a wave of preemptive exhaustion flooded my forehead and shoulders. I knew what Tina needed to talk about, and I knew that it would be hard to hear. I knew it would be hard to hear because I heard some version of it at least once a week. On some dreaded nights, I would hear numerous versions of the story on one shift.

Tina was coming to talk to me about her childhood. She had been raped by her stepfather over a period of six years starting at age ten. She had married at age seventeen to escape her house, only to find that she was trapped in a house with a new man who would demean, beat, and rape her for the next five years. I knew

---

1. Tina is based on one woman from the prison at which I work. I have changed some of the details of her story to protect her identity. At all places in which details were changed, I tried to use the details of other women who have been harmed by the church's simultaneous silence regarding sexual assault and simultaneous loud condemnation of homosexuality. In this way, Tina is a composite character representing a number of women with similar stories.

that Tina was coming to talk about this because she had recently joined our sexual assault and domestic violence support group. Her courage had been building, and Tina was ready to break the silence surrounding her life of abuse.

I am a chaplain at a minimum security women's prison. Most of the women in my congregation are victims of sexual assault or domestic violence.

As a chaplain, I plan programs, walk with people through death and illness, and attend to the usual spiritual questions. But in the prison, much of my pastoral care is focused on helping women recover from experiences of violence done against them in their own homes. The stories are so many and so similar that they begin to blur together.

But some haunting details refuse to blur. Like Kia trying to stab her uncle with a pair of child safety scissors while he raped her. Or that Jane was preparing a felt board for the three-year-olds in her Sunday School class the first time her pastor propositioned her. Or Lou forgetting to put on her shoes when she ran out of her house at midnight to escape her husband. He was violating a restraining order by forcing his way into the home they once shared.

My congregation, comprised entirely of incarcerated women, is disproportionately plagued by sexual assault and domestic violence, but the plague of violence against women is by no means contained within the prison walls. I also worship at a well-respected and well-loved Baptist church. While I have never heard it discussed on a Sunday morning or around a Wednesday night supper table, I can safely assume that some 30 percent of the women in my congregation have been beaten, raped, or sexually assaulted at some point in their lives, many of them in their own homes.

I can assume this because some 30 percent of women in the United States are victims of sexual assault or domestic violence. Imagine what would happen if 30 percent of the women in our congregations contracted chicken pox. In my church, the prayer warriors would put on their armor, the casserole dishes would start flowing to the affected families, and our politically active members would be picketing outside Congress calling for funding to end the chicken pox epidemic. But when the women and girls in our congregations are beaten and raped by their caregivers and partners at a rate that can easily be called epidemic,[2] we find it hard to say anything at all.

I have never heard a sermon on domestic violence or sexual assault. The biblical passages that address rape have been conveniently omitted from the lectionary. There is only one biblical rape story that I have ever heard preached or talked about in a public setting. This text is preached loudly and often. But the sad irony is that amidst the din, this biblical rape text is not used to condemn rape.

Genesis 19 tells a story of a family that graciously houses two angelic visitors. As night falls, a crowd gathers around the family's home. The crowd demands that the visitors be sent out so that the crowd can rape them. The father of the family urges the crowd not to commit such a violent action. When the crowd refuses to be swayed, the father offers his own daughters as replacement victims for this impending gang rape. God responds by blinding the crowd, saving the daughters, and destroying the town.

Christians call this the story of Sodom and Gomorrah. We seem to agree that God's response to the scene indicates judgment. When I read the story, it seems that the sin being condemned is rape. When I'm feeling more specific, I name the sin in the text as gang rape. Sometimes I wonder if the sin is prostituting one's daughters for the safety of one's home.

But the public discourse surrounding the text suggests something else. From listening to sermons, gatherings, and internet media sources, I have learned that by and large, Christians agree that the sin in this text is homosexuality.

While I haven't heard any sermons condemning rape or sexual assault, I have heard more sermons than I care to recall condemning

2. Intimate partner homicides account for 30 percent of the murders of women and 5 percent of the murders of men. The Centers for Disease Control and Prevention does not have a specific percentage of deaths that always constitutes an epidemic; the percentage changes slightly for each disease. But as a measure, the flu is considered an epidemic when it causes more than 6 to 8 percent of the total deaths in an area in a given day or week. (Bureau of Justice Statistics Crime Data Brief, Intimate Partner Violence, 1993-2001, February 2003. Bureau of Justice Statistics, Intimate Partner Violence in the U.S. 1993-2004, 2006.)

homosexual relationships. As a Baptist minister who affirms the dignity and worth of my LGBTQ brothers and sisters, much of my pastoral care both inside and outside the prison has been devoted to offering a safe space for people to process lifelong histories of rejection by the church concerning their sexual orientations.

Tina came back to my office a few months after our first conversation. The weather had turned, and now I wished that the thin walls of the trailer were a little better at keeping in heat. The women at the prison are allowed to crochet, so Tina was wearing a colorful scarf and cap atop her prison garb.

Her face was again tense, but this time I wasn't sure why she wanted to meet. Tina began to tell me about how she had finally found a healthy relationship. She was with a woman who saw her gifts, made her laugh, and cared about her physical and spiritual well-being. It was the first relationship in which Tina had ever felt truly cherished. Just as her smile was beginning to break through, Tina dropped her head.

She mumbled something I couldn't understand.

"I'm sorry Tina, what was that?" I asked.

She looked up at me with a tired face, and looking straight into my eyes she said, "I just can't get over being a disappointment to God."

I looked in front of me and saw a deeply faithful woman who actively participated in Bible studies almost every night of the week. I saw a beautiful woman who led our prison's dance team and ministered in our worship services. I saw a woman who had faced decades of horror in her own home and had come out on the other side with a fierce belief that God is still a God of love. I also saw a woman who had received a strong message from the church that a decision to engage in a loving relationship with another woman was unacceptable in the sight of God. For the first time, Tina was in a life-giving intimate relationship, and all she could hear from the church was condemnation.

Tina's story of abuse is common, but Tina's story of feeling rejected by the church as a lesbian woman is also common. Gay and lesbian stories of rejection and persecution by the church are so numerous that they too begin to blur. But as with stories of rape and abuse, some heart-wrenching details just refuse to soften. Like Dan and Paul's persistence in praying in their home before a wall full of crucifixes, even after three decades of being too scared to enter a church. Or Gail and Jane's hopeful insistence that a row be kept open in the front of the church just in case Gail's family made the unlikely decision to appear at their wedding ceremony.

We who persist in being Christian learn to live between the church's loud and public condemnation of gay and lesbian people and the church's deadly silence about sexual assault and domestic violence. Until recently, I never noticed how the two are connected; I never noticed that our condemnation of one rests on our willing silence about the other.

But as Tina sat in my office, I realized the horrible paradox that the texts we use to condemn homosexuality more aptly describe rape and molestation. Looking in her face, I realized that our biblical case against homosexuality requires our willingness to lay aside the biblical case against rape and sexual assault.

The interpretive choice we must make between condemning homosexuality or condemning rape is not limited to the story of Sodom and Gomorrah. The Greek words that we translate as "homosexuality" in other biblical passages refer to ancient practices in which men of status used young boys, effeminate male prostitutes, or men of lower economic status (like slaves) for their own sexual gratification. All of these situations involve men of greater power using and abusing men and boys of lesser power. Today, we call these situations molestation, prostitution, and rape. And yet we continue to accept translations of Scripture that call these acts "homosexuality." We continue to accept translations that render invisible the sins of rape and molestation. Victims of sexual assault and domestic violence have become collateral damage in the church's war against gay and lesbian people.

The damage in this war reaches farther than we like to admit.

This reading regime in which the church has so heavily invested makes double victims out of people like Tina. Victims of sexual assault are 26 times more likely to abuse drugs than people who have not experienced that sort of abuse.[3] Children who are exposed to domestic violence are more likely to exhibit behavioral and physical health problems including depression, anxiety, and violence toward peers. They are also more likely to attempt suicide, abuse drugs and alcohol, engage in teenage prostitution, and commit sexual assault crime. Sixty-three percent of males incarcerated between the ages of 12 and 20 are there for assaulting or killing their mother's abuser.[4] Men who witness violence in their childhood homes are three times as likely to batter their wives and/or girlfriends.[5]

In short, victims of domestic violence and sexual assault are much more likely to end up in prison. These abused women, men, and youth spend years, decades, and lifetimes forced into environments in which their only options for intimacy are same-sex ones. The church that was previously silent to their experience of abuse becomes painfully loud in condemning the only intimacy available to them.

We must ask if our current interpretations of Scripture are the most faithful ones available to us. Will we continue to read the Scriptures according to our taboos around homosexuality and domestic violence, accepting interpretations that maximize violence? Or will we move toward biblical interpretations that mobilize us to protect victims of violence and free us to welcome our gay and lesbian brothers and sisters?

Tina was released from prison a few months ago. A few weeks after her release, she called the prison to give me a report on her new home, recent job opportunity, and dance team pursuits. We exchanged emails and agreed to keep in touch about how her life was unfolding. A few weeks later, I got an email from Tina. It began "Dear Chap," and it ended like this:

3. Statistics from the RAINN, the Rape, Abuse, and Incest National Network at http://www.rainn.org/get-information/statistics/sexual-assault-victims.
4. Statistics from the Midshore Council on Family Violence at http://www.mscfv.org/dvstat.html.
5. Ibid.

"I'm never going to forget your example or your advice or your prayers. You looked me right in my eyes on a day that I felt like I was one of God's biggest heartbreaks and told me I do not displease God. And during this season while God is strengthening and preparing me for what is to come, I want you to know that I am not afraid; I am ready. Let's go change the world."

So may it be. Amen.

No Women Need Apply
by Gina Messina-Dysert

GINA MESSINA-DYSERT, PhD, is visiting assistant professor of theological ethics at Loyola Marymount University and cofounder and codirector of Feminism and Religion, an international project that explores the "F-word" in religion and the intersection between scholarship, activism, and community. As the author of multiple articles and the book *Rape Culture and Spiritual Violence*, and coeditor (with Rosemary Radford Ruether) of the anthology *Feminism and Religion in the 21st Century*, Gina has given serious attention to issues faced by women in relation to religion and social justice. Her research interests are theologically and ethically driven, involve a feminist and interdisciplinary approach, and are influenced by her activist roots and experience working with survivors of rape and domestic violence. She continues to be active in movements to end violence against women and explores opportunities for spiritual healing for those who have encountered gender-based violence. Gina can be followed on Twitter (@FemTheologian) and her website can be accessed at http://ginamessinadysert.com.

There is a war on women and it has been waged by the Catholic Church. It is not a new war, but one that has persisted for nearly two millennia, executing its attack in multiple ways. Excluding women from ordination has been a key strategy. Although many women have been called to the priesthood, according to the Vatican, God must have called the wrong number. Their gender excludes women from this role.

Growing up in the 1980s, there were no altar girls in the Catholic Church. My brother was an altar boy, and I found myself jealous that he was able to participate so intimately in mass while I had to observe from the pews. I often asked, "Why can't I be an altar server?" The response I would receive was always accompanied by a laugh: "Because, you're a girl!"

Recognizing that I was excluded from being an altar server because of my gender also led me to understand why there were no women priests. I was deeply troubled by this since it was the women in my life whom I believed truly embodied the Spirit of Christ: my mother, my grandmothers, my aunts. These women worked tirelessly to support the Church, to teach their children the values of Christ, and to carry out the mission of Christianity in their communities, and yet the "man-made" rules of the Church denied their right to the priesthood.

The Vatican has been clear in its position, affirmed in the 1976 "Declaration on the Question of the Admission of Women to the Ministerial Priesthood." The Church argues that women cannot be ordained priests for three reasons: 1) Jesus intentionally did not ordain women in his ministry; 2) the Church's continuous tradition has excluded women from the priesthood; and 3) priests represent Christ, who was a man; thus women are physically unable to fulfill this role.

This position clearly ignores the women who played a vital role in Jesus's ministry as well as those who were leaders in the early Christian Church. In addition, the continued claim of infallibility for the Church, along with its focus on the sacramental relationship between Christ and maleness, is disturbing, highly problematic, and according to some theologians, heretical.

My experience of being excluded from altar service and the priesthood because of my gender caused serious self-esteem issues throughout my childhood and early adult life. I reasoned that if my gender excluded me from embodying the Spirit of Christ, then my gender must be subordinate. I felt unworthy to speak up in the classroom, to participate in activities, and even to hold conversations and interact with peers. I was confused about what I could contribute to a community where my gender was not valued—a message that was continuously reinforced through family, religion, and society.

Being raised in a strict Sicilian Catholic household, these messages were supported by my family, including the women in my life. My self-esteem was poor and mirrored the lack of self-worth I saw in my mom. She was raised to recognize her gender as limiting and often told me that book smarts were not important since the only roles I would achieve in life would be wife and mother.

Likewise, attending Catholic schools and weekly mass, I was bombarded with messages about the expectations and roles of women. I learned about the matriarchs who all struggled with infertility and only found happiness once they bore children; the virgin saints who were canonized for their willingness to give up their lives rather than their chastity; and of course, Mary, the mother of Jesus, who was a perpetual virgin impregnated in order to serve God. Women's lives were of little worth (particularly if their hymens were broken), their only value carried in their wombs. It wasn't until I was in college that I realized I could question the problematic teachings of the Vatican that had worked to tear down my self-image for so long.

Although I struggled over time with the question of whether or not I could still identify as Catholic, I have come to realize that I am my own agent, and I will not allow anyone to tell me what my religious status is based on my refusal to accept discrimination. Catholic social teaching calls for the affirmation of the full humanity of every person. How is refusing a person the right to participate in the priesthood representative of this? By standing up to sexism in the Church I affirm my Catholic identity.

As a self-identified feminist Catholic and a theologian by training, I find myself in a constant struggle between my beliefs and my profession. I have been warned behind closed doors about the risks I pose to my career by speaking out. Some warnings have been friendly while others were coupled with a reprimand; all cited risks to my professional future. It has been clear to me that a culture of fear is alive and well within Catholic institutions when it comes to speaking out about women's ordination.

The most shocking thing of all is that the act of pedophilia can be excused, but to call for women to be ordained is such a threat that it can lead to termination of employment or expulsion from the Church. Is the idea of a woman embodying the Spirit of Christ more terrifying than the act of raping children? Regardless of the warnings, friendly and otherwise, I cannot be passive on this issue. Having received a Jesuit education in the tradition of social justice, my conscience will not allow me to be silent. I have lectured and given public talks calling for women's ordination, organized events and participated in rallies, and have documented my stance through blogs, articles, and radio/video interviews. I will not be bullied into submission.

Some claim that the Vatican *is* the Catholic Church, that I am excluding myself from the tradition by calling for women's ordination and taking a stand against the Vatican's position. While the Vatican is a part of the Church, so is the community of Catholics of which I am a member. I believe that to claim the hierarchy of the Vatican as the true Catholic Church is not only dangerous for women's emotional and spiritual health but also for that of the entire community.

To be Catholic is to be part of a dynamic, historical tradition. The Church is not one static entity, but rather a community that encompasses many representations of identity within the tradition. Catholicism is represented by the parishes, organizations, and base communities that take Catholic social teaching, the mission of social justice, and the ministry of Christ seriously.

I believe that it is the duty of every mature person who identifies as a Catholic to bring the innovations of the world to the tradition so that it may grow. We all have a responsibility to leave our mark on the Catholic Church. In this way, we allow the Church to develop, expand, and continue in an ever-changing society. My mark will be made by demanding the end of sexism and the refusal to ordain women. Working for justice is the act of a true Catholic.

While I am not called to the priesthood, I am called to end discrimination. Many believe that women's ordination is a Catholic issue, or a women's issue; however, we must recognize it as a human issue. Denying women the right to be ordained does continue a Church tradition—it is called sexism. This war against women has waged on for far too long, and we must work to put an end to this violation of the mission of Christ. As long as women are refused any role, our full humanity continues to be denied.

Now I am a mother raising a daughter. It is more important than ever to me to interrupt the sexist messages that damaged my esteem for so long. I refuse to allow my daughter Sarah to have a mother with low self-worth, and I refuse to have her exposed to destructive messages. My husband and I tell our daughter daily that she has the ability to do anything she wants in life, including being a priest. We tell her that she embodies the Spirit of Christ and that it is her choices and her actions that affirm her full humanity, not her gender.

Recently, during a family dinner, Sarah, who is three years old, threw her arms up in a victory position and out of the blue shouted, "Ordain women now!", a phrase she picked up from participating in rallies. Our continued efforts to end sexism in the Catholic Church are making an impact on Sarah. It is never too early to start teaching our children to reject the injustice in the world.

A Woman of Many Questions
by K. D. Byers

K. D. BYERS grew up the daughter of a Methodist minister in Wisconsin. She earned a bachelor of arts in English from the University of Iowa and a master of divinity from Duke University. She is working on a master of fine arts in creative writing from Seattle Pacific University.

"You need to stop talking so much," Jill says through thin lips as she pulls me aside during the break in our Bible study.

I swallow. I know I do this—talk too much, go off on tangents, and lose my point. I try to avoid it, but it happens. On the other side of the room is the rest of the Bible study. Men and women, my friends, mingle over cookies, and someone talks about the upcoming football game. We attend a large, vibrant college ministry at the University of Iowa and most of us live in the same dorm. We eat together, play on the same intramural teams, and study side-by-side, so it feels natural that our two small groups have gotten together for a onetime coed Bible study.

"I don't mean to," I say. "I'll keep it shorter."

Jill is my Bible study leader. A junior, she is dedicated to walking alongside me through my freshman year. Jill is real and fierce and fun, but now she levels me with a steady gaze. "No, you just need to answer less."

Someone calls us back to the group, but Jill wraps her fingers around my arm. She wants me to understand, "We're here to encourage the guys to be spiritual leaders. When you answer all the questions it makes them feel dumb."

Words perch on my lips, but for once I am speechless. Her censure is neither fair nor right. Why would these men, whom I know to be smart and capable, need me to stay silent in order to feel confident?

When we stop for the break I don't follow everyone to the kitchen for snacks. I sit on my hands and rock. I grin. I love asking the questions that come with faith: *why, what if, perhaps, maybe* and teasing out possible answers. But according to Jill, when I speak I trespass on something that belongs in the realm of men. In my head I know my voice is not a threat to them, but when we sit back down I nevertheless stay quiet with my hands folded politely in my lap. I am rendered silent in this multi-gendered group not because I agree with the rebuke, but because I've run out of answers.

I believe the church fails to teach her daughters how to ask good questions.

Any Christian woman worth her salt can come up with a laundry list of answers common to women's "issues." The church feeds them to us like medicine. We regurgitate them to one another over coffee and at women's retreats. Men don't respect women who have too many guy friends, one retreat speaker explained to me in college; it tells them you aren't a biblical woman. Christians love to turn the Bible into an adjective; we sprinkle the term *biblical* around as if it will render our advice holy. If we can tack a bible verse onto it, then it is the godly answer. (Once I was given a pamphlet of "biblical" guidelines for modest dress that advised women to avoid purse straps that went across our chests lest it further emphasize our breasts and cause a Christian brother to stumble. Someone rightly pointed out that seat belts do the same thing.) All of these answers are mere shadow rules, half of the equation, of what a Christian woman looks like. Like a corset, they give shape to us while also suffocating us.

But answers are not the problem.

The church feeds women answers when what we need are questions. A question is elemental, like hydrogen. A good one unearths foundations and cracks open something that previously had no entrance into our lives. In grammar school we learn the elements to a good story: *Who? What? Where? When? Why? How?* As adults we return to these basic questions in order to understand our own story: *Who* are we? *What* is our purpose? When we encounter suffering we look at God and ask *why?* Every young woman wonders *how* she will get where she wants to be. We cannot know ourselves until we can face these questions. The question is fundamental to knowing. It is the beginning of understanding.

The summer after sixth grade I attended a Four Square Church camp. The female counselors gathered all the girls together for a special afternoon session. There was a table with chocolate cheesecake and fruit tarts. Someone put on a Point of Grace album. We stood, gangly and awkward preteens, in a circle while the female counselors demonstrated the godly way to dance.

"There is a right way and a wrong way to do things," they said. Here are the rules for how to move your bodies so your new curves won't tempt a young man beyond what God says is holy: Keep room for the Holy Spirit, don't tip forward so he can see down your shirt, and never let his hands wander. No undulating hips, they shouted. We danced, held hands and spun with one another like some sort of Christian coven free to do in private what was forbidden in public. My bunkmate taught me to shimmy and I remember feeling wild. Laughter bubbled up as I shook and dipped and rolled those hips. "Most of all," the female counselors shouted over the music, "remember there is a right way and a wrong way. Know the answers and you'll stay pure and holy. You'll be a good girl."

As I edged toward adulthood these answers were my map for questions about what kind of woman God wanted me to be. I learned the first charge was to temper myself. The most important thing in God's eyes was not who I was, but what I didn't do.

When I went to college, the litany of answers exploded in my life. I am the daughter of two United Methodist ministers, and even though I grew up in the church, even though I knew Jesus loved me and I prayed to him every night, I didn't know the Bible. No one had ever taught me to read it until Jill suggested we start with 1 Peter. My freshman year was spent huddled over scripture waiting for answers to disseminate like dewdrops scattered in the grass. I wanted to scoop them up and hold them in my hand.

"I am lonely." Answer: When you are satisfied in Christ, *then* He will bring you a boyfriend.

"What is godly dating?" Answer: Do not let hands go anywhere a soccer uniform covers.

"What does God want me to do?" Answer: Read Proverbs 31.

"Who should I be?" Answer: Be a mother or a nurse or a teacher. Become a missionary. Have you considered that?

And then something happened that had no answers. A woman in my life was raped. She was young, and when I found out all I could think about was how she still slept beneath a blanket covered in neon aliens holding up the peace sign. She was still made of sugar and spice and everything nice. In the aftermath I listened to her cry, read her testimony against her assailant, and watched *Bridget Jones' Diary* with her a dozen times. Privately, I groped for answers, but there were none. The only words of scripture I could stand to read were Psalm 6: "Have compassion on me, Lord, for I am weak. Heal me, Lord, for my body is in agony. I am sick at heart. How long, O Lord, until you restore me?"

You cannot go back to a life of answers once you begin to question.

I questioned why God would let this happen. I questioned my doubt and my anger and my overwhelming sadness. I was disappointed that I didn't have an answer, just a fist full of tears that I shook at God. One night I curled up on a bench beneath a starry sky and dared those pinpricks of light to come down and fix this. I was done. As my friends dated, I questioned why I wasn't doing the same. I slept on a friend's futon because I couldn't stand to be alone in my dorm room. I developed ulcers, couldn't eat more than boiled chicken, and had to buy my jeans in the juniors department. My parents told me if I didn't go see a counselor they would stop paying for school.

It took another year-and-a-half before I admitted that I could not fix myself. By this time I had dropped out of my church ministry and routinely skipped class. I hadn't made a new friend in a year and hadn't been on a date in two. I didn't go crazy and rebel. Instead, I did something worse. I stopped living.

And then one morning I hit a parked car in my rush to get to class because I was late, again. It was a wet December day and I sweated in my parka as I got out to check for damage. When I got back into my car, I leaned my forehead on the steering wheel and told God I was done trying. I was not the person I wanted to be. I had run out of answers.

This is the shadowed, gray place where so many women fall away from the church because no answer can stand in the place of a question. When the church fails to teach her daughters how to ask good questions we sign their fate. I consider it a miracle, a work of the Holy Spirit, that I have anything to do with God after my depression. I questioned because I was desperate.

The church suffers from an overabundance of answers in general, but I think it is particularly detrimental to women. Proverbs 31 is touted as a literal and complete list of what makes a godly woman. She "will not hinder [her husband], but help him all her life." She looks for bargains, spins wool, and prepares breakfast before dawn. She does not worry about charm or beauty, but always fears the Lord. She is strong, dignified, and laughs with no fear of the future. She is a Christian superhero!

The church has romanticized womanhood into a fairy tale. I worked for a church that used the popular "Princess with a Purpose" curriculum for their fourth- and fifth-grade girls retreat. While receiving pedicures, the girls were taught Jesus loved them. The mistake is not in pampering our daughters but in teaching them that Jesus is like a holy prince. In *Captivating: Unveiling the Mystery of a Woman's Soul*, John and Stasi Eldredge call the godly woman a warrior princess who "yearns to have an irreplaceable role in a grand adventure." But the Christian walk is not a Disney fairy tale. Jesus is not your boyfriend and He is not going to rescue you like a knight in shining armor.

We have sentimentalized Jesus into a prince who saves our dreams this side of heaven. And we have sentimentalized the woman in Proverbs 31 by turning her into the woman worthy of such a prince. She is the woman who can fix anything, a woman who has all the right answers. Answers winnow women down to warrior princesses who stay silent and bake bread. But questions open up our possibilities. Questions are the making of our character.

When we ask a question we are saying we do not know. We are but lowly sinners and we seek God's wisdom. The power of a question lies in its prophetic possibility. In the Bible, prophets were not fortunetellers. Like John the Baptist, they were a voice in the wilderness. They questioned the reality the world called good and named God's vision for the way things ought to be. A prophet is not someone who stays silent and accepts the given answers. A prophet bows low before God and asks those elemental questions: *Who? What? When? Where? Why? How?* And in the Bible there is a tradition of women prophets—Miriam, Deborah, Huldah, and Anna, to name a few. These are women who asked questions, had visions, and spoke up.

That morning in college when I hit the car and finally told God I was done trying to fix my life was when I finally admitted that I could not save myself. I needed a Jesus who hung on the cross and died for my sins, not a prince from mere fairy tales.

The Proverbs 31 woman is a woman who repents, who struggles, and who questions, more than she is a woman who has all the answers. We become the disciples and prophets God seeks to raise up when we move beyond the answers of our youth and embrace the questions, for questions shift our foundations, break open new possibilities, and allow the Holy Spirit to enter un-trespassed parts of our souls.

I know this to be true because I have witnessed it. Answers did not satisfy, but questions brought me low before God and God has done a good work in me. He restored my heart, and He has given me a voice that cannot remain silent.

Hinges and Doors

by Andrea Palpant Dilley

ANDREA PALPANT DILLEY grew up in Kenya as the daughter of Quaker missionaries, and also spent the rest of her childhood in the Pacific Northwest. Her memoir, *Faith and Other Flat Tires: Searching for God on the Rough Road of Doubt* (Zondervan), tells the story of her faith journey. Her work has appeared on cnn.com, huffingtonpost.com, and christianitytoday.com, as well as in *Rock and Sling*, *Geez*, *Utne Reader*, and the anthology *Jesus Girls: True Tales of Growing Up Female and Evangelical* (Cascade Books). She lives with her husband and two daughters in Austin, Texas. For more information, visit Andrea on Facebook or at www.andreapalpantdilley.com.

I don't remember the story. But my mother does. I've heard it so many times that it seems like part of my own memory. One morning while she was sitting in the living room of our house in Kenya, our friend Joy Panicker came running through the front door with bad news. "The Lord has given and taken," he said. "The baby stopped moving two days ago." Joy and his wife, Mercy, were missionaries from India serving in western Kenya with my parents, also missionaries, whom they adopted as surrogate family.

When Joy came through those doors with news of his baby's death, my mother welcomed him in his grief. I imagine her pulling out a chair, inviting him to sit, breathe, and cry. It might have been a very private moment. Except that he wasn't alone in the living room. Our neighbor Mama Rosoah had come to visit and was sitting in one of the wicker chairs in the corner. Not long after she came, a beggar had knocked. Kenya had almost no infrastructure for mental health patients, so the mentally ill wandered homeless and aimless and were sustained by the hospitality of their community. The beggar was the second person my mother hosted that morning. Joy was the third. They all came walking through the French doors of our house in need of something—food, comfort, or friendship.

I still remember those doors, and the house, too. We lived in a cement-block house on the edge of the Quaker hospital compound where my dad worked. In retrospect, I associate the front doors not with the house, really, but with my mother. She left them open all day long, partly because of cultural convention—hospitality was paramount in rural Kenya—and partly because she was an American hippie born and bred on civil rights and a Christian who believed it was her God-given duty to care for anyone who came walking through those doors. Everyone was welcome: the beggar, the friend, the bereaved father. There were others, too. Sometimes foreigners from Germany and other European countries showed up out of nowhere in need of a place to stay for the night. My mother fed a meal to the beggar, prayed for the mourning father, and found a bed for the traveler.

Even after we returned to the United States for good, my mom continued her commitment to hospitality, public service, and volunteerism. She was the Patron Saint of Meatloaf, taking food to tired firefighters, new mothers, and lonely immigrants who moved to eastern Washington from Russia. She visited the elderly shut-ins from our church and hosted foster kids from all over the world who flew into our city for donated medical care. Although she followed American convention and left the front door of our house closed, it was for all intents and purposes open to anyone, anytime, the way it had been in Kenya.

My mother wasn't alone, either. Other women in the Presbyterian Church we attended were like-minded in their commitments. As a girl growing up under their collective influence, they embodied the feminine Christian identity and became my role models for what it meant to practice God's scriptural mandate to care for others. If you took your faith seriously as a woman, you served the poor and underprivileged. A woman without a service banner—Save the

Children! Stop the Wars! Feed the Hungry!—was a woman without purpose. It was that simple.

When I went to college at age eighteen, I carried this model with me. In the grandiose idealism of youth, I developed dreams of saving the world by volunteering in the American inner city or starting an orphanage in Honduras. I would be "that woman," the one wearing long skirts and gaiting through the hallways of my well-run orphanage, the one they wrote glowing biographies about after I was dead and buried. My name would be remembered along with Mother Teresa, or at least uttered solemnly by a few Christian mothers telling stories to their daughters before bedtime.

In the summer after my senior year of college, that vision changed. I volunteered in a Sisters of Charity orphanage in the Kibera slums that rim the southwest edge of Nairobi. Every week, once a week, I rode with other volunteers in a van that took us down the dusty, narrow roads of the slums—past aluminum shanties, wild dogs, and hungry children. Before I even arrived at the orphanage, I felt overwhelmed by the sheer magnitude of human need all around me. Although the orphanage in some ways was a small oasis in the middle of the slums, it was, like the slums, a wellspring of suffering.

The AIDS nursery, in particular, troubled me. Located on the edge of the orphanage campus, the nursery was housed in a small room with a cement floor, white walls, and one bank of windows facing south. The afternoon sunlight filtered through the windows while Kenyan nuns scurried around the room, going from baby to baby, changing diapers, feeding, holding. They couldn't possibly tend to them all at once. At times, half a dozen babies were left crying. Waiting. Needing.

One morning while I was standing in the AIDS nursery trying to figure out how to be helpful, an infant in a crib nearby started to cry. The cribs were lined up in five or six neat rows, white metal cribs with curved frames and vertical bars. I leaned over the crib railing and picked her up. She was tiny, a little shell of a person swaddled in a white linen blanket. I put my index finger next to her hand and then watched her curl her preemie fist around my finger with a frail but firm grip. I still remember the feel of that grip. Watching her there and listening to the babies around me crying, I thought to myself, "How can I possibly do any good here? What's my role? And where's God in all this?"

In the process of doing what I had dreamed about for years—working in an orphanage—I found myself stumbling into a major identity crisis. It wasn't my first encounter with suffering. But it was one of the most significant. As I stood there in the AIDS nursery holding a motherless infant, I felt the floor drop out from underneath me. Everything I believed growing up—that serving others made the world a better place—seemed idealistic and ridiculous. I had in mind that I was supposed to feel fulfilled as a Christian woman, acting out my call to serve the poor and needy, but all I felt was overwhelmed.

At some point in her adult life, I'm sure my mother experienced similar disillusionment. But she survived it somehow and pushed through in service of God and the greater good. I wasn't so tenacious. When I got back from that summer in Kenya, I felt my identity shift and falter. Like many Christian women, I felt the expectation to serve, give, and volunteer. A disengaged woman was a woman without vision, without purpose. But for my part, I couldn't be "that woman." I couldn't be my mother, couldn't practice the kind of service that she had practiced. Moreover, I wasn't even sure I could be a Christian. Roughly eight months after working at the orphanage in Nairobi, I left behind not just the Christian church but everything I associated with it, including volunteerism. I closed the door and walked away.

Ten years later, I've returned to the church. But I'm not running an orphanage in Honduras or working in the inner city. I live in the inner suburbs of Austin, Texas and spend most of my time changing diapers, sweeping floors, and tending to my garden. Managing a "crisis" in this setting means calling the plumber when the sewage backs up into the bathtub or trying to explain to my anxious three-year-old that no, a bug will not eat her.

When I was eighteen, I used to think of suburban family living with utter disdain. It was the antithesis of the Christian service model—tending to an isolated little kingdom of backyard grills and gas mowers rather than going out on the global front lines to fight for justice, equality, and food for the hungry. I believed in a hierarchy of Christian vocations. If you didn't go off to be a missionary, a pastor, or a social worker, at a minimum, you committed to volunteering and giving yourself to the cause of alleviating suffering in the local community.

Back then, I felt sure of my calling as a Christian woman. Now I'm not so sure. The Capital of Texas Food Bank is only half a mile from my house and I can't even muster the energy to volunteer there. I wonder sometimes, have I completely failed my mother, my faith, and my community?

I still feel a particular kind of pressure burning at my back. It tells me: You're not doing enough. You're not giving enough. You're not fulfilling your Christian duty as a woman. I don't know where the pressure comes from, honestly. It doesn't come from my mother—she's too gracious for that. Maybe it comes from the insecurity that arises when comparing myself to others. Maybe it comes from hearing too many sermons on public service. Or maybe it comes from a Christian community's unspoken expectation that every woman worth her weight should be out there doing the good stuff, the big stuff, the significant, amazing, headline-worthy stuff.

Regardless of where the pressure comes from, I struggle with it. Three limitations in particular continue to challenge me:

First, the limits of work. Until recently, I was employed part-time from home by a television and film production company. My husband and I needed extra income. Although the work itself was modestly purposeful—I was marketing video services to universities and other nonprofit organizations—it wasn't exactly the kind of dramatic work that I once envisioned. My uninteresting desk job did not itself provide an essential public service and furthermore did not allow time for outside volunteer work. I had only so many hours in a week. Although some women manage to pull it off, I couldn't make extra income, be a parent, *and* volunteer.

Second, the limits of motherhood. I have a three-year-old and an infant at home. Even with a supportive husband who practices co-parenting, the demands of motherhood are still prohibitive.

Instead of going off to volunteer with the Red Cross in an earth-quake-shattered region of another continent, I'm scrubbing urine off the futon in my living room. I'm schlepping diaper bags, filling the kiddie pool, and frying fish sticks on the stove. "Think more local, think smaller," I say to myself. My mother somehow managed to incorporate her kids into the volunteer work she did at the hospital in Kenya. Every week, she took us on visitation to see my dad's patients. Why can't I do something like that?

Because of the third limit—perhaps one of the most important—known as "compassion fatigue." It stands as my final boundary point and blocks my ability to give. It means I'm tired. After growing up as a missionary kid and volunteering for years as a young adult, I'm experiencing now, in my mid-thirties, that compassion burnout. Every time I see a person in need, I dive into a cycle of guilt, grief, and responsibility. I feel guilty for my good life. I grieve their pain. And I want to save them from their pain at the same time that I feel completely overwhelmed by the prospect of helping them.

A few months ago, I started seeing a counselor to figure out why seeing the world's suffering draws out in me some deep, debilitating grief, and why volunteering has become such a life-sucking experience. To a former Christian missionary kid, counseling seems privileged, frivolous, and bourgeois. I'm sorting through high-level psychological pain while people all over the world go without basic needs like food. It feels equivalent to sweeping floors while there's a war going on outside your window. And yet here I am, faced with the very real limitations of my ability to volunteer.

Twenty-some years after watching my mother open the French doors of our house every morning in Kenya—the doors of ministry and service—I realize that my own doors don't open that wide. My hinges have limited range. Only recently have I felt some measure of peace with my half-closed doors. Although I have great admiration for my mother, her meatloaf, and her big heart, I'm beginning to accept our differences. I'm beginning to put up healthy boundaries. If I don't, I risk burnout.

For me, this means saying "no" to the church-wide volunteer activity of hosting a service for homeless people under the downtown freeway. It means stepping out of Sunday school when the female priest with a PhD in educational psychology starts telling a heartbreaking story about neglected children in the neighborhood two miles away and how we need to help them. It means picking up the list of potential volunteer places that I put together a few years ago in a fit of ambition—a list which includes the food bank half a mile away—and setting it aside for the future.

Being okay with my limitations, though, is only part of the solution. I have to revise my view of what it means to be a Christian woman. I have to redefine the traditional conception of volunteerism and broaden my vision of "giving." More importantly, I have to move beyond the perceived taboo that a woman without a service banner—Save the Children! Stop the Wars! Feed the Hungry!—is a woman without purpose. Christian women (and men) are called to serve others—that much hasn't changed—but serving others might not *look* the same for all of us. My doors are open, albeit in a less traditional sense.

I take comfort in the Parable of the Talents as told in Matthew chapter 25: "The one who had received the five talents came and brought five more, saying, 'Sir, you entrusted me with five talents. See, I have gained five more.' His master answered, 'Well done, good and faithful servant! You have been faithful in a few things. I will put you in charge of many things . . . The one with the two talents also came and said, 'Sir, you entrusted two talents to me. See, I have gained two more.' His master answered, 'Well done, good and faithful servant! You have been faithful with a few things. I will put you in charge of many things.'"

I'm the one, not with five talents, but with two. I don't have much to give or to invest. But I'm doing what I can with what I have. Here's what "being faithful with a few things" looks like for me:

One, I tithe money to a nonprofit organization that equips young people to serve overseas and in the inner city, young people who have become proxy volunteers doing what *I* once thought I would do myself. Writing checks is not nearly as sexy as laboring on the front lines. But I've come to appreciate it as an important, albeit hidden, form of public service.

Two, I engage in writing projects and also support my husband's professorial scholarship. Although intellectual activities like writing are not always high on the list of laudable Christian giving, I view it as a service to the inner life of others. For example, after writing about my spiritual journey of leaving the church during a crisis of faith, I find myself corresponding with readers who struggle with doubt. I feel called to respond to them, not because I view myself as some self-ordained pastor, but because I know what they're going through. I feel their struggle. And I believe sharing stories in a spirit of transparency can mitigate that pain.

Three, I try to practice hospitality to the best of my ability. Sometimes when the doorbell rings, it's the eighty-three-year-old widowed neighbor that I invited over for dinner. Sometimes it's the twenty-something guy selling forty-dollar all-purpose soap, which I buy because I feel sorry for him and sorry for the state of a world where young men have to sell schlock door-to-door just to scrape up enough money to pay the rent. And sometimes it's the divorcée from across the street who rings the doorbell claiming that her Chihuahua *really* wanted to come over and visit my three-year-old. She comes in, sits down in my rocking chair, and talks for half an hour.

I'm no Mother Teresa. From what I've heard, she closed the gates of her compound once a week to give herself a break. My capacity is the reverse. And even though I could never compete with my own mother in sheer quantity of volunteer activity, we're both in our own way trying to serve God and others. For my mom, that meant hosting foster kids and feeding beggars. For me, it means something less traditional. It means sending checks. It means writing. It means listening to a lonely neighbor go off about her broken lawn mower while her dog races around the living room on the heels of my eldest child.

I still struggle with the expectation to be out there serving on the front lines. I still feel guilty sometimes for not volunteering at the food bank half a mile away. But for now, I try to follow the Parable of the Talents by being "faithful in a few things."

Gender Confusion: Navigating Evangelical Discussions of Gender Roles

by Sharon Hodde Miller

SHARON HODDE MILLER grew up in North Carolina, where she earned her BA in religion at Duke University and her master of divinity at Duke Divinity School. She is currently pursuing her PhD in educational studies at Trinity Evangelical Divinity School. Sharon has worked for Proverbs 31 Ministries and has served as a college minister, but she feels her primary call is to writing. Today she is a regular contributor to *Christianity Today*'s blog for women, *Her.meneutics*, Ungrind.org, and CultivateHer.com, in addition to her own blog, SheWorships.com. Sharon currently lives outside Chicago with her husband and their son.

I am a woman, I am an evangelical, and I am called to ministry. I know that about myself. What I don't know is how those three elements square with one another. That piece of the puzzle has taken me on a journey that has been both long and lonely, though not in the way one might expect.

To understand the tension created by these three strands of my identity, it is helpful to understand what evangelicalism is to me. The term itself is difficult to define because it includes such a wide swath of people, and the label has been used to describe everything from born-again Christians to political voting blocs. Historically, evangelicalism is marked by an emphasis on Biblical authority and sharing the good news of Jesus Christ through word and deed. These markers, however, make "evangelicalism" nearly as specific a term as "American."

I personally claim the label because I value the tradition's core principles, but I also love the intangible aspect of evangelical life that can only be described as sheer passion for God. That invisible yet palpable aspect of the tradition is what drew me and continues to draw me today.

Although I was not raised in the tradition, I have spent the last decade attending several evangelical churches. At each church I felt like I was home, like I was among my people. And yet, each church has been starkly different from the others I attended. The Southern Baptist church I once attended is very unlike the non-denominational church to which I now belong. Some of those differences might be cultural or geographical—the former is in North Carolina whereas the latter is outside Chicago—but other differences are far more basic.

While evangelicals unify around principles like Scripture and evangelism, there are a number of issues that also divide us. Some profoundly so. In particular, evangelicals are polarized on the topic of gender roles, there being great disagreement about what it means to be male and female. Within the debate there are two dominant voices: the more conservative perspective, which believes in divinely prescribed gender roles; and the more liberal perspective, which places no limits or concrete definitions on either gender. As an evangelical woman with a call to ministry, I have found myself sitting in the thick of that debate.

Now, my story is not that of a woman who cannot find a church in which I can serve or be accepted. As I mentioned, there are many evangelicals who fully support the calling and gifts of women in the church. That is not to say that evangelical women have not been hurt by their churches. Many have, and their stories need to be heard. Fortunately, there are safe communities within evangelicalism that provide refuge for these wounded souls. But my story is a different one. I have not been silenced by a narrow view of gender. Instead, I have found myself silenced by the debate itself.

Unlike many evangelicals who have firm convictions about gender, I am sympathetic to both sides of the discussion. I recognize the limitations and dangers of prescribed gender roles, but I also believe that God created two distinct genders for a purpose, and I desire to honor God's design. In this way, my position is a moderate one, and it has not been easy to hold. Margaret Thatcher once said, "Standing in the middle of the road is very dangerous; you get knocked down by the traffic from both sides." That has been my experience. In fact, I would argue that one of the only taboo positions in evangelicalism, as it relates to the topic of gender, is the middle ground.

I first noticed this strange "alienation of the moderate" about a year after I graduated from college. I had joined a Southern Baptist church that I loved. The community was strong and committed to the faith, and I felt right at home. However, a small group of male members within the congregation was more radical than the rest, particularly in their views on women. They espoused an extremely conservative position, believing that women should refrain from even speaking in the church, let alone preach or teach.

Although I was by no means a rabble-rouser in the congregation, this band of men somehow sniffed out my less conservative views on gender and began to target me. Their attacks culminated at a church league softball game when a female member was asked to open in prayer. For reasons I cannot explain to this day, the men singled me out as the reason for this show of "liberalism," and they publicly rebuked me on the spot. It was humiliating and infuriating, and I fled the field in tears.

To the church's credit, the incident was handled swiftly and sternly, and the men eventually left the church. Even so, I cannot help but marvel at the entire experience. I had done nothing to incite the ire of these men, save being a Christian female who taught and led in the college ministry, and yet I somehow came to symbolize a leftist position on Scripture and gender.

Nearly ten years later, I live in the Chicago area and attend a nondenominational evangelical church where women are free to preach and be ordained. I also write for an evangelical women's blog whose readership is diverse but tends toward the progressive end of evangelicalism. As I have continued to work through my own beliefs about what it means to be a woman in the church, I have experienced resistance from progressive evangelicals as well. One writer has even targeted me on his blog multiple times. In the same way that my conservative friends are uncomfortable with my "liberal" views on gender, my progressive friends and readers are often concerned about—or even offended by—my conservative views.

As an evangelical who has sympathies with both sides of the debate, the middle ground is a difficult place to inhabit. Whether in the company of my progressive friends or my conservative ones, each sphere has its own in-group language and its own unique convictions, each narrow and slightly alienating in its own way. Adherents to both sides are passionate about their views, and both have Scripture to back their stances. Both also believe that the integrity of the church is at stake, and with such high stakes there is little room for mutual understanding, let alone charitable dialogue.

It has been difficult to find a community where I can safely wrestle with my questions about gender. Among my conservative friends, I am reluctant to challenge the socially constructed views that purport to be "biblical," for fear of being perceived as one who does not revere the Word of God. Among my progressive friends, I am hesitant to voice a position that seems "backward" and oppressive to women. In admitting to differences between genders, I don't want to be accused of promoting overly simplistic gender distinctions that are more cultural than they are scriptural.

As a result of this personal conflict, I have learned to be careful about my word choice if the topic of gender roles arises, especially if I don't know where my conversation partner stands. I listen for cues that indicate where he or she falls on the spectrum, and I tailor my own words accordingly.

Whenever I take a step back, it is clear to me that these gender role negotiations are unhealthy. Neither are they very Christian. As important as the subject of gender roles is, Christians should be able to have honest and thoughtful conversation with one another. In 1 Corinthians 12, the Apostle Paul describes the church as a body with many diverse members, all equally necessary to its function. From Paul's perspective I have concluded that even when

I vehemently disagree with another Christian, there is an extent to which I *need* her perspective. Without her, my own understanding of God and my ability to serve God is handicapped.

Despite this biblical teaching and others like it, the issue of gender roles raises barriers and stifles civility faster than almost any other. It is a category with which evangelicals pigeonhole one another with the label of "conservative" or "liberal." In fact, the above description of my own conversational tap-dancing is evidence of that practice. As much as I don't like to be pigeonholed, I am prone to pigeonhole others quite easily.

Although conservatives bear the brunt of criticism for being too judgmental, it is my experience that both liberal and conservative Christians alike contribute to the breakdown in communication. I suspect that this phenomenon within the church reflects the larger political climate in the United States. Many conversations are dominated by a vocal few who represent polarized positions, all while a "silent majority" finds neither pole to be wholly sufficient.

When it comes to the topic of gender roles, I don't know whether I belong to a silent majority or only a minority, but no matter our numbers there seems to be little space for us to work through the complexity of gender. As I explore the arguments for each perspective and discern the direction of my calling, my wrestling is interpreted as narrow-mindedness, liberalism, or even naiveté, but rarely as earnest reflection.

At a time when public discourse is so divided by partisan politics and civility seems an endangered discipline, I hope the Church will strive to have a different witness. Whether the subject is gender roles, same-sex marriage, or contraception, there should be grace enough in the community of Christ for wrestling with the complexities of our world. Wrestling should not be seen as lack of conviction, but the very evidence of it. For me, struggle is a sign of great investment.

Being a Voice for the Stranger
by Jenny Hwang Yang

JENNY HWANG YANG is the Vice President of Advocacy and Policy at World Relief. In this position, Jenny works with U.S. government officials to improve refugee and immigration policy. She also frequently speaks at churches and conferences educating and mobilizing the Christian community on immigration. She previously worked in the refugee resettlement program of World Relief and at one of the largest political fundraising firms in Maryland managing fundraising and campaigning for local politicians. Jenny has researched refugee and asylum law in Madrid, Spain through the United Nations High Commissioner for Refugees. She is co-author of *Welcoming the Stranger: Justice, Compassion and Truth in the Immigration Debate.*

I used to watch Connie Chung, a famous Asian-American news anchor, on television and think to myself that one day I would be a journalist like her. I've always felt a deep compassion for those suffering from pain, war, and conflict, and I wanted people to see and feel the way I saw and felt the world.

What I experienced while studying abroad in Madrid, Spain, derailed my aspirations of a career in journalism. I was riding the subway on a crowded train when I saw a young African mother tenderly interacting with her two children as they waited to get to their destination. After a few stops, a group of young, rowdy Spanish teenagers got into the subway car and started to graffiti its walls. They wrote in Spanish, "Get out of our country, black people." I had experienced such blatant racism myself in Spain when people called out *"China, China"* as I walked by. But to see these hateful remarks written on the walls in front of this young family, along with the lack of reaction from the people in the subway car with me, was disturbing.

That summer, I volunteered at a nonprofit organization dedicated to combating racism in Spain, organizing rallies, and coordinating events to raise awareness. I also worked at the United Nations High Commissioner for Refugees (UNHCR) office in Madrid. When I came back to the United States, I wanted to work specifically with refugees. Refugees are among the most vulnerable people in the world, their very lives in danger as a result of fleeing their homes, often after being attacked for something fundamental to their identity, their nationality, or their beliefs.

A few years after college, I started working with World Relief, a Christian humanitarian organization that provides relief and development overseas and resettles refugees to the United States. Eventually, I started working in Washington, DC as their director of advocacy and policy for the immigration and refugee program. During one of the first few days in this new position, my boss called me into his office and said, "The immigration debate is reaching new heights, and as an organization serving immigrants throughout the United States, we have to speak up for better policies. We are officially supporting comprehensive immigration reform, and we need you to lead our advocacy on it. This will mean advocating for not only border security and a more flexible visa system, but earned legalization for immigrants who are undocumented in the United States. Would you be willing to do this?"

I thought to myself, Could we really be advocating for thousands of people who had broken the law? Would this difficult, unsavory issue take me away from advocating for refugees overseas, a people who I thought were even more vulnerable than immigrants in the United States? And would the fact that I am a minority embroil me in a debate I wanted to distance myself from?

As a Korean-American woman, I hadn't thought much about the debate surrounding immigration, because it didn't affect me or the people I knew personally. My parents had come to the United States legally, but I started to wonder whether people would question the reason I was speaking out for immigration reform as one of personal gain instead of conviction and truth. I wanted to advocate on an issue that was easy to understand and care about, not an issue that was more ambiguous and took a full five minutes to explain coherently. As I tiptoed into the debate, I sought to answer the many controversial questions I heard swirling around in the news about why immigrants don't always enter the country legally or how immigrants contributed to the U.S. economy.

What was most startling to me at that time, however, was that when I talked to Christians and non-Christians about immigration, the conversation was the same. It revolved around economics or politics, but little mention was made of Scripture. In fact, it seemed to me as if everyone, Christians included, hated immigrants.

Through my own study of Scripture, I realized that immigrants are mentioned ninety-two times in the Old Testament alone, and often as particularly vulnerable because they didn't have family to lean on or their own land to farm for sustenance. God thus commanded His people to take special care for them and even legislated such care into law. Deuteronomy 24:19-21 says that the Israelites were to not go over their fields twice when picking crops in order to "leave what remains for the alien, the fatherless and the widow." I also realized that almost every major biblical character had some kind of migration experience, and that migration experience was fundamental to his or her experience and love of God. Abraham, for example, was called to leave his homeland and "go to the land I [God] will show you" (Genesis 12:1), while Ruth followed her mother-in-law into a new land where she would meet her future husband, an ancestor of Jesus. I wondered whether these heroes of the Bible had to get visas before traveling or were ever unwelcomed guests in their host communities. It was clear to me throughout Scripture that God cared for immigrants, and He wanted His people to do the same.

I also realized that the prophets of the Old Testament and Jesus Himself didn't just care about the individual needs of people but also wanted to address the root causes of oppression. Isaiah 58:6, for example, says, "Is not this the kind of fasting I have chosen: to loose the chains of injustice and untie the cords of the yoke?" And Jesus said in Luke 11:42, "Woe to you Pharisees, because you give God a tenth of your mint, rue and other kinds of garden herbs, but you neglect justice and the love of God." The more I learned about U.S. immigration policy, the more I realized our immigration laws weren't functioning for our country or for the immigrant.

I've seen how a broken immigration system creates broken people. One young man I met in Mexico had been picking grapes in northern California for eight years but had recently been deported. "I am never going to see my daughter again," he said to me despondently while pushing his fork into a bowl of salad, telling me his father and wife are now taking care of his daughter. I have met youth who didn't know they were undocumented until they had to apply for college, and their parents finally told them they could not afford the out-of-state tuition. While immigration laws are important, laws can and should be changed if they are not working for the common good.

This realization posed a particular problem for me. I wasn't just responsible for advocating for immigration reform on Capitol Hill, but for taking the message of why immigration reform was needed to the evangelical community in the United States. On the Hill, I could make coherent arguments about why immigration reform was needed for the good of our economy or national security, but now I was supposed to take this message to white evangelicals. From various polls I learned that only 16 percent of this group had ever heard about immigration from their pastors, and that they were the most inclined, among faith groups, to view immigrants in a negative light.[1, 2]

I found myself uncomfortable at times when I traveled to speaking engagements throughout the United States and realized that I was the only minority in a room full of Caucasians or people who were mostly older than me. I wondered, Will they reject the message because of the messenger? Would they feel more open to hearing what I have to say if I were more similar to them?

---

1. The Pew Forum on Religion and Public Life, "Few Say Religion Shapes Immigration, Environment Views" (September 17, 2010), accessed on August 12, 2012, at <http://www.pewforum.org/Politics-and-Elections/Few-Say-Religion-Shapes-Immigration-Environment-Views.aspx>.
2. Smith, Greg, "Attitudes Toward Immigration: In the Pulpit and the Pew," Pew Research Center, April 26, 2006, accessed on April 25, 2012, at <http://pewresearch.org/pubs/20/attitudes-toward-immigration-in-the-pulpit-and-the-pew>.

I have always valued being a woman and a Korean-American. In the immigration debate, however, I feared the parts of my identity I treasured could in fact become reasons to detract from what I was saying or writing. The more public I became as an advocate, in fact, the more personal the attacks became. One guest column I wrote for a Christian magazine online about Arizona immigration bill SB1070, for example, had almost 300 comments—mostly negative, and many demonstrating readers' wrongful assumption that my Asian identity was the reason I advocate for immigrant-friendly policies. One comment writer, for example, said "You can tell an immigrant wrote the 'story'!" Another said, "Tell me, Jenny Hwang, who in your family is illegal?" Others have written "Is Jenny a Christian? It doesn't sound like it," and "The author seems to be taking a liberal approach rather than an evangelical approach." My personal identity as a young Asian-American woman had seemingly become a public liability that discounted my voice.

In order to convince the evangelical church in the United States, I had to start sharing my own personal story of how I came to understand immigration scripturally so people would know I was speaking out of my knowledge of the Bible first and then immigration policy second.

While I initially thought that having a personal stake in the debate would detract from my arguments for immigration reform, I realized all of us have a personal stake in this debate. By supporting immigration reform, we are not condoning the breaking of the law but making the law more functional for the good of all. More than the economics of the debate, I believe our response to people who look different and often speak a different language will define our values as a nation and who we will become. It also tests what we fundamentally believe about whether God's sovereignty extends over the movement of people, that it is not an accident, but, as Acts 17:26-27 says, "He marked out their appointed times in history and the boundaries of their lands. God did this so that they would seek him and perhaps reach out for him and find him, though he is not far from any one of us." Immigration has a moral dimension and tests our ability to include, rather than exclude, others.

My faith has been integral in helping shape not only who I am as a person but also my role in the public sphere because I'm compelled by what I believe to be true in Scripture and what God has personally revealed to me about His heart. I can listen to the detractors and be discouraged to dampen my voice, but I realized my utmost allegiance is to carry out what I believe to be right in the eyes of God. After several years of feeling like I was one of only a few evangelical voices on the Hill that were advocating for immigration reform, there have emerged many prominent evangelical leaders who are now speaking up to say that the status quo cannot continue. We are creating an echo chamber for many others to do the same. Proverbs 31:8, which says to speak up for those who cannot speak for themselves, must be true of the Christian church today.

It's easy to listen to cable news television or radio personalities and have what they say be the sole basis for our worldview. As Christians, we have a higher calling to constantly reread Scripture and ask God to shape our hearts and minds on any issue that has a tendency to divide and create hate. It is also our responsibility to turn what we know into action in order to be good stewards of our God-given influence, to speak up when we see injustice even though everyone around us may be saying something different. We must constantly be reminded through the reading of Scripture and prayer how He would like us to respond as individuals and as a nation, recognizing that the grace that God bestows upon us every day is a grace we should extend to others.

While my dream of being the next Connie Chung has not been realized, being a voice for the voiceless and leading the church to be the hope of the world is a calling that fulfills who God created me to be. In a struggle to constantly separate my personal identity from my public one, I realized that God wants to use me wholly to make an impact for His kingdom. As a woman and an ethnic minority in the United States, I thank God for using all of who I am to impact the church and politics in order to influence decisions that affect the most vulnerable in our society.

The Pastor has Breasts

by Rebecca Clark

REV. REBECCA GIRRELL CLARK is an ordained clergyperson in the New England Annual Conference of the United Methodist Church. Now in her ninth year of ministry, Becca serves as pastor of Trinity United Methodist Church in Montpelier, Vermont, where she also volunteers as cofounder and president of a nonprofit organization dedicated to providing for people's basic needs. She views her ministry as a calling to live as her authentic self, while advocating for justice and sustainability in the local, global, and online communities. Building relationships, creating something new, and sharing reflections feed and sustain Becca, and she enjoys gardening, time with loved ones, and writing (including blogging at www.pastorbecca.com). Becca enjoys spending time with her two children, Arianna and William, who keep her honest and on her toes.

"It just makes me nervous."

My congregant blushed a little, an almost comical sight on the face of a middle-aged man. I was twenty-five and in my first year of service as a pastor. I was also in the third trimester of my first pregnancy.

I found out I was pregnant my first week at the new church. I had been public about it from the beginning, eschewing the traditional wait-until-twelve-weeks-to-tell-people thing. At first it was great; it helped me set healthy boundaries and prioritize my health and my home life, and it helped both my husband and me bond with the congregation. There were a few bumps in the road—congregants were sure this meant I would leave after nine months and become a stay-at-home mom—but there were also moments of beauty and wonder. Advent and Christmas took on new meaning as I celebrated the season with a round belly and a heart full of anticipation.

Now I was in the eighth month of pregnancy. Already an imposing woman—five feet nine inches tall with more curves than people know what to do with—I was starting to resemble an ancient fertility statue. It was this body that my congregant had found . . . distracting.

He swallowed his fear and said what was on his mind. "I don't like having a pregnant pastor. It just makes me nervous."

I asked why. He said it made me look too vulnerable. "Besides. It's like I have to think about—." His blush deepened as he trailed off.

"But what if the pastor's wife is pregnant?" I pressed.

Different, he assured me.

I'd been aware that my sexuality as a young woman was always in the room, so to speak, in my role as a pastor. When I presided at my very first memorial service, I wore a modest skirt suit. After the service, a dear friend of the deceased thanked me for the service in the receiving line and then leaned in and whispered, "And you have the nicest legs I've ever seen on a pastor."

That suit went to the back of the closet when I returned home. I can take a compliment, but I don't want people focusing on my body while I'm trying to proclaim hope in eternal life.

My pregnancy put my sexuality on display in a deeper way; it was as if my body now had a big, bulging neon sign above it, screaming, "The pastor has sex!"

Why was a male pastor's pregnant spouse not as disconcerting as a female pastor's pregnancy? In my experience, it wasn't the knowledge that the pastor had sex that made people most nervous; it was that the pastor was a powerful woman who did so.

I never apologized for breastfeeding once my daughter arrived. I never wondered if it was okay to do in a particular place. The church building was my home and workplace, and my baby came with me wherever I went when I returned from maternity leave. I nursed her in my office, in the nursery, and during meetings. We spent hours in the rocking chair in the back of the sanctuary, me nourishing her from my body in the most sacramental, sacred moments I'd ever known.

If my blushing congregant—or anyone else—was uncomfortable, I never heard about it.

My second congregation journeyed with me through pregnancy, loss, and joy in different ways. Where my first congregation had been quietly supportive, if somewhat nervous, my second seemed to embrace my embodied experience so much so that I was the one who felt more reserved. I felt a sometimes disconcerting loss of boundary between the very personal and the very public.

As with my first pregnancy, my husband and I announced we were expecting around eight weeks. I shared the due date—the end of September—and there was a pause. Then a quick-thinking math teacher crowed from her pew, "Happy New Year!" We'd been trying to conceive for over a year, charting body temperatures and ovulation cycles, and so I knew she was right. I blushed, a deep enough shade for Pentecost when the church decorates the sanctuary in flaming red fabrics.

We never saw that due date. Four weeks later, at eleven weeks and five days, I miscarried. We told the congregation that, too. I never regretted that they knew we'd been pregnant since their love and support were so meaningful. My body was the center of a tragedy and a place of healing. My sexuality was gone for the moment, absorbed into the often-shared experiences of loss, grieving, and yearning for hope again.

When we conceived a third time, the feeling among this same congregation was one of cautious joy. As my body took on the visible signs of pregnancy, the lines between personal and public grew blurry again. My belly was touched and poked, my weight gain the topic of conversation. This was almost *our* pregnancy now. Perhaps that's why no one within the congregation expressed discomfort; we had become like family, and from our shared experience there was enough comfort to hold both the pastor / preacher / prophet and the expecting mother.

Outside the congregation, I still encountered surprise and confusion. My favorite question was "Can pastors *get* pregnant?"—as if one's ovaries are removed as part of the ordination process. But in my progressive, close-knit community, these reactions were few. I carried my son to term, delivered, and nurtured a beautiful child. As I did with his older sister, I brought my son to work with me for the first year of his life. I received a little critique here and there for it but managed to hold it together.

When my son was almost a year old, the realization that my body was still sexualized came crashing down upon me.

One day, a young man came to visit me in my office and asked to speak privately about his lack of housing. Sitting across the desk from me, he unfolded the story of his past, which included abuse and abandonment and struggles over boundaries with the women in his life. It was lunchtime, and my son sat next to me in his high chair, playing with his food.

The young man paused in his story, looked at my son, and then back at me in my ill-fitting nursing top and asked, "Do you breastfeed?"

I forgot. I forgot that for some people, this is not a question about nutrition or feminism or raising a child in community. I forgot that for a young man who has already named struggles with boundaries, this was a comment about my breasts.

"Yes," I said.

"What's it like?" he asked.

"It's a wonderful and life-giving way to nourish my son," I said. "But we were talking about your travels and how you are looking for some shelter while you are in the area . . ."

The conversation re-centered on those concerns until he again focused on my torso, this time pointedly staring.

"I just get distracted," he said, almost apologetically. "I like women with big breasts. And you're breastfeeding so they're even bigger . . . a pastor who has breasts."

Ten minutes later, shaking and crying, arms folded protectively over my chest, I poured out the story to an older male colleague. How I had told the young man it was time to leave. How he had looked out the window into the church office and seen it empty (our administrator having stepped out for a moment). How he had come toward me around the desk, and I had stood to meet him, placing myself as a shield in front of my son. How he had tried to embrace me, hold on to me, get his face and his hands close to my body. How I had pushed him away, forcefully, thrust his backpack at him, and showed him the door.

More vulnerable, that first congregant had said, during my first pregnancy six years ago. More sexualized, he'd hinted.

I had been so committed to living out the fully authentic, fully embodied witness of being a woman in leadership while pregnant and breastfeeding that I neglected my own boundaries. I was so intent about not letting other people's discomfort dictate my actions that I wasn't listening to my own discomfort.

I find the balance a tenuous one to walk: unapologetically claiming my sexuality, sensuality, and embodied nature, all epitomized in the big-bellied, big-breasted mother, while at the same time preserving enough of my privacy to keep my body safe and my heart intact. I don't have answers for how to walk this tightrope; like our bodies, our comfort with the public and private is unique to each one of us. What I do know is that the way we see women's bodies—the way we see our own bodies—challenges us to live in this tension. The female body, especially accentuated in pregnancy and the postpartum period, conjures powerful feelings of protectiveness, nurture, and sexuality. I refuse to see this as something at odds with what it means to be a Christian minister and a leader in the faith community. In fact, sexuality is at the very heart of what it means to me to be a powerful woman. For those of us with female bodies, this can neither define nor confine us. I'm more than a pastor with breasts, and a belly, and a baby.

My daughter is seven and my son is two. My body looks almost like it did before the miracle of nature filled me and distorted me like a funhouse mirror. I won't be making any congregants blush with the thought of my protruding pregnant belly again, but I will surely still make people nervous from time to time. My balancing act continues; the tension between my authentic and embodied self and the professionalism and safety of my role in the church and community remain.

It's a little top heavy. The pastor still has breasts.

Joiner

by Alena Amato Ruggerio

ALENA AMATO RUGGERIO is an associate professor in the Department of Communication at Southern Oregon University, where she has also served as interim director of Women's Studies. She holds a doctorate in communication and culture from Indiana University. She is the editor of *Media Depictions of Brides, Wives, and Mothers* and the author of *You Get a Lifetime: The Chronicle of a Semester in Greece*. Her work has also appeared in *Feminist Media Studies, Christian Century,* and the *Encyclopedia of Christianity*. A life member of the National Communication Association, she is an officer for the Feminism and Women's Studies Division. Her teaching specializations are persuasion, argumentation and debate, advanced public speaking, rhetorical criticism, and feminist rhetorical theory. She is an active member of EEWC: Christian Feminism Today, an organization she has served as coordinator, assistant to the editor of *Christian Feminism Today* magazine, and a frequent speaker. She lives in Medford, Oregon, with her husband, three cats, and her collection of rhinestone tiaras.

A religious publication needs 200 subscribers to maintain its nonprofit bulk mailing rate with the U.S. postal service. I know this obscure fact because *Christian Feminism Today* has 211. If twelve people fail to renew their subscriptions, the Evangelical and Ecumenical Women's Caucus, an organization founded in 1975 to promote a biblical approach to gender equality, would no longer be able to afford to mail our quarterly magazine. This situation leaves me, as the assistant to the editor of *CFT*, feeling mystified and sorrowful. Are there really only 211 people willing to subscribe to a magazine covering the stories of people striving to live as both Christians and feminists? This is just one symptom of an economic downturn in which all nonprofits have sustained massive financial hits. It is also the result of a taboo among people under forty against becoming "joiners."

I identify as one of the Gen Xers—those born between approximately 1965 and 1982 who were shaped by Reaganomics, MTV, and the AIDS pandemic—but I do not share my generation's distaste for organizational affiliations and accepting labels. At the same time, young Christians are fleeing church pews in alarming numbers and the college-aged women in my courses are often unwilling to call themselves feminists. "I'm spiritual not religious" and "I'm not a feminist but . . ." should be tattooed across the knuckles of the post-Baby Boom generations who have dealt a one-two blow to my most beloved sources of religious shelter and renewal: Christian Feminism Today and my local church. Sometimes I feel like one of the only joiners my age in those organizations, and although I have reaped the benefits of belonging, I've also seen firsthand the devastation my generation has inflicted by their absence.

It's not that GenXers and Millennials (those Americans who don't remember a world before the Internet) don't want community. But who's got time to attend a chapter meeting? Our individualistic dislike of committee work is so strong that small-group communication scholars began describing the phenomenon of "grouphate" as far back as 1981. It's just easier to wear a silicone bracelet or post our favorite causes to our Facebook walls. Our digital usage demands nothing of us but consumption, and by that consumption we declare our political and religious affiliations, enact our activism, and present our identities.

So then what's wrong with me? Why do I feel like one of the few oddballs of my generation who enthusiastically join? Maybe it goes back to my nerdy childhood. I never learned to make friends easily or mingle at parties. Now I'm more comfortable interacting with people in the structured environment of an organization. Or perhaps it's because I don't have children. I look for belonging outside my nuclear family and find ways to connect with people other than through parenting. More likely, being a joiner is just part of my personality. I have some kind of weird compulsion to volunteer to be every group's secretary: I'm highly organized, I can type like a pro, and I long to be a part of the inner circle of leadership without being the figurehead on the chopping block if things go awry.

Becoming a joiner has allowed me to forge a family of choice when I moved two thousand miles away from my family of origin. After I lost my college gang to the graduation diaspora, I didn't find my new tribe until I became a member of Christian Feminism Today and joined the committee that plans our biennial conference. It was the intense shared task that drew us together in friendships I hope will be lifelong, particularly with Sharon, who picked me up at the bus station every weekend when I traveled an hour to the planning meetings. Often there would be enough time for breakfast before the meeting, and Sharon would describe, over omelets and pancakes, what her life looked like before feminism. She told stories of sex-segregated want ads in the newspaper and being fired from her job when she got married because her employer assumed she would just quit anyway upon getting pregnant. She taught me much about what we were standing up against.

Two more members of CFT, Letha and Linda, invited me to join them in a Bible study conducted via conference call across three states, a standing date we've kept for three hours every Friday for nine years. They have become my dearest friends. I wish we had transcripts of all the adventures we have during those phone calls, like when Linda falls asleep when we talk too far past midnight, or I put my cat on the phone to purr. Sometimes Letha announces she's spent the past thirty minutes exercising on her step machine and she wasn't even winded during the conversation. On the other hand, I'm glad there aren't recordings of the terrible low points we've gotten each other through. Even when I taught in Greece for a semester, Linda and three other CFT members flew to the other side of the planet when I needed them. Living in Athens was a remarkable experience, but it was also unnervingly lonely maintaining a professional distance from my students and being separated from my husband, who was unable to travel with me.

When Linda, Louise, Arlynne, and Janet arrived and I told them how I had been hanging on by my fingernails until they got there, Louise proclaimed, "Your people are here now." My homesick heart dissolved with relief.

Being one of the few joiners my age has meant building these friendships with other joiners who are significantly older than I am: Letha by forty years, Sharon by thirty-six, and Linda by twenty. At feminist conferences and church meetings there is much talk about "intergenerational dialogue;" I live it every day. These women are wiser, more forgiving, more stubborn, more hilarious, more lippy, and more generous than anyone I've ever met. I've learned how to handle illness from Letha, who kept breast cancer and three joint-replacement surgeries in perspective as inconvenient distractions from her passionate ministry. I've learned how to handle profound grief from Sharon, who fought to make decisions in her own right time after the death of her husband. I've learned self-care from Linda, who managed depression and seasonal affective disorder by limiting her computer time and admitting her vulnerability. My life path would have never crossed with any of these spectacular women except within the organization.

The valuing seems mutual. The older members of Christian Feminism Today have repeatedly created spaces for me to speak, write, and lead. It's not like grad school, where although you apprentice under the rock stars of feminist theology, you're always below them on the academic hierarchy. Joining makes you an equal. My organization has never experienced the generation gap strife that has been so overblown between second- and third-wave secular feminists. Perhaps it's because my group is so small they cannot afford to turn the young away with any Electra Complex drama where the daughter must fight to differentiate herself from her mother. Sometimes we chuckle at the years that divide us, like the time I tried to define the slang of *squee, slash,* and *squick* I'd picked up online (I'm not going to share which websites I was frequenting). Other times, the age gap is more serious, such as when some of the less web-savvy older members feel excluded and anxious when we talk about the technological intricacies of our biblical feminist website and listserv. Regardless, CFT's commitment to the radical inclusivity of Jesus provides us with a way to communicate together despite our generational differences.

Seeing myself as a joiner unexpectedly led me back to an institutional church. Like many of the post-Baby Boomers, I had let my membership lapse after high school. Barna Research Group polling reveals that young Americans leaving the church find it too judgmental, irrelevant, hypocritical, and obsessed with the "pelvic sins" of homosexuality and abortion. I don't blame anyone for leaving. The church has perpetrated so much homophobia, sexual abuse, misogyny, and domestic violence that healing those wounds is often beyond human capacity. "I'm spiritual not religious" is shorthand for the understanding that religious faith and church involvement are two different things, and as a sociological trend, those under forty have kept the former but dropped the latter.

For ten years, Letha, Linda, Sharon, and my other biblical feminist friends were the face of Jesus to me, and our conference calls were my church. But I missed the in-person contact I only got with them once every year or two, and I worried about what would happen if my husband and I faced a crisis so far away from our family and friends. We found our kindred at the progressive United Church of Christ a few blocks down the road. Thanks to my experience with Christian Feminism Today, we were unconcerned that the congregation skewed heavily toward our elders. Sure, it's awkward when the minister calls for children's time and only two kids walk to the front of the sanctuary. Some of the church events I wish I could attend are scheduled for the convenience of retirees. I'm on a list of congregants whose knees can handle the three steps up and down from the altar dais to help serve communion. But I intentionally chose to join where I fit theologically, not demographically, and I have no regrets. My minister's sermons are brilliant and challenging, and the church is growing at a time when the other Protestant denominations in the area are dwindling. When we share communion or pass God's peace during the worship service, I am reminded of the irreplaceable power of spiritual practices meant to be observed together in a living, breathing community.

Of course there are downsides to being a joiner. More is expected.

I have served on the boards of both my biblical feminist group and the local church. At various times, I have worked as an editor, conference planner, fundraiser, scholarship coordinator, layout designer, secretary, teacher, listserv administrator, transcriber, and envelope stuffer. I have endured endless business meetings and entertained wild fantasies of shutting up a few blowhards with tranquilizer darts. To be a joiner, you have to be willing, even among people with whom you have something in common, to deal with differences and disagreements.

But the hardest thing about being a joiner of organizations full of those born in earlier eras is the dread of losing them. Historian and theologian Nancy Hardesty. Feminist psychologist David Abbott. Gentle congregant Roger Johnson. Gone. It's possible I could get hit by a bus tomorrow, but statistically speaking, these people are likely to be the first in a long string of losses I will endure. Joining is so taboo to my generation that once the Depression Babies and Boomers have all passed on, I fear the institutions they supported will no longer be viable. I mourn the day I might be one of the few left behind to close the doors.

Thankfully, today is not yet that day, and we're doing what we can to change that fate. But carrying the hopes for the future of an institution is a heavy burden, and I am baffled as to how to produce the droves of new members under forty that CFT and my church would need to keep them solvent in the long term. Both institutions have experimented with changing their names, music, and services to entice younger people. At some point, however, you have to cater to those who do show up instead of chasing a demographic that has demonstrated no interest in you.

The magazine *Christian Feminism Today* will cease print publication at the end of the year, and we are shifting those resources to our extensive online ministry. If no post-Boomers join in the multitudes that my biblical feminist organization and local church would need to stay afloat in the coming decades, that's okay. I pray that other kinds of community in forms yet unimagined will arise to meet the needs of younger generations, and our message of equality will reach those who need it on the wings of a Spirit greater than ourselves.

Free to Believe—Breaking with Biblical Authority

by Jennifer D. Crumpton

JENNIFER DANIELLE CRUMPTON spent thirteen years as a corporate advertising executive for major global brands before graduating in 2011 with a master of divinity from Union Theological Seminary in the City of New York. There she immersed in feminist theology, social and structural ethics, and social justice initiatives. Jennifer is a public speaker, a writer for Patheos and Huffington Post, and a contributing author to *A New Evangelical Manifesto* (Chalice Press). She has worked as a playwright, and a theater, commercial, and indie film actress. Jennifer resides in New York City and is Vice President for Strategic Partnerships of the International Center for Religion & Diplomacy, based in Washington, D.C. Ordained in the Christian Church (Disciples of Christ), she is a pastoral associate of Park Avenue Christian Church in New York City.

Growing up in Birmingham, Alabama, I kept the Bible on my bedside table and read from it every night before falling asleep. Raised Southern Baptist, I believed every word was the direct, infallible word of God—however that translated in the tender bud of my imagination. Intense Psalms, quirky Gospel characters, the sci-fi of Revelations; I felt like an insider even as I interpreted people and events I couldn't possibly comprehend, bereft of context for its complexity and history. With the faith of a child, I believed.

If I read tales of mass murder and rape in some of these bed-time stories, they didn't concern me. Authoritative voices of my childhood assured me I was on the right side. I had accepted Jesus. I was saved. It was explained that unbelievers provoked God's predatory rage by immoral living. Besides, Eve's apple affair had started it all by bringing sin into the world, so it went. God was only violent because we drove "Him" to it. Rather than ask questions, I should concentrate on making sure "true love waits." I succumbed to slumber those sultry, Southern nights, protected by a mighty "heavenly Father" who watched over me from above. With the faith of a child, I believed.

If I internalized the submissive levity and dismissive brevity with which female characters were often portrayed in the Bible, it didn't upset me. I expected no different. At family dinners my grandmother cooked all day, then called out. "It's ready! Now let the men get their plates and go first." At the time I didn't realize this was a remnant of old, deeply entrenched Southern cultural norms. A generation before, in towns just an hour or two outside our city, women labored on farms for equal hours as men but also got up earlier to make breakfast, then cooked and served dinner for the men during their rest time. But a few decades later, I caught on that men were still more important and more worthy than women. Men apparently had some unknowable yet unquestionable quality that made them the ones we were to serve and revere. I just had to accept it, and assume there were dynamics at play I wasn't smart enough to understand. With the faith of a child, I believed.

This seemed to make sense since in the broader evangelical world of my Bible-belt youth, white men were the right hand of God. The Bible stated that men were the head of women and all creation. So it was innately understood that their "naturally superior competence" upheld the status quo just like Christ's existence kept the universe from collapsing. Mystically prequalified men decided what the Bible meant; we followed. This was supposed to be for my good. With the faith of a child, I believed.

Everything changed in my twenties, when the gap between inculcated, enforced beliefs and the newly emerging, hard-won space to think for myself became too large to cross back and forth. As I embarked upon new experiences, met different people, read more diverse books, worried less about pleasing others and developed a mind of my own, I sidelined the scriptural sedative—and only then did I begin to awake to my own female experience of faithful belief. It was a slow process of discovery, but in my quiet time, alone, I began to notice that a *living* God was meeting me where I was: in a female heart, mind, and body in twenty-first-century America. While the religious lessons of my youth—which taught literal, inerrant biblical authority—imposed a mighty, mercurial male voice of vertical command, the God I began to hear speaking connected with me in my gut and encouraged me to become the unique individual I was created to be. Despite my best attempts, I was not turning out like the women around me who fulfilled traditional expectations.

Although I cannot pinpoint how and when things began to change in my relationship to God and the Bible, I can pinpoint the prayer that put that journey in motion. After graduating from a small, private religious college in my hometown, I married and tried to live a suburban life just a couple miles from my childhood home and alma mater. Within a couple of years I realized that, unlike my husband, I did not want kids. Instead, I desperately wanted to raise the sheltered child still within me. I yearned to be a writer but realized I had no idea what I personally thought about anything because I had always been told what to think and say about everything.

Then 9/11 happened. Even as people left New York City in droves, I felt an irresistible desire to be there. After much heartfelt discussion over our drastically different needs, my husband and I began an amicable divorce process. People close to me warned I would elicit serious anger from the biblical God, potentially damning me to hell.

Alone in my own apartment for the first time, and frustrated by my inability to happily follow the rules, I sat on my sofa in the silence and prayed my first actual authentic-to-me prayer: "God, I don't know what to do next, and for the first time in my life, I have no idea who you really are. I'm handing it over to you, someone I feel I'm meeting for the first time, but who has been here all along. Just lead and I'll follow."

That prayer began the wildest ride of my life—a beautiful yet difficult roller coaster that drew out my own true voice and personality, one that reshaped me completely. I realized that churches, pastors, family members, politicians, community leaders, and others who authoritatively interpreted and quoted the Bible did not actually have everything figured out, did not have a direct line to God any more than I did. The distinct whispers of the living God became stronger and more frequent. This God was not asking me to believe anything that did not make sense within my real experience of being. This God did not tell me that women could not be religious authorities or outspoken leaders. This God was telling an entirely different story, and one that did not exactly echo the Bible. This voice instead insisted that my assessment of the world was just as legitimate and my voice was just as authoritative as a man's. I began to imagine that my ideas and choices, my talents and work, were of equal consequence and importance.

After a period of incredulous doubt and guilt over trusting my own instincts, I began to recognize this voice of the living God from some of my earliest memories. It had been silenced for quite a while, but it was a spirit that had been with me since birth, who knew me, a constant companion. I knew it back before I even realized whether I was male or female, whether people enforced God as male or female, before ever reading the Bible. I would hear it especially when I was outside alone, feeling the grass under my feet and the sun on my face, becoming friends with birds, butterflies, and wise, old neighborhood cats. I would hear it in the wind rustling up a song of sighs in the tree tops, the leaves glittering as they danced in the sunshine, and it was her. God was simply there, with me and in me—no questions asked, no explanations needed, no sacraments or statements required, no seeking or interpreting necessary.

After reacquainting with the voice, I started paying close attention to the Bible stories that supposedly revealed undeniable truths. Despite the inspired nature of the Bible I had been taught, the plain truth was that the female characters in the Bible had actually been written by mortal male authors. Most women in the Bible had truncated roles and over centuries of patriarchal interpretation developed polarized personalities—either saint or whore. Their voices felt forced and were often used to express dangerous political ideas of the time, like Mary's Magnificat in Luke 1, where the innocent, impregnated virgin declares that God has brought down rulers from their thrones and denied the rich and powerful—something an uneducated peasant girl would likely know little about. Their stories, both written and unwritten, suddenly seemed to cry out for liberation.

I also began to reassess the importance of feminist ideas. I had been taught that feminists were loose, bitter women who lacked faith and just didn't get it—that Christian submission was God-ordained for the good of women. But then *I finally got it*: The treatment of women in the Bible's ancient stories was directly connected to my modern feelings of being inconsequential, unworthy, voiceless. I felt guilty for even thinking it. But the whispers did not stop; they became more urgent, more guttural.

I moved to New York City in 2003. In summer of 2008, I was accepted to study at historical Union Theological Seminary in New York.

Before graduate school started, I visited family back in Birmingham and checked out a popular megachurch where a twenty-nine year old pastor had been hired, which seemed a progressive move. The congregation was nominating elders and deacons, and, to my shock, the young pastor preached, based on his literal interpretation of 1 Timothy 2:11-15 and 3:1-13, that God did not allow women in these roles. I had to laugh; after all this time and growth I was being put back in my place by biblical authority. But then I realized why the voice was leading me to seminary, and my purpose.

Over the next three years at Union, I learned all aspects of Christian theology, Christian social ethics, and faithful global justice. I read the Bible in Hebrew and Greek, learned the derivations and intentions of the original words. I read it via historical, literary, and redaction criticism. I studied church history and the process of canonization of the Bible in depth, read the spectrum of spiritual, academic, and religious thought on biblical authority. It all started to come together for me as—wholly questionable.

This became clear: The Bible's good news of the Gospel of Jesus, on which Christianity is based, is not that individuals can recite a prayer for personal salvation and then be magically on the "right side," sanctioned to interpret and enforce biblical authority, as I had been taught as a young girl. Actually, the *euangelion*—Greek for the evangel, or good news—was Jesus's announcement fulfilling Isaiah 61:1-3 that he was anointed by God to bring good news to the poor. He had come to "bind up the broken-hearted, proclaim liberty to captives, and freedom to prisoners." But more important than Jesus's statement of purpose was the action that followed. He commenced the greatest social protest of all time, ironically against religious leaders and politicians who claimed to speak for God and used the "word of God" (the scriptures) to keep their own power unchecked and unchallenged.

I realized that Jesus died on the cross not because I was a terrible sinner in the lineage of the woman who had brought sin into the world, and not because an angry, bipolar God would only be satiated by one last bloody sacrifice. Jesus was nailed to the cross because he had the blasphemous courage to speak out against the misguided authorities of his time, who interpreted and enforced the scriptures in oppressive and abusive ways and as such took grave advantage of the vulnerable and voiceless. Jesus risked everything to try to lead people from death-dealing religious jargon and ideologies back to the authentic voice of God—a God who is simply love, the love felt by a tiny, unwitting girl child standing quietly outside in the breeze. I wondered if Jesus had heard the same whispering voice that had spoken to me, challenging me to go against the grain, to be what I was created to be no matter the consequences.

In my role as a pastoral associate and in my work with nonprofits that champion human rights, I have begun to understand women around the world as being those broken-hearted captives Jesus spoke of when reading from Isaiah 61, collective prisoners to a global social system that generally exploits us, second-guesses us, and oppresses us. I have increasingly become exposed to the stark reality for many women around the world—that the same horrors of objectification, domestic violence, rape, slave trafficking, and second-class citizen status ascribed to women in the Bible is still prevalent, and our world suffers greatly because of it.

Religious communities don't often recognize that long-standing, male-dominated ideologies of literal biblical authority entrenched in the human consciousness contribute to—if not justify—the denigration of women's well-being and the denial of opportunities for self-sufficiency and growth.

Today I am leading a charge called Femmevangelical, to take back the core meaning of the evangel and allow Jesus's promise of freedom and wholeness to extend fully and globally to women. I am convinced that Christian women must not only question, but also redefine biblical authority in order to uphold holiness within our traditions. We must reject Bible stories being used to teach women how to endure trauma gracefully or to stay silent through atrocities. We must re-imagine Bible stories for the women who were written into them, for ourselves, and for the girls coming behind us. We must ensure that girls are allowed and able to hear that still, small voice that tells them they can be change agents with important truths to shout from the rooftops—and the pulpits, and the floor of Congress, and the bench of the Supreme Court, and the Board room, and wherever else they want to put their belief into being. But most importantly, it should resound in our own feminine hearts, right where the voice of the living God lives on.

God in the Bedroom: Does Jesus Care How You Make Love?

by Anna Broadway

ANNA BROADWAY is a writer and Web editor living near San Francisco. The author of *Sexless in the City: A Memoir of Reluctant Chastity*, she is also a contributor to the anthologies *Faith at the Edge* and the forthcoming *Disquiet Time*. She holds an MA in religious studies from Arizona State University and has written for TheAtlantic.com, *Books and Culture, Christianity Today, Paste*, the *First Things* and *Sojourners* blogs, *Relevant*, and The Journal of the *History of Sexuality*, among others. She also contributes regularly to the Her.meneutics blog. Someday she hopes to make actual jam (not accidental syrup) with the prickly pear fruit in her backyard and use up most of the yarn and fabric in her stash. Find her on Twitter: @annabroadway or visit sexlessinthecity.net.

When the folks who mapped out "read the Bible in a year" programs thought to promote them in churches across the country, I'm pretty sure their goal was something other than introducing nine-year-old readers to Song of Solomon, the short book of erotic Hebrew poetry included among the wisdom books of the Old Testament. But that is almost certainly why I discovered the Song, one Sunday afternoon at church, while waiting for the rest of my family to join me in the car.

It did not take long for a sense of illicit glee to seize me. *I'm reading this in the Bible! This counts as reading the Bible!* Yet despite the immediate sense that erotic poetry sure beat Leviticus in interest value, I didn't make much connection between the book and weddings I'd attended, or certain things I'd sometimes overheard from my parents' bedroom. Reading the book felt like I was getting away with something.

Had my parents made a practice of discussing each day or week's reading with me, perhaps we might have talked about why Song of Solomon seemed so different from the other books. It could have been the perfect way to also have a first sex talk. But that didn't happen.

Though my parents knew I was reading through the whole Bible that year (as I would again the next two years), devotions of that sort were not discussed much. Mom did her own reading alone, and Dad must have done his before I got up in the morning, so I, too, read my three- or four-chapter daily allotment alone without discussion. Family Bible times with my three younger siblings tended to focus more on Psalms, and especially Proverbs.

When I thought about romantic relationships in those days, it was all about the courtship leading to marriage, never sex. Most nights I talked myself to sleep, whispering the latest installment of the story about how I'd meet and fall in love with my future husband, whose name was usually cribbed from a favorite read like the Laura Ingalls Wilder series. The first time I encountered a story where even a hint of sex figured in (two teenagers went skinny dipping), I sensed something amiss. Uncertain of what to do, I consulted God and told Him that I would take a hairclip lying beneath my bed as a sign He wanted me to alert my mom about the skinny dippers. In the book of Judges, Gideon asked God to wet and then dry a fleece before he proceeded on a risky mission God asked of him. The hairclip was as much as I felt confident asking for, but I found such a fleece without difficulty and my mom sent the book back to the library, unfinished.

But the second time I encountered sex, I kept reading. And when Mom found out, I started sneaking more books like that home, making sure to check out when she was not in sight and then hiding my stash behind other books on my bookshelves. Sex in these books almost always led to marriage, but it happened long before. In fact, it was usually the start of a couple really beginning to "see" each other. This confused me. My basic understanding of God's ideal came from the story of Adam and Eve, in which they consummated their divinely appointed marriage with sexual union and never shared their bodies with anyone else. My father, too, deemed theirs the right approach, saying he regretted relationships he'd had before he met Jesus and, later, my mom. His previous sexual experiences, though forgiven, had made the already-challenging task of building a good marriage that much more difficult.

Romance novel authors did not agree. For them, a man's past lovers were key to the prowess that almost always produced prompt orgasms from the very first time he slept with the novel's heroine. Though I eventually tired of the most simplistic romance-novel plots, in which the first sexual encounter was the climax of the action, followed by some sort of misunderstanding and then reconciliation sealed with a proposal, I never questioned the plausibility of such sexual omniscience. Eventually, I decided God was untrustworthy when it came to sex and offered second-rate advice at best.

Around the same time, my church youth group was going through Josh McDowell's book *Why Wait?*, the leaders encouraging us to think about where we would draw the physical line on a date. I don't remember them tying this to emotional intimacy or any other aspect of the relationship, nor do I remember what, if any, other general teaching there was on romance and dating except the avoidance of sex. But I wish now that there had been other lessons, too.

I wish we'd talked about what it means to show love for another person, even when they receive love in different ways than you may like to show it—whether by listening or kissing, writing love songs or helping with chores.

I wish we could have talked about how to *talk* about where your physical boundaries are—if you're ready yet to kiss someone or willing to being touched there. How do you find the essential courage to say, "I'm not comfortable?"

Years after I had rejected my earliest standards as impractical—while still holding onto the ideal of premarital abstinence—I found myself struggling with just such dilemmas. Too often I submitted to embraces and caresses I didn't want, at least from those men, granting them grossly undeserved access to my body because it felt somewhat nice and was far easier than awkwardly interrupting things to defend my emotional integrity.

The last time someone tried to kiss me was probably the first time I really stood up for wholeness, refusing to say with my body a sentiment nothing else in me felt. And it *was* awkward. But I went home afterward feeling honest, whole, and free of regret. Perhaps you could credit the confidence of age for that change, but in the years since my first slightly unwanted kiss, I've also come to trust God with my body far more deeply than before. Part of that increased trust has come from realizing that He cares about far more than just with whom I have sex, which means He also cares *how* we share our bodies.

Though my Bible reading started early, I was probably too young at first to see how all those sixty-six books fit together to tell one story. It's taken adulthood and several good teachers for me to see that they do. But as I've read the Bible in that holistic, cover-to-cover fashion, several themes emerge.

One of the most important themes is the ideal of self-giving love, perfectly realized in the life and death of Jesus. Though the Bible doesn't make a particular point of this, nearly all the ways one demonstrates self-giving love are embodied. Jesus washes the disciples' feet—a task involving sight, smell, touch, and maybe sound. Jesus gives his life by submitting to a brutal execution that must have nearly overwhelmed his senses.

Love is embodied. Love at its best is sacrificial. Love is perhaps most radically demonstrated in the covenantal relationship of marriage (possibly one reason the Bible begins and ends with weddings). Though this wasn't addressed in our *Why Wait?* course, it seems pretty clear to me that sex is just another means of showing love, which means Jesus must care how I do that, too—not just with whom, but how.

By those lights, sex becomes much more daunting in some ways. I imagine it's one of the hardest settings in which to deny self and put another first. But the biblical ethos for relationships also makes me much more hopeful of someday experiencing a bit of the mutual delight depicted in Solomon's song. If self-giving love as an ideal applies to sex, too, then I feel safer about letting someone have such intimate access to my body.

You don't practice chastity very long without people raising objections—whether they're men who would otherwise pursue you, or friends who think you're taking an awful risk with your life. And they don't just think you run a risk by missing out on sex, they think you're skipping a terribly important qualification for potential mates. Would I really marry someone without having first checked our sexual compatibility?

For a while that stumped me. It did seem like a risk, I had to agree. Then one day it dawned on me that sexual compatibility assumed a fairly selfish approach to things. If you're looking for someone who meets your needs, then, yes, you'd want to know that their way of getting *their* needs met meshes pretty well with yours.

But if both my potential husband and I are seeking to put the other person before ourselves, why should I worry about our sex life? We don't have to know in advance what brings the other person pleasure; as long as we're both willing to learn how to love each other well—in bed and out of it—sex will work out fine, even if things aren't romance-novel perfect at the start.

It's one thing if other people, whether through carelessness or selfishness, harm my car, laptop, knitting, or finances. But my body is the most precious thing I have, aside from my life. I only want to share it with someone whom I trust profoundly.

I don't know what would inspire greater trust than a solemn, lifelong commitment and endeavoring to love in the self-giving manner Jesus did.

Created for Pleasure

by Kate Ott

 KATE M. OTT is a feminist, Catholic scholar addressing current questions of sexuality, children/youth, and the role of public, activist theology. She is assistant professor of Christian social ethics at Drew University Theological School in Madison, New Jersey. Her writings include *Let's Talk about Sex: A Progressive Christian Parent's Guide from Toddlerhood through the Teenage Years* and *Faith, Feminism, and Scholarship: The Next Generation*. She is the editor of the Feminism in Religion blog at www.fsrinc.org/blog. Prior to Drew, Kate was the deputy director of the Religious Institute, a nonprofit committed to sexual health, education, and justice in faith communities and society. There she led the project and publication of *Sex and the Seminary: Preparing Ministers for Sexual Health and Justice*. She was born and raised in the Midwest as a "cradle Catholic," and now lives on the East Coast with her husband and two children. She attributes her theological journey and development to amazing Roman Catholic women religious teachers and feminist mentors.

Masturbation? That's not something "good" Catholics, especially women, ought to talk about. As a teen, everything I knew about the topic was hearsay (or should I say, heresy). I remember hearing that boys could become obsessed with masturbation, go blind, or become stupid from its excesses. In comparison, I can't remember hearing anything positive *or* negative about masturbation for girls.

I grew up attending Catholic schools through high school and participating in a Catholic campus center in college. Sexual health and reproduction were addressed two times in my health classes: once as a fifth grader and again as a sophomore in high school. Sexual pleasure and masturbation were not on the top of the "positive behaviors to promote" list in either of these classes. In fact, masturbation is still categorized in the Catechism as an "intrinsically and gravely disordered action" (a.k.a. sin).

I was taught that there is one kind of sex; it is for having children, and only when you are married. The lessons were technical and the messages were clear—sex was to be purposeful, contained, and directed, not pleasurable. We were warned that sexual pleasure was something to regard with caution. It might at any second take over, sending you down a slippery slope of uncontrollable sexual behaviors. Of course, I knew this was not entirely true. I had watched enough MTV and movies to know there had to be something positive about sex; otherwise why would so many people make such a big deal about it?

Still, I wondered, *What did faith have to do with this?* There was no positive message about my sexuality as part of God's good creation or even the beauty of sexual expression in marriage. The reigning religious education opinion was (and still is) that if we were given more information we might experiment, when in reality the lack of information often increased, rather than stifle, curiosity. The rest of the information we figured out along the way, often through fumbling, confused, and embarrassing firsthand experience.

As a twenty-something seminary student, I had traversed the journey of sexual self-education fairly well. I had come to love and appreciate my own body (most of the time). The women's health movement, which published the first and subsequent editions of *Our Bodies, Our Selves* starting in the 1970s to educate women about their bodies, empowered me to be a well-informed feminist, proactively taking responsibility for my reproductive health. I had not experienced sexual violence or emotional trauma like many of my female friends had. To boot, I was married and having "good sex" sanctioned by the religious teachings of my tradition.

Then, in my seminary sexual ethics class, I was assigned to read *Body, Sex, and Pleasure: Reconstructing Christian Sexual Ethics* by Christine Gudorf, a Roman Catholic moral theologian. It changed me. Not because I hadn't learned about sexual pleasure in other contexts, but because I had never heard a positive religious, let alone Catholic, perspective in favor of sexual pleasure. I read the line, "If the placement of the clitoris in the female body reflects the divine will, then God wills that sex is not just oriented to procreation, but is at least, if not more, oriented to pleasure." A light bulb went on in my head and a garment of guilt was lifted from my shoulders. Sexual pleasure could be something God intended? And the evidence for this is women's bodies? Is the clitoris? No wonder we never teach girls or boys about the clitoris! And why some try to alter it, in the case of female circumcision, to prevent women from experiencing pleasure. It is the only body part created for no other purpose than our enjoyment.

Women's bodies and their sexual empowerment have always been a threat to a church built on male bodies as the height of perfection, the only ones eligible to be "ordained" leaders. For thousands of years, the church teachings have tried to control sexual behaviors by labeling them as sinful if they are not open to or directed toward a single good—procreation. Following these teachings comes a stridently reinforced view of women's primary purpose as child bearers and rearers, complementing the men's social, political, and religious leadership. Sex for pleasure, not procreation, removes the cornerstone of carefully crafted scaffolding that holds up a worldview in which family, heterosexual marriage, and women's natural role as mothers are central. It also creates the possibility that we might appreciate bodies, women's bodies, for more than childbearing and affirm a variety of sexual behaviors. It might in fact even lead to judging sexuality and relationships on the basis of how bodies are respected, not just whether a sperm and egg can meet.

Sexual pleasure, in particular masturbation, is not an easy topic to talk about openly. Most of us share a lack of comfort when talking about sexuality apart from euphemisms or innuendos. And then there's the ever-present fear of going to hell for not only sinful behavior or talk, but also thought. My revelatory reading of *Body, Sex, and Pleasure* didn't really change my behavior—I was already in the two-thirds of women in the United States who masturbate and enjoy sexual behaviors with a partner for the purpose of pleasure and not just procreation. What did change were the judgment and guilt, discomfort and silence that could unexpectedly creep into my sexual self-image. I had a renewed sense of conviction that God intended us to express our sexual selves in a variety of ways. Reading about the self-pleasuring design of the clitoris made me believe even more strongly that God designed the love and intimacy I knew my single and same-sex coupled friends experienced. Sexual pleasure of any kind, but especially masturbation, was lifted from moral caution—or worse, the depths of sinfulness—to a form of self-empowerment and aid in relationship building. In this sense, it could actually be morally good!

It isn't difficult to figure out, either from medical studies or personal experience, that masturbation can serve physiological as well as emotional goods in our lives. I just had never considered them moral goods. Self-pleasuring can reduce tension in our bodies and alleviate stress. More importantly, it helps us better understand our body's unique desires and sexual arousal cycles, which might assist in building self-confidence and owning our bodies. For women, this is particularly important. We are often taught that our bodies are sites of temptation and our only value is to produce children and take care of husbands. While many of us enjoy caring for and loving others, we are prone to a posture of self-sacrifice that is reinforced by religious teachings about the complementarity of men and women's roles and by the denial of women's clerical leadership. And yet, it is undeniable that loving the self is a core aspect of the greatest commandment:

> [Jesus] answered: "You shall love the Lord your God with all your heart, and with all your soul, and with all your strength, and with all your mind; and your neighbor as yourself." Luke 10:27 (New Revised Standard Version)

In a society and religious tradition that often sees women as sexual objects, rather than subjects, masturbation is a practice of self-love, self-knowledge, and self-empowerment. Just consider how many mainstream films and songs in the United States show or reference male masturbation, and how few have female examples. And how often the female characters are "being watched" by a male gaze, as though the masturbation is for men's, not women's, pleasure—think of scenes with characters like Nadia in *American Pie* or Beth in *The 40-Year-Old Virgin*. There are few depictions of masturbation as education, a self-knowledge that brings empowerment. One notable example is the scene in *Pleasantville* when Reese Witherspoon's character, Mary Sue, tells her mother what masturbation is; the mother later experiments in the bathtub, experiencing orgasm for the first time. The black and white world of Pleasantville is dabbled slowly with color; as her orgasm approaches a tree catches on fire. With this new experience and knowledge her world is set ablaze.

Knowledge of our bodies can help us better communicate with a partner about what we find pleasurable, thereby enhancing the physical and emotional aspects of our relationships. Masturbation can also provide sexual fulfillment if one is single or trying to reduce risks like STDs or pregnancy. Knowing and being comfortable with one's body may also help us say "no" to particular behaviors and relationships that are detrimental to our well-being. In other words, we do not need to look elsewhere for affirmation and acceptance.

There are times when self-pleasure can stand in the way of mutual pleasure, like when we become so self-centered we stop responding to the needs of others. After all, love of self is balanced by love of neighbor and love of God, as the commandment expresses. For women, however, I would argue that tipping the scale toward increased self-love is overdue. As I started dating, I thought a girl kept a boyfriend by giving in to his sexual needs (or what he claims they are), that if I were to stand up for myself and say what I wanted or needed—from holding hands to kissing, or touching the clitoris to trying a different sexual position—I would be considered a slut. It took me a while to value myself and my body enough to be confident about sharing my sexual desires and asking for those to be met in return. We contend with a daily barrage of negative sexualized messages and the astounding rates of sexual violence and abuse women suffer; the time is long overdue that women hear the news that God intended pleasure to be part of *our* experience of sexuality. Mutual pleasure should be a moral standard for relationships, not a wishful illusion.

Religious affirmation of sexual self-pleasure can seem like a selfish and almost petty concern in the face of issues like ecological degradation, violence, war, and poverty. Aren't there more important things to worry about as a Christian? I believe that encouraging empowerment of women, even in small ways, slowly chips away at the very foundation of these larger injustices. It is women and their children, after all, who are most affected globally by ecological degradation and toxins, who are predominantly the victims of sexual violence often used as a tool of war, and who are the poorest of the poor. Religious teachings against sexual pleasure and masturbation perpetuate the idea that women are not created as equals, and that sexual behaviors are only to be valued for their procreative potential.

What would the world look like if every girl and woman knew exactly how her body worked? What would the world look like if every girl's and woman's body was respected and her enjoyment of sexual behaviors was as important as that of her partner? What would the world look like if every girl and woman could choose her partner freely and plan her pregnancies? That would be the world God intended. God did not create women to be sexual objects for someone else, to be self-sacrificial to the point of erasure, or to be ruled by a sexual ethic completely counter to their own creation. God created us to experience pleasure for the sake of knowing and loving ourselves better, so that we can know and love others better, including God.

A Thing of Beauty
by Katie Anderson

KATIE is passionate about communicating the dignity and worth of women from all backgrounds apart from patriarchal constraints, especially those related to limited portrayals of women in media. Since graduating from Duke University, Katie has pursued a fulfilling mix of traveling, working, and writing the manuscript for what she hopes will eventually become a book. Katie is currently a student at Duke Divinity School where she is pursuing a concentration in gender, theology and ministry. Katie's hope is that God will use her words to give readers a renewed perspective on the intersections of gender and the Christian faith, as well as to stir them toward intimacy with the One who can redeem their hearts and minds.

"Pain is beauty, beauty is pain."
You usually hear the expression whispered among groups of women, a quiet agreement that eventually erupts into bubbling laughter. Older women impart the phrase into the eager ears of young girls with the light-hearted assurance that "this is just how things are for us." Growing up in middle-upper-class America, I, too, dismissed the phrase as a silly summary of the beauty work all girls were destined for. I didn't understand the "pain" part until I got older.

I can pinpoint the moment I became aware that this mantra applied directly to my own life. The inadequacy of my appearance stared back at me in the gaze of Kirsten Dunst, the blonde, blue-eyed cover model on my first *Seventeen* magazine in sixth grade. She looked sort of like me, but she was a prettier, flawless version of me. Her smoothed hair was more elegant than my self-cut bangs, and her slinky dress revealed a stick-thin figure, one that seemed to laugh at the last layer of childhood flab lingering along my legs and arms. Maybe I needed to look more like her, even though she represented an ideal my chubby cheeks and freckled face couldn't measure up to.

A few months later, I remember taping a poster of a bleached-blonde, midriff-bearing Christina Aguilera on the back of my bedroom door. I would stare blankly at her smoky eyes and tiny tummy every day after school, pulling my own bedazzled Limited Too shirt above my belly button to examine how my stomach compared. At twelve, I trusted in the promises of my pink butterfly clips and shiny lip balm, hoping that they would someday give me the idealized glamour that stars seemed to so effortlessly possess. I even brought my compact mirror on a school camping trip. My made-up reflection offered a dream to hold on to, an appearance of perfection that seemed just within reach.

While the awkward stages of middle school are normal and expressing yourself through your appearance can be healthy, magazines and movies often set an unattainable standard that young girls literally and figuratively buy. The effort to emulate media images of beauty has become a religion, one whose followers worship the golden goddesses of models, actresses, and pop stars. Along with many other girls, I found solace in suntans and scarlet-stained lips, donning the priestly garments of bronzer and bikinis before entering the tabernacle of the tanning salon. The pounds we shed were sacrifices offered at Hollywood's altar, fueled by a vague hope of somehow being sanctified. We performed the sacred ritual of treadmill running and the liturgical rhythm of sit-ups on the living room floor. Adhering to the latest fad diet was a kind of sacrament, while calculated calorie counting was the pinnacle of spiritual progress—not to mention skipping a meal every few days, a fashionable form of fasting.

I obeyed the canons of media-constructed beauty standards throughout middle and high school with even more fervency than my own Catholicism. I was accustomed to the daily humdrum of beauty work, refining the edges of my lip-liner and scrutinizing my sweaty reflection at the gym. But underneath my slender shape, my heart was shrinking as much as my stomach. I didn't see a girl who had reached the pinnacle of self-actualization or who had inherent worth. Instead, I saw a girl who still, no matter how hard she tried, couldn't compare with the women in magazines. Even though family and friends had always affirmed my beauty and value, their words dissolved in the storm of glossy photos and rainbow fonts that told me I would never quite be enough.

I didn't start getting serious about the messages conveyed in the New Testament of Scripture until college, but even then the theology presented in sermons and Bible tracts couldn't quell my constant compulsion toward physical perfection. I wanted to believe that the way I viewed the world and myself could be transformed (Romans 12:2), that my beauty didn't come from my outer appearance alone (1 Peter 3), and that Jesus could offer me some form of freedom from the snare of messages I was caught in (John 8:32). If having a relationship with Jesus was supposed to liberate me, why was I still ridden with these insecurities? Bowing down to airbrushed goddesses had become so ingrained that I could hardly identify my own enslavement to their demands. It didn't feel like freedom when I wasn't confident enough to talk to a guy I liked without concealer on. It felt like a pair of invisible hands carelessly stamping out my image with a cookie cutter instead of carefully molding my individual uniqueness. I was so focused on projecting the "right" image of myself that I ended up losing myself somewhere along the way.

I continued to comply with the normalcy of body criticism for the first three years of college, but by senior year something inside me shifted. I was in the middle of my makeup routine one morning and preparing to finish covering up my second eye. I leaned into my reflection, brush in hand, mouth gaping open, and suddenly caught sight of my naked eye in the mirror. I hadn't yet lined the bottom with brown or fluffed the lashes with mascara. The image took me by surprise. It looked so undone, so vulnerable. It was so unlike all the made-up eyes in advertisements I was used to comparing it to. I found myself thinking that my eye looked beautiful without any makeup as it floated freely on my face.

I just sat there, staring at my eye in my mirror for four or five minutes, as if I were seeing it for the first time. I marveled at the way the lashes seemed to dance in different directions, how delicately the curvature of my skin shaped the outline of my eyeball. Why had I never noticed such exquisite beauty?

It was one of those profound, poetic moments when you feel like you can press the "pause" button on life for a few minutes because time seems roomier. I decided that maybe I didn't need to wear eye makeup that day after all, that for once my whole eye should be allowed to see the sun.

Simple as it may seem, my decision to forgo eye makeup that day spurred me toward a deeper understanding of my faith, and it started with asking what it meant to be worth something as a woman in my world. Questions raced around my mind as I began to recognize the web of lies that had entangled me and other women: Why haven't I been able to appreciate my imperfect features, or any part of my body for that matter? Why does my belly have to be completely flat? Why should I care if my boobs aren't big? What exactly is it that makes me valuable?

My questions led me on a journey through academia. In the year following my epiphany, I discovered feminism, abandoned my plans to enter the business world, devoured every book and documentary film possible on media beauty standards, shed my own reliance on beauty work, wrote a senior thesis about the topic, led discussion groups about my findings, picked up a women's studies minor, continued coursework in Boston, and finally landed back at Duke Divinity School to try to reconcile all I had learned with my Christian faith.

The voyage was exhausting and energizing all at once. I was slowly finding liberation from the unrealistic standards of beauty that had once held me captive. But it wasn't until the discussions ended and the papers were turned in that my newfound knowledge moved from my head to my heart. The tears that flowed that day were cathartic, covering my cheeks so they glistened like streams in the sunlight. It was in this exposed face that I grieved for myself and other women like me. I wept for all the times I had sized my body up against deceptive images. I wept for my ignorance, that the whole time I had been running around in darkness Jesus had been waiting for me to look up from the scale and see his face, to put my pain into his gentle, opened hands.

Jesus hadn't wanted me to carry the burden inflicted by the beauty industry. In fact, he was against all those forces that had convinced me that life was only found in a perfect body. When any woman is reduced to the way she looks, he too is reduced; when media forces distress us, he too is distressed. He knows our hurt, as he, too, was devalued in his humanity. Scripture tells us that under the weight of his oppression, "He was a man of sorrows, well acquainted with grief" (Isaiah 53:3). Jesus knew my pain. He had taken it for me on the cross, and he wanted to take it from me now.

Every battle with food, every airbrushed image, every one of the devil's patriarchal deceptions that devalues the full humanity of women is nailed to the cross with Christ. The resurrection of Jesus overcomes any message, practice, or mentality that robs my capacity for life. He offers me freedom to experience the fullness of my created body, spirit, and mind apart from standards that would otherwise confine me. His gives me comfort that I am enough because I am "fearfully and wonderfully made" (Psalm 139:14), because my beauty and worth rest in my belovedness.

It is a wonderful feeling to love my body.

After spending much of my young life being critical of my "flaws," learning to like my thighs and my less-than-generously-endowed chest felt unnatural at first. But I've managed to scatter the remaining pieces of my image-crazed past. I am finally allowing the magnetism of God's love to pull me forward into a freedom that lasts.

The beauty industry no longer dictates the way I see myself; God does. I don't weigh myself anymore. I eat healthy foods because I want to feel good physically and avoid health problems. I indulge in a little bit of chocolate each day, and I don't always pass on dessert. I enjoy eating because it is pleasurable to my taste buds and nourishes my body. I exercise regularly in order to nurture my body's health, to recharge my mind, and to delight in fresh air. Physical activity keeps my body strong and energetic, instead of weak and lethargic. I want to take care of my body because it is a creation of God.

The same attitude carries over to the ways I adorn my body. I wear makeup when I feel like it, but I don't need it to feel beautiful anymore. I can use makeup to highlight who I am, not to hide who I am. I can enjoy picking out outfits that complement my body type as a means for self-expression without obsessing over whether they make me look "fat." That word hardly enters my vocabulary anymore—except to talk about the good kind in almonds or avocados.

Even if I do notice my jeans getting a little tighter around the waist, I feel no anguish. My body is no longer my identity, its appearance no longer my source of life. Of course there are times when I catch myself surveying a stretch mark on my leg or cringing at a zit planted on my chin. But these things are drowned out by God's whispers of love. These things can no longer condemn me. Instead, they are a gentle reminder of my humanness. And to me, being human is a thing of beauty.

Tattooing My Faith
by Robyn Henderson-Espinoza

ROBYN HENDERSON-ESPINOZA (una Tejana y queermeztiz@) is currently finishing a PhD in philosophical ethics. Robyn identifies as a Christian Agnostic and uses doubt as an important analytic and social tool in considering theology and ethics. Robyn's research interests reside in interrogating the Mestizaje Body, particularly its materiality. Robyn uses Critical Spatiality, Queer Theories, and the Thought and Theories of Gloria Anzaldúa to conceive of a much more robust notion of bodies, Mestizaje, race, and the epistemological importance of the Mestiz@'s moral agency. Robyn situates this work as queer\Ethics.

I knew from an early age that tattoos were for some an act of rebellion and for others a way to retain a sense of cultural memory. I grew up in a culture that held the purity of the body as something sacred, and my parents socialized me to think that tattoos were mostly on the bodies of those on the fringe. Then I learned that my father had a tattoo.

I first saw his ink when I was a child. He had gotten his tattoo while serving in the Navy in Vietnam. As a young person navigating her way through various modes of faith, I did not know where tattoos fit in the church, or if they did at all. Growing up, I had multiple experiences in churches—from attending a Southern Baptist church on Sundays and a Catholic school during elementary and middle school to being confirmed Lutheran in the eighth grade and, finally, returning to a Southern Baptist church while in high school. Through them all, I grew to love this thing called "church." Church was where I came into being, where family and community made sense to me.

When I left home to attend college, I chose a Baptist university in Texas, deciding to study in the school's department of theology. One of the requirements was that I had to choose an ancient language. I decided to study both Greek and Hebrew. It was during my first year of studying Greek and its plethora of vocabulary words that I returned to thinking about my dad's tattoo. I suddenly wanted one in Greek. Perhaps it was the novelty of learning a new language or the pure love I developed for the ways in which Greek was affecting me. I recall seeing others with Bible verses or images tattooed on their bodies, and I wanted to follow suit. Although I knew my decision would not go over well in the Southern Baptist church I was involved in at the time, I felt this sense that my body was asking for ways to "show" itself to the world, to be recognized authentically. However, I also had this sense that my decision to get a tattoo would somehow violate the sacredness of the body, or the theology that describes the body as a temple of God. I was nervous but excited nevertheless.

And so, I went to the Happy Dragon in Abilene, Texas and asked for ιχθυΣ (which is transliterated as *ichthus* and literally means fish) to be tattooed on my ankle. I learned in my Greek language class that this term was used as an acronym for "Jesus Christ God Son Savior" during the early church. A year later, I returned to the same tattoo shop to have another tattoo placed on my right ankle. This time I got the Chi/Rho, traditionally interpreted as Christ my Shepherd. Both tattoos were in plain sight only if I was wearing shorts, as I continued to straddle the lines of being committed to Baptist life and learning to literally embody a more encompassing Christian identity.

I remained closeted about my tattoos for years because of my involvement with the church. Eventually I began leaning into the possibility of leaving the church after growing disenchanted with the community, their theologies, and commitments. While I left Texas shrouded in uncertainty, the ink on my ankles permanently reminded me of the way I wanted to live my life: decidedly Christian. I wanted a way to remember myself, the moments where I believed. The traces on my body helped me retain a commitment to a culture that affected me in deep and meaningful ways. Although the church I was attending had begun focusing more on evangelism and conversion, I turned my heart and mind to the margins of society. Christianity's work on behalf of the poor and suffering had captured my heart and compelled me to follow the ways of Jesus even with a tattooed body and a doubting heart.

I remained mostly closeted about my tattoos for many years, only occasionally wearing shorts. The importance of the body as a temple of God had been so ingrained in my mind that "coming out" in Church as a person who embraces body modification and artful ink made me incredibly nervous. Only in private would I be reminded of how my tattoos informed my identity as a Christian. My feet had the markings of a Jesus follower, a reminder that I always wanted to walk the way of justice. My lower neck was a reminder that I desired that my mind continue the rigor of theological scholarship that would also remember the margins. But I knew I needed to find a space and place where my body would be accepted and recognized as something other than taboo.

My migration from Texas to Chicago for graduate school offered me a much more open context to consider a place for my tattoos. I found a church in the area and began to slowly expose my tattoos, because I now saw people like me in the pews, those who perhaps felt on the "fringe" of society, too. I returned to my practice of permanent ink. This time, I was drawn to the three transcendentals: Truth, Beauty, and Love. My third tattoo began to create a sort of map of my faith journey, a cartography of my theological wanderings, in light of my ever-doubting heart.

It was in Chicago that I found the space and place to think critically about theology and my own mixed-race body—my mother's family is from Mexico and my father was Anglo. It was there that I began to think about what a mixed-faith body could be. I decided on Christian Agnosticism prior to leaving Chicago, a choice that helped pull together the tattoos on my body and salved my doubting heart and mind. I was Christian in my practices and Agnostic in my beliefs. The tattoos were important to this new identifier.

I was surrounded by folks who asked many questions about religion, the Christian church, and how to live a faithful life in such a chaotic world. Perhaps part of the reason I decided on Christian Agnosticism was that I sensed that in the stories I read about the disciples, they struggled to make sense of the mystery of Jesus and the challenges they faced in being different (or fringe) in their world. I decided on Christian Agnosticism because I saw it as a real option that would help me continue to live a life committed to Jesus' principles while enfleshing a particular orientation to doubt. I saw Christian Agnosticism as a way to speak to the real darkness I experienced when trying to make sense of faith and Christianity. I knew I was committed to the ways of Jesus, but believing in the human construct of the Christian religion challenged me. It was the tattoos that helped me negotiate my ongoing doubt and questioning.

When I left Chicago to pursue a doctorate, I landed in Denver. I brought with me my doubting heart and mind with my radical Christian leanings—radically committed to the ways of Jesus and radically committed to eradicating poverty and suffering. Having left the Baptist church while living in Chicago and embracing my doubt as an important feature of my Christian faith, I was in search of a space and place where my body would be accepted with its ink. The reality that I am a mixed-raced person became incredibly important as I continued to think about my body, its recognition, and its markings.

It was in Denver—a city much more accepting of body modification—where I decided to get my first visible tattoo representing the commitment to both an indigenous faith and Christianity, and the complications of a mixed-race body in the art of Frida Kahlo. Inked during the deep winter, I ventured into Sōl Tribe, a local tattoo and piercing shop owned by an indigenous woman. My tattoo artist drew my tattoo freehand: a sparrow wrapped in thorns in honor of a necklace worn by Kahlo. Kahlo's choice represented her commitment to indigenous faith and Christianity, while also making a statement about race and politics. I knew that this was the image that I needed as my first visible tattoo. And so, I emerged with visible ink representing both indigeneity and Anglo sensibilities.

The tattoo inspired by Kahlo's artwork compelled me to think further about race and religion, faith and doubt. This thinking culminated with a trip to the border the following winter for a class on ethics. There I learned of the "Man in the Maze" painting. This painting depicts the chaos of life and the maze that we all must engage in each year. In the center, should we make it through the chaos of our life, the Sun God meets us to give us all our hopes and dreams. The "Man in the Maze" was my second visible tattoo on the cartography of faith, race, and religion I was building, a different kind of embodied temple than the one I had been instructed to keep "pure" in my youth.

My tattoos create a landscape of art on my body, but they also map out my theological wanderings and attempts at what the monastic tradition called "faith seeking understanding." The church silenced me as a woman and effectively forced me into the closet with its inability to accept my body and its tattoos. It was through my own desire for recognition that I mapped out my own faith. Tattoos gave me a voice as a woman to better articulate my faith and my ongoing doubt.

Inscribing ink has been a way for me to negotiate cultural and religious memory. My body speaks about both race and religion, and I am reminded of my commitments, along with the ways I've changed and shifted in my Christian thinking. I continue to doubt, and that, perhaps, is what my mixture of tattoos speaks the loudest.

Perhaps the tattoo that sums it up best is the one that resides on my hands. It reads: "Divine Doubter" in English on the outside of my hands just below my pinkies. Visible and memorable, the ink on my body speaks beyond itself and is my attempt to embrace the fringes of my own faith, full of doubt and mystery, and full of a commitment to the ways of Jesus.

Recovery from the Porch
by Pilar Timpane

PILAR TIMPANE is a freelance producer, writer, film editor, and photographer. She was associate producer and assistant editor for the award-winning science documentary *Atlantic Crossing: A Robot's Daring Mission*, which aired on PBS in 2011. She was also a producer of *Finding Our Pathways*, a collaborative interview project with Rutgers Writers House and the Institute for Women's Leadership at Rutgers University, a video archival project that continues to provide young women with video skills and opportunities to make films about women in leadership. Most recently she has produced films in Uganda and the United Kingdom for churches and the academy. Pilar graduated from Duke Divinity School with a Masters in Theological studies and an interest in multimedia storytelling, theology and the arts, and social change. Pilar has lived in various locations including France and Mexico, but currently resides in Durham, North Carolina. More of her work appears at http://pilartimpane.com.

"We can't let Pilar graduate," said the vice principal.

The high school classroom was silent. My mother sat, her mouth parted slightly in pain. I sunk into my chair, dug my heels into the linoleum floor, and said nothing.

"Why not?" my mother asked.

"I would give her an A," said my history of film teacher, "if she would just come to my class." I had taken several Adderalls and smoked pot that day and my mind was a hazy mess. I didn't want to miss graduation, but I had lost all ability to care about any events in life other than drinking and drugs. I could not stop myself anymore; something greater had a hold on me.

One night, shortly after that meeting, I drove to buy cigarettes and got in a verbal fight with a cop, which turned into a sobriety test, which got me arrested. From the arrest came court mandates, from the court mandates came twelve-step meetings. And in meetings there was coffee, prayer, and community. And in meetings there was God.

For the first year of my recovery, I smoked cigarettes on the wrap-around porch of a big white house in Highland Park, New Jersey with a bunch of other addicts and alcoholics. When we weren't attending meetings at this house, we were on that porch facing the street. Only a few of us had jobs that gave us more than five hours of work a day.

My friend Samir was an Ishmaelite junkie twenty years my senior. He lived in the big white house, and so did Cathryn who had a stubbed finger blown off from a careless rocket one Fourth of July. She was a woman who grabbed you to dance and held you so tight against her that you felt like she was doing something naughty—that's just the way she liked to have fun. Cathryn smoked more cigarettes than anyone in the group, and she drank more coffee than anyone, too. She also wore long hippie skirts, had a short ginger hairdo, and loved everyone around her. She smelled like patchouli oil, cigarettes, and coffee; after she hugged you, you smelled like that, too.

I was nineteen then and she was thirty; I had used alcohol and methamphetamines and she had used heroin. I'd only ever had one real romantic relationship, and she'd had more than she could count on her one hand with that stubbed pointer, but we were the best of friends. All of us were.

There was a bunch of us: young people coming into recovery, some new and some trying it out again after a relapse, every one of us tattered and emotional, needy and lost. Any one of us would have given anything to be loved, and for the time being, we were that love for one another: Ben, the sardonic classics scholar / dropout who could not stay out of rehab or find a permanent place to live; Rianne, the bipolar who had grown up in hospitals and who sucked cigarette smoke and rubbed her potbelly; Clark, the gay redhead who could never decide whether or not he really wanted to get sober; Samir; and me, the not-even-twenty-year-old with an interest in writing, and a heavy habit of reading and talking about God.

The first time I saw Ben he was wearing hospital scrubs and had just walked out of a detox center. A bunch of us were congregating on the street after a nighttime meeting held in the coffee-tinged multipurpose room of a church that none of us attended.

"Can I have a cigarette?" Ben asked Samir. Samir's ex-wife approached Ben and gave him a hug. Ben cooed and caressed her, stroking her hair.

"I'm *so* glad to see you," she said, "*When* did you get out?"

"About four hours ago," said Ben, with the cigarette hanging off his lip. "I don't have a place to stay tonight." His eyes shifted around in his head, and he jumped from foot to foot in his blue scrubs.

"That's okay, man," said Samir. "You can stay with us if you want. This is Pilar. She's new."

I put up a hand, "Hey." Freshly detoxed from heroin, he was still ruddy and attractive. He had big, unconcerned gray-blue eyes and a scruffy face, and his eyes lay on me real strong and just stayed there a while as he dragged on a Marlboro Light. Then he smiled, mumbled, "Hey, *welcome*." I felt accepted. He went back to talking fast and moving his hands around.

With the addition of Ben, floating among our houses, needy, but adorable, we became a very close-knit group. Often, as we all sat on the porch, Ben entertained us by oscillating wildly between speaking poetically about Dostoevsky and Blaise Pascal to asking for money while nonchalantly scratching his crotch. We laughed a lot in that year and learned to be happy. Some of us fell in love with each other. But most importantly, we stayed clean. For as long as we lived in that tight-knit community, not one of us used. We were smelly, weird, and emotionally distressed, but we were *clean*, saved from an impending death. Some of us went on to find God. We were miracles.

I wasn't living on the street before I found that porch. I was a wannabe criminal with an expunged record living in the suburbs. I was sick. I did criminal things and thought criminal thoughts and had friends who were criminals. I had been in fights, wrecked several important relationships, terrorized my parents, driven drunk, and endangered myself and others. I had drug dealers' numbers programmed into my cell phone. I had a psychiatrist who wrote me scripts for anything I asked him for. I had a court mandate to make twelve-step meetings.

In Alcoholics Anonymous there is a saying that all active addiction dead-ends in one of three places: jails, institutions, or death. I never went to jail, and I'm still alive. But if I had not attended AA meetings, I'd be in jail or dead before I turned twenty-five. I am blessed to have gotten clean so young. Little did I know, however, that AA would be the very place to guide me into the arms of God, to a new and faithful life as a sober Christian.

I came to know God through the prayers of AA and through reading the Bible by myself on that porch, chain-smoking. I sat there consuming the Word of God, taking God into my heart as much and as often as I could. I made meetings seven days a week, and there I encountered this little ragtag community. I begged God for his presence, surrounded by a community of funky misfits and vagabonds who were on their own journeys as well.

Early recovery can be painful. Some people don't make it past the beginning stages. The stinging emotional and mental pain drove me to my knees. I learned to cry out. I learned to pray. There in my weakness, I found the stirrings of life creeping up within me and around me.

There is a saying in AA that healing happens sometimes quickly, sometimes slowly. After getting sober and coming to belief in God, I experienced real and unexpected healing in my life. After years of barely being able to speak civilly to my family, I spent long hours amending my ways to them, having tear-soaked conversations and listening to them describe the ways they had been hurt by my actions. I hoped again for the first time in a long time that my dreams would someday be realized. I saw the ways that forgiveness was possible—and necessary. I got into college and excelled. I served, volunteering in food banks, with the elderly, and talking to other young recovering addicts and alcoholics to help keep them sober. And, slowly, after many tantrums, I joined the Church.

When I had an adult baptism in the Atlantic Ocean, my pastor wanted me to share some of my recovery story with our church. I explained to the small group gathered to celebrate my baptism on the beach that I was an alcoholic in recovery, but I used to be a drunk. I shared that, like the woman at Jesus's feet in Luke 7,[1] I have been forgiven much. God came so far down to save me. How far, then, should I go to be by my brother or sister in need? How much love and worship should I then show a God who gave me a second chance at life? I tried to focus on the changes God had produced in me, how I considered it a *gift* to have come through all of those awful things. Since then, I have shared my story with other congregations and privately with small Bible study groups and individuals.

Inevitably, no matter how much I talk about the fact that God has made me new, remark on how he has refreshed and restored my dignity, even point to all the clear signs that God has pulled me into a Christian vocation as an artist and made me a living witness through ministry, I will have someone come up to me and say:

"I'm *so* sorry for what you went through."

"I really can't believe that ever happened to you. You're so different now!"

"You know, you really don't have to call yourself an alcoholic. That's in the past. God gave you a new life."

And this one gets to me a little bit: "Don't be so hard on yourself," accompanied by a pat on the shoulder.

As welcoming and loving as church congregations are, as understanding as Christians can be, there are ways the Church's perspective on healing can stifle someone's recovery. Such remarks throughout the years help me see that alcoholism is not something the Church as a whole really knows how to deal with. Should a true "healing" mean that you function like a normal person now? If you don't drink anymore, do you really need to go to meetings?

---

1. In Luke 7:36-50, a woman comes to Jesus, weeping and wiping his feet with her hair. Some of his opponents ask why Jesus is allowing this sinful woman to come close to him, since "uncleanness" was a very dangerous thing at that time. But Jesus replies that the woman has loved much and will be forgiven much, but whoever loves little will be forgiven little.

The truth is, I don't have an answer to those questions. I only know what has worked in my life and what I have learned from the experience of others. People who lack experience with alcoholism and addiction think of these as problems with obvious solutions. But alcoholism is a hereditary disease that has a treatment and a recovery period. It can flare back up again if the addiction is fed.

Consider what it's like for an alcoholic, trying to quit, who goes back to drink. The best description I ever heard was from a fellow alcoholic who quoted a passage out of the Gospel; it's where Jesus describes a demon as a man leaving a house and returning to it to find it clean, only to take it over to bring it into a worse condition than it was before (Luke 11:24-26). It's always possible that an alcoholic can use again and find himself or herself addicted worse than ever, even after *years* of healthy living and sobriety (I have seen this happen numerous times). Naming ourselves as *alcoholic* is meant to remind us of our continuing, potentially unfinished, relationship with alcohol.

Given my experience, developing faith through recovery and *then* coming into the Church, I've thought a lot about what they both mean to me, what they have done for me, what they can learn from each other. As a recovering addict and alcoholic Christian, I think it would do the Church good to acknowledge not only that many people in twelve-step programs experience healing through total sobriety and spiritual discipline, but also that, for many people, programs like AA have become safer places to confess and heal from sins than even the Church itself.

Non-alcoholics have seen the ways that AA "shows up" the church in this regard. Remarking on how AA functions, author and pastor Frederick Buechner wrote in his 1992 book, *Listening to Your Life*, "They simply tell their own stories. . . . Sometimes one of them will take special responsibility for another—to be available at any hour of day or night if the need arises. There's not much more to it than that, and it seems to be enough. Healing happens. Miracles are made. You can't help thinking that something like this is what the Church is meant to be and maybe once was before." It's easy to see that as the Body of Christ, we struggle to do these things with competence and grace: taking responsibility for one another, confessing openly to one another, allowing the other to be free to share, telling our own stories, and coming willing to listen.

As Buechner said, it seems to be enough to tell our stories, to confess our sins, to be reminded of what we have been through. Sometimes, as my friends on the porch in early recovery exemplified to me, that is the best we can do for one another. It is has been enough for me to say, "I am an alcoholic. I am imperfect, human, close to the edge of my own will. I am not guaranteed a life of love or peace or even sobriety." It is enough for Christians who struggle with any deep issue or brokenness in their past or present to say, "I am a sinner. I am imperfect, human, close to the edge of my own will." These are words that challenge us and bring us into interdependence with one another. These are words that are the beginning of healing, non-judgment, of turning around.

As an addict in recovery, I know this will be a lifelong process. In Christianity, we call this process—of becoming more whole and spiritually centered throughout life—*sanctification*. I live in gratitude for what has brought me healing, even when it hurts. Recognizing extended sobriety, the power of God, communities like the one on that porch, and working the twelve steps as powers of help, I stay humble. I go to church. But I need to go to meetings.

Sex, Shame, and Scarred Knees
by elizabeth mcmanus

Currently a member of the class of 2014 at Mount Holyoke College, ELIZABETH fills her time with rereading Harry Potter, longing for the sweet tea of her North Carolina homeplace, being a nerdfighter, and doing far too much reading for her religion major. Her academic interests within religion are centered in feminist/womanist theology and the praxis of nonviolence—fields of thought she works to apply in her work as a peer writing mentor at MHC's speaking, arguing, and writing center. She is a voracious cat lady in training, but in order to support her feline habits she intends to pursue a PhD in theology. Her primary passion, however, is adventuring in global travel; she lived in Uganda, fell in love with London, attempted to speak French in Rwanda, and dreams of the day when she thrives on what only a battered suitcase can provide. She lives to write. Should you like more of her work, check her out at wanderingwrites.com. *Author's Note: In order to daily confront structures of linguistic oppression and to remind myself that the ego can be a dangerous license for selfish behavior, i choose to not capitalize my name nor the pronoun "i" when found in the middle of my sentences.*

I am perched at the kitchen counter, running my finger over the granite surface. The memory of a friend's snappish words sits, like a haze, over my eyes. My mother heaves a sigh. In her exhale there is a sympathetic tone, "Well, honey." Her eyes have that minister-look in them. She's about to have a teaching moment. "The Church is for the broken." I nod, thinking about how my skin feels taut, like there is too much of me to be contained within it. Thinking too that i need to be better, that i need to be better at loving the people in my middle and high school youth group who sometimes leave me feeling like a pin stuck to the wrong map.

I've always liked my mother's quips. Her quirky sayings age like fine wine: the older i grow, the more i can appreciate them. The clever oxymoron in my mother's statement is that we are all, of course, broken. The Church ought to be a place that embraces all of us in spite of it.

Sex is broken too. To expect perfection from sex is to expect perfection from our bodies, and from all the thoughts encased within our minds. And i tell you freely now, i am an imperfect soul with an imperfect body image. I am broken by the expectations of society to be thinner, to have un-scarred knees, to be more blonde and to be apologetic. I am broken because sometimes i lie, i think terrible things about the people whom i love, and sometimes i even doubt that faith in Christ is worth all the frustration and exclusion.

The men who led my youth group were the best sorts of people in my eyes; they listened attentively, took us out for milkshakes, and cared deeply for our well-being. It was one particular Sunday, though, that our white, heterosexual, cisgendered (someone whose gender identity corresponds to their biological sex) youth pastor explained why we had to wait until we were married to have sex.

"Guys," he addressed us all, sitting on a stool with Bible in hand. The room, teetering with self-conscious teens, suddenly felt considerably stiffer. "We're going to talk about the tough stuff today. We're going to talk about sex, and why we are called, as Christians, to save it for marriage." As he continued, an uncomfortable silence fell with the weight of our unsaid thoughts.

"Sex is a holy thing. God gave it to us to show His presence in a covenant between a married man and woman who love each other." He went on to enumerate how our culture treats sex as something merely for pleasure and that, in doing so, misses the point of the emotional power intercourse has in a relationship.

"Guys, I know it's especially difficult for you," he continued. Somehow, though i knew he had first used *guys* in a gender-neutral sense, it now carried with it the implication of males-only.

"You *really* have to control those urges." The older boys shifted uncomfortably. His face earnest and vulnerable, he concluded, "I'll be totally honest with you. I'm really glad I waited. It's been really rewarding for my wife and me."

In the void between the clamoring voices of abstinence-only sex education in my public high school and *Seventeen Magazine*, here was someone who was being real about sex in his life. There was never a doubt in my mind or body that what he said about the holiness of intimacy was true. The shared, physical space of the sex act alone spoke to the level of trust it required. If i wanted to let someone know me that deeply physically, i would want to trust them as deeply in my heart.

What chipped away at my conscience and heart was the presumption that sex could only be holy in its most perfect state: heterosexual marriage. I couldn't help but feel the expectation of perfection from any human act was inherently ignoring human brokenness, as my mother had reminded me over the kitchen counter. And besides, did this mean there was not real love between people who weren't married? What if i didn't want to marry a man? Were we to judge *everyone* having sex outside of these covenants bound by church doctrine and secular law? And why—*why*—was waiting to have sex until marriage supposedly so much more difficult for the guys in the room? Was i a freak for having a vagina and wanting to use it for pleasure?

I was not the only one whose convictions clashed with my youth pastor's. My best friend in high school furtively came out to me on the bus our freshman year. "It's not that I only like girls," she said. Her face flushed. "I feel like I'm going to end up with a man. But I, I kind of . . . I kind of have a crush on her. Like, majorly." Her freckles were deep chestnut on her pale face, the color behind them drained in sudden realization of what she had said aloud. In a tumble of words, i assured her that i thought she should love whomever she wants.

A year later, we were seated in her kitchen when she exclaimed, "I just—I feel like if I were to get married to a man and he weren't a virgin, it wouldn't be that big of a deal in society, you know? But *why* is that? Why do I, as a woman, have to be a virgin and he doesn't? And what if I have sex with a girl—does that make me still *technically* a virgin?!"

She was right. There was a profound double standard. Women are either to proselytize their chastity or be deviant whores with whom straight guys relieve their balled-up tension. And good God, what if you weren't even attracted to the opposite sex? Or what if you identified as intersex or trans*? There was no gray space, no arena in my church for these questions to be validated.

The Church had taught me that only God can judge the human heart. The idea that all premarital sex was wrong felt like an undue judgment from the mouths of humans who could not, by virtue of being human, speak for God's judgment. If i felt that the holiness of intimacy would be best preserved in a partner with whom i wanted to spend the rest of my life, then that should be my *own* choice. How could i judge other people without presuming to know their innermost heart?

In the same year, my (also white and cis-male) English teacher both clarified and muddled my thinking when he assigned "Oppression" by Marilyn Frye. In the essay, she articulates why a myopic focus on one bar of a cage doesn't enable the onlooker to see the entirety of the prison. It is only when we step back, observing the bar in tandem with the others, that we see the whole cage for what it is: a system of injustice.

Frye's words consumed me. They revolutionized my life. Her essay was the liberation i needed to introduce myself to the world with the f-bomb: i am lizzie, and i am a *feminist*. I saw, with new eyes, the macroscopic view of my youth pastor's sex lecture. His implicit, if unintended, shaming of me for being a woman with sexual desires was a bar on the cage. The expectation that sex was perfect only in a heterosexual marriage was another bar on the cage.

Where i had support at church in building a relationship with God, there was no support for building an understanding of my body or physical desires without shame. Going to youth group felt claustrophobic, and so i stopped going altogether.

This was a devastating decision. I valued my faith before all else. To feel that my faith was less valid because i disagreed with so many church doctrines made me feel inadequate. Outside of the church, it felt taboo to say i thought intimacy could be sacred in a culture that called it merely pleasure. But inside of its walls, it felt taboo for me to express my libido as a woman within a patriarchal framework.

As i matured in my faith and developed my critical thinking, the feelings of being excluded lessened. Frye's article was only the beginning; i swam in the literary company of Audre Lorde, Mary Daly, bell hooks, and Phyllis Trible. In awakening to feminist/womanist literature, and in specifically uncovering feminist Christian theologies, i began to see the cage did not have to bind my tongue forever.

Through it all, i fell in love. And whatever my partner and i decided to do or refrain from doing was our business and ours alone. If i felt right with God, who was God's church to judge me?

In knowing even the emotional intimacy that can exist between two people, regardless of physical intimacy, i came to know what it truly means to have your brokenness on display. I came to realize that intimacy is not perfect and neither is sex, even if it is first experienced by a woman and a man on their wedding night.

It is this raw, human exposure that allows sex to be sacred. When we come before God, we are not able to withhold our past, our wants, our worries from God's omniscience. We trust God to love us in spite of our depravity as we work to live into the fullness of being created in God's image. The trust in my partner's love for me stands on shakier ground than the trust i have in God. It is, after all, subject to its earthly context. But for me, this trust is what makes intimacy holy. My scarred knees are exposed, and i love and am loved in spite of my inequity.

To be naked in body and soul is not a complacent or lightly undertaken act. To have the courage to share my naked self is a gift from the Divine. But when the pulpit of judgment tells me i am wrong to love someone with my body, i am left to believe it is wrong for me to trust them with my soul.

I do not need condescending scrutiny from the church for decisions concerning my body. I am not merely an object of desire.

Nor am i going to buy into a virgin/whore dichotomy that stems from the idea that men have a stronger sex drive than women. I can make my own decisions with prayerful consideration, and these decisions do not require my youth pastor's—or anyone else's—approval.

My mother's quip that the Church is for the broken rings more true now than it did even then. If she, a divorced mother, can preach the Gospel as an ordained minister in a rural North Carolina church, i can have faith. I can have faith that God transcends our brokenness. I can have faith that when we actively listen to the Messiah who calls us to *love* one another above all else, that constructive dialogue can occur. I can have faith that the trust and mutual respect that makes intimacy between people in love sacred can be what empowers us, as a collective, to love one another— scarred knees and all.

Flesh and Blood
by Ashley-Anne Masters

ASHLEY-ANNE MASTERS is a pastor, chaplain, author, and theologian in Chicago, Illinois. She is ordained in the Presbyterian Church (USA) and received her master of divinity from Columbia Theological Seminary in Decatur, Georgia. She is coauthor of *Bless Her Heart: Life as a Young Clergy Woman* and author of *Holding Hope: Grieving Pregnancy Loss During Advent.* Currently, Ashley-Anne serves as a PRN pediatric chaplain at Lurie Children's Hospital of Chicago, where she is passionate about providing education and support to families during their hospital stay. She also serves as an event planner for various Presbyterian Church (USA) events. She blogs at revaam.org.

There is not even a word in the English language to describe a parent who has lost a child, as there is for a child who has lost a parent or a spouse who has lost a partner. A parent outliving his or her child goes against the perceived natural order of family life.

While grief over the death of a child of any age is complex for parents, the grief of miscarriage and stillbirth may be even more so due to the reality that nobody ever met the child. For instance, when a parent loses a toddler or teenager, often their community rallies around them in support and shared grief. However, when a parent loses an infant due to miscarriage or stillbirth, the grief is not necessarily shared in their community, as members of the community do not yet have a strong relationship with the child.

As a chaplain, I work with parents who have lost children due to miscarriage or stillbirth. Their grief is often accompanied by feelings of guilt and shame. Some feel guilty that perhaps they didn't eat all the right things, do all the right exercises, or take all the right vitamins. Others feel embarrassed that their bodies are not up to par to carry a child. Many feel awkward grieving at all since their pregnancy ended before it was even public knowledge. Even worse, some feel shame and wonder if God is punishing them for past failures or present sins.

In my early experiences as a chaplain, I learned not to ask patients, "How are you?" as I entered their hospital room. Instead, I asked, "What are you feeling right now?" This allowed them to name the emotion of the moment and served as my theological GPS for navigating our conversation. Frequently my question was met with the responses, "I am angry. I am devastated. I feel guilty. I feel like my body isn't normal. My heart is broken." I was informed of past mistakes, prior relationships, and current stressors that contributed to these feelings.

After I heard their story I told them that they were not alone, that they were not any less of a woman for not bearing children, that they were not being punished by a higher being for being imperfect, and that they did not cause their loss simply by missing a day of prenatal vitamins. I recited Romans 8 and reminded them that nothing, not any imperfection or any loss, absolutely nothing, can separate them from the love of God. I reminded them that God loves them even more than they loved their child. I told them that even while living life in the midst of death, we belong to the God of unconditional love.

But my words—no matter how theologically sound or biblically based—were not enough. While they were powerful words, they were still, in those moments, just words. And just as there is not a word for a parent who no longer has a child, there were no words adequate enough to fill the sighs too deep for articulation.

After months of being with several grieving parents, I felt the need to do something, anything, to give tangibility to the words. I wrestled with what that might be, and a few weeks later I received my answer.

I met a mother, alone in a stale smelling hospital room, just after her dilation and curettage procedure. Her significant other was out of the country. When she responded to "What are you feeling right now?" with "More alone than I ever have been in my life" she reached out for my hands. I held them with my left hand and wiped her tears with my right hand. She asked if I would sit on the hospital bed with her and hug her. As I crawled over the cords and railing and onto the bed, we hugged for what seemed like forever. Neither of us spoke. There was nothing to say. At some point I started humming the tune of "Amazing Grace," and she started humming along with me. As we hummed we began to rock and hug, as a parent would rock and hug a baby to soothe him or her to sleep. In fact, she did fall asleep. So I gently let go, tucked her in, and quietly sat in her room. If she woke up, she would know that she was not alone.

While she slept, I thought about how our encounter was not exactly compliant with my seminary and clinical pastoral education training on boundaries. I typically did not so much as touch a hospital bed out of great respect for patients' privacy and space. However, I had also learned how to embody the "Word Made Flesh" through studying the life of Jesus. And I believe Jesus would have rocked her to sleep too, because that's exactly the kind of seemingly odd yet entirely personal type of pastoral care Jesus offered. In that moment, she and I were no longer strangers. We shared a more intimate afternoon than either of us had probably shared even with our closest friends. All manners were null and void because the natural order of life had been turned upside down. Social graces did not matter because only divine grace could see her through that day and strengthen her for the days ahead.

I continue to experience the Word Made Flesh in the unorthodox intimacy of shared grief between strangers, and perhaps that's precisely the point of the Gospel. I remind parents that when Jesus said, "Let the children come to me," he did not specify a gestational or geriatric age limit. I close my prayers for deceased children with, "In the name of Your child, who welcomes all children home, we pray, Amen." All of us, especially grieving parents, need a tangible representative of God, our parent, to rock us to sleep in the middle of our darkest night.

Sadly, more often than not, the church is not the place grieving parents feel the most comfortable sharing their grief. Parents frequently tell me that they shared the news of their miscarriage with their family or close friends, but not with the church because they were ashamed. Or, they did share the news with their church and the pastor told them it was all part of God's perfect plan, which made them feel even worse. Some have shared that church members told them they could just have another child or that God must have needed another angel in heaven. Ergo, they turn to support groups instead of the church, rather than *in addition* to the church, in order to have a safe place to be authentic in their grief.

Not long after a miscarriage of my own I was asked to officiate a baptism. At first I was thrilled, as I love officiating baptisms of healthy children, but the closer the day came, the more sick I became at the thought of it all. I was nauseous every time I thought of the baptism. My former morning sickness had been replaced with dread. I was dreading the baptism because I thought I might not be able to get through it emotionally. I was dreading dipping my hand into the waters that have always sustained me because I was grieving my own child's baptismal vows that never were. I was dreading the journey to the font, not because I was scared of the waters, but because I did not feel comfortable going to those waters publicly in case my own tears fell freely.

On the morning of the baptism, I was overcome with a sense of peace that can only come from the One who commands the waters, "Be still." As I held the perfect and healthy baby, I asked the baptismal questions of the parents, "Relying on God's grace, do you promise to live the Christian faith, and to teach that faith to your child?" Then I asked the congregation, "Do you, as members of the church of Jesus Christ, promise to guide and nurture this child by word and deed, with love and prayer, encouraging them to know and follow Christ and to be faithful members of his church?" As the parents and congregation affirmed, "We do," I was filled with gratitude to be a part of the village vowing to raise this child in faith. I felt great joy when I had the privilege of cupping the waters in my hand, pouring them on the baby's soft head, and proclaiming, "You are a child of the Covenant. I baptize you in the name of the Father, and of the Son, and of the Holy Spirit." I felt grace overflow while I held fresh life in my grasp.

It is my great hope that we as people of faith will take seriously our baptismal vows to nurture, love, and guide one another, so that our brothers and sisters who grieve may feel welcome to cry at the font. For the streams of grief are also necessary in the waters of baptism. I hope we do not create obstacles which prevent a grieving parent from feeling welcome at the font with their family of faith. The Apostle Paul teaches that we are all new creations in Christ. As new creations, I hope we strive to embody the broken body and shed blood of Christ, who promises the day when mourning, crying, miscarriage, stillbirth, and parents outliving their children shall be no more. Until that day, may the salty tears of grief continue to guide us to the font of life, community, and hope, as we pray:

> Lord, in your mercy, hear my prayer for parents and those who want to be.
>
> For those who got pregnant right away and those who have been trying for years . . .
>
> For those who entrust their babies to the care of another family . . .
>
> For those who cannot wait to welcome a baby into their home and those who are terrified they are not fit to be parents . . .
>
> For those whose child will get a soccer scholarship and those whose child will never run . . .
>
> For those who proudly pose for pregnancy photos and those who shamefully hide their bellies . . .
>
> For those who are proud to be fathers and those who hope the DNA tests are incorrect . . .
>
> For those who pay child support and those who need child support . . .
>
> For those who fight with teenage daughters and those whose daughters have run away . . .

For those who cannot pay for college and those who cannot pay for medical care . . .

For those who homeschool and those who fear their children won't make it home from school . . .

For those who think their son is the best surprise of their life . . .

For those whose children are in prison and those whose children want to be corrections officers . . .

For those whose baby doesn't live outside of the womb and those whose wombs are empty . . .

For those taking hormones and those who feel exhausted from hormone changes . . .

For those grieving what will never be and those amazed by what life has become . . .

For those who are single parents and those who are now stepparents . . .

For those who have an empty nest and for those whose nest was never full . . .

For the couple who is closer than ever and the couple getting divorced . . .

For all of your children of all ages, hold them close and give them life . . .

Amen.

Finding My Voice
by Sarah Thebarge

SARAH THEBARGE is a speaker and author who grew up as a pastor's kid in Lancaster, Pennsylvania. She earned a masters degree in medical science from Yale School of Medicine and was studying journalism at Columbia University when she was diagnosed with breast cancer at age twenty-seven. Sarah's writing has appeared in *Christianity Today*, BurnsideWriters.com, *Relevant*, TheOoze.com, *Raysd*, and *Just Between Us*. Her writing for *Christianity Today*'s This Is Our City project won first prize from the National Evangelical Press Association. Her first book, *The Invisible Girls*, was published by Jericho Books in April 2013. Sarah currently lives in Portland, Oregon.

When I was a little girl, my family moved from Pennsylvania to New Jersey so my father could pastor a small Baptist church there. Before my three brothers and I could enroll in the new school, we had to take math and English placement tests. And then we had to meet with a psychologist and a speech therapist.

The only negative finding on all of our evaluations was something the speech therapist noted about me. "You lisp when you say words with 's' in them," she said. "If we'd gotten to you earlier, we could've fixed you. But it's too late now."

With those words, I was thrust into a new school—the preacher's daughter who had no friends, wore homemade clothes, and lisped when she said her own name. It was embarrassing that while my father made his living as a gifted speaker, I couldn't say a single sentence without my sibilant "s" giving me away.

The church my father pastored applied a literal interpretation to the New Testament, and so because the Apostle Paul said in 1 Corinthians 14:34, "Let your women keep silence in the churches: for it is not permitted unto them to speak" (KJV), women in our congregation were not allowed to preach. They weren't even permitted to read the Scripture aloud or lead the hymns during Sunday services.

I was frustrated not only by the limitations our church placed on women, but also by the seemingly random hermeneutic used to divine these standards. During lunch one Sunday afternoon when I was in junior high, I asked my father why our church applied 1 Corinthians 14 literally, but didn't enforce 1 Corinthians 11, which mandated women to wear head coverings in church. My father's explanation that the former was an absolute standard while the latter was an irrelevant cultural tradition was exasperating to me.

But between our church's conservative culture and my speech impediment, I was too intimidated to speak up against the restraint I perceived as an injustice. So instead of protesting, I fell silent.

And in my silence, I started thinking. Why did it matter so much? Why did I care so deeply about having a voice? Even though I couldn't ever be a biblical superhero, my culture did offer me the opportunity to be a sidekick—a beautiful female companion who took few risks and made no independent decisions and was always along for the ride. That was enough for scores of women in history. Why wasn't it enough for me?

Because silence that is not self-imposed is punishment. The thought came to me one afternoon when I was in high school, reading the story of Zechariah being struck mute because of his lack of faith. Throughout the Bible, silence was a sentence. It was a punishment. It was a threat. And, judging from the fact that Jesus healed people from muteness, it was a disease.

It was one thing for Paul to recommend that women in the early church be silent so they could absorb teaching about God they'd been excluded from in the past. It was wise to let women have the opportunity to catch up on the education they'd been denied before they began to teach others. But applying the verse beyond that context, and insisting that women need to continue to be silent in spite of the advances our culture has made in women's equality, is a dangerous misuse of authority.

Forcing women to be silent in the church not only perpetuates what was likely a limited restriction, but it also perpetuates the *need* for the restriction. Deny women the chance to enroll in seminary, to earn advanced theological degrees, to participate in a church's eldership, or to preach from the pulpit, and soon you will have created exactly the misogynistic culture Jesus came to lead people out of. He came not only to heal individuals of congenital muteness, but also to heal the broken culture that condoned men who oppressed women's voices.

Those who don't think imposed silence is a burden need only look at the evolution of the word "dumb" to see the implications muteness has for those who cannot speak. I understand the pain well, because I lived with it for much of my life.

As a girl, I was too shy to raise my voice against the men who believed that God not only condoned but mandated their domination, and so I began writing instead. At night I'd sit on my bedroom floor near the nightlight and scribble poems and ideas and notes into a journal that I kept hidden in a box beneath my bed.

After I graduated from high school, I left the box full of journals in my parents' attic and flew to California to start college. I was still shy and only spoke when it was absolutely necessary. One afternoon a student sat down next to me in the cafeteria and asked me a question about a class assignment. As I answered him, he leaned in close, brushed aside my long blonde hair, and looked behind my ears.

"What are you doing?" I asked.

"Looking for your hearing aids," he said. "You talk like you've never heard the sound of your own voice before."

That afternoon I sat in my dorm room with my Bible, looking for the passage with the most "s" sounds in it.

I settled on Psalm 23, and began to read it aloud.

> *The Lord is my shepherd; I shall not want.*
>
> *He maketh me to lie down in green pastures:*

he leadeth me beside the still waters.

He restoreth my soul. (Psalm 23:1-3, KJV)

I read it over and over again, making myself repeat the words that began with "s" until I said them correctly. Every day for two semesters, I sat in my dorm room reading Psalm 23 aloud, trying to give myself the speech therapy I'd been denied as a child.

I went on to finish college, and then grad school, and then I moved to Portland where I met a Somali refugee mom and her two little girls on the train. I nicknamed them *The Invisible Girls*, because the day I met them, no one on the train seemed to see them but me. I didn't have nearly enough resources to meet all their needs, but I gave them what I could: my friendship and my gift for writing.

As I helped them get settled in America, I wrote a blog about the adventures we had together. This year I compiled the stories into a book and sold it to a publisher with the hope of using the proceeds to send the Somali girls to college.

When my pastor in Portland, Oregon, heard what I was doing, he called and asked if I'd like to preach about God's love for Invisible People at church one Sunday. And that is how, a few weeks ago, I ended up standing on a stage in front of thousands of people, preaching the story of Hagar.

After God pursued this penniless, pregnant Egyptian slave girl in the desert and spared her life, she became the only person in the Bible to name God. She called him El Roi, The God Who Sees.

As I told Hagar's story, I was reminded that not only did Hagar name God, but God named Hagar's unborn child. God named her son Ishmael, which means, God Hears.

When I finished preaching, I stood at the front of the sanctuary, praying with dozens of people who came forward to encounter El Roi. And I wept tears of thankfulness and relief, grateful that in all of his mercy, God not only saw refugee girls who were lost on the train and a fugitive slave who was abandoned in the wilderness; He also heard and answered the prayers of the preacher's daughter with a sibilant "s," who had been trying all her life to find her voice.

A Pregnant Silence
by Katey Zeh

KATEY ZEH is an advocate for reproductive justice in faith communities. Raised in southern Georgia, she struggled to connect her faith with her progressive values. She began studying theology while at Davidson College, where she wrote her honors thesis on theology, ritual, and motherhood. In 2008, she graduated from Yale Divinity School with her master of divinity. Currently, she directs a grassroots education and mobilization initiative, focused on improving global maternal health for The United Methodist Church. Katey serves on the board of directors for the Religious Coalition for Reproductive Choice in Washington, DC. She lives in North Carolina with her husband Matt and their dog Lucy.

I met Alice Wasilwa Otieno on a crisp October evening at Dulles International Airport. She'd been traveling for more than a day from her hometown in Kenya. As we greeted each other with an embrace, she nearly collapsed into my arms with a mixture of exhaustion and relief. The next morning we embarked on a journey across the United States, visiting the halls of power in DC, the Rocky Mountains of Colorado, and the cool ocean waters of southern California with a single mission: to share her story.

Earlier that year I'd begun building a grassroots advocacy project for The United Methodist Church called "Healthy Families, Healthy Planet," aimed at educating and mobilizing people of faith on the moral tragedy of maternal mortality. Although I had facts and statistics to support my claims, what I lacked was the direct connection to women's suffering on the ground. What my work lacked was a certain authenticity that only an advocate like Alice could bring.

Alice directs a health clinic in a rural area of Kenya called Kopanga, a short distance from the banks of Lake Victoria. For the 40,000 people who live in the surrounding area, Alice's clinic is their only access point for healthcare. During the week, Alice lives apart from her husband Kephas, a United Methodist pastor, and their two young daughters. On the Friday evenings when she isn't on call at the clinic, Alice flags down a taxi to take her the long, exhausting journey home so that she can spend the weekend with her family.

Despite the many hardships that this distance creates, Alice is passionately committed to her work. Ten years ago she started her health ministry, working without pay in a small rented room in a house with only a few basic supplies donated by local churches. One day a woman came to her with a baby who was sick with bronchitis. With only a bed sheet, a steaming pot of water, and a few menthol crystals, Alice delivered the simple yet miraculous relief that the young child needed, and his breathing immediately cleared. As if lifted out of a Gospel healing story, the young mother went back to her community, declaring her son had been made well.

Since that time, Alice has become a leader in the community. She purchased a piece of land and secured donors to build the clinic in Kopanga. Now each day more than thirty patients come to Alice's clinic seeking her care. Her proudest achievement is that every child born in the community is now vaccinated for measles, preventing countless infant deaths each year. But there are still many challenges in her work.

Throughout our travels across the United States, the story that Alice repeated time and time again was that each day, a dozen or so women come from their work in the fields seeking family planning counseling and services. Every three months, Alice receives one hundred vials of Depo Provera, a contraceptive injectable that is discrete and effective for three months. The demand for the injection is so high that after only two weeks, she has completely run out of it. The injection costs less than two dollars per vial, but the clinic simply does not have the financial resources to keep a supply on hand.

The women Alice is forced to turn away are part of the more than 220 million women worldwide who want to delay or prevent pregnancy but cannot access the services that empower them to do so. The consequences of this unmet need are tragic. One in three of these 220 million women will get pregnant this year, and for thousands of them, it will be a death sentence. Every two minutes somewhere in the world a woman dies from complications during pregnancy or childbirth. Nearly all of these deaths occur in the developing world.

Further, nearly a third of the women who die in childbirth did not want to get pregnant in the first place. Women are dying from pregnancies that they never wanted, not because we lack the information and services that would save their lives, but because we have failed to ensure that every woman has access to them.

Given this global tragedy, it is puzzling to me why a person's access to contraception would be at all contentious in the United States. At the very least the idea of family planning should be commendable. Pastors and politicians alike claim "family" as central to our values as Christians and citizens. Similarly, the concept of planning—striving to have forethought in decision-making—is considered wise. Why is it that when we piece together these virtues of family and planning that we suddenly encounter resistance and even aversion? Simply put, the phrase "family planning" is much more than the sum of its parts.

In reality, the term "family planning" shouldn't be just about planning a family. It should be used to talk about what parenting books to read, or what foods to feed our kids, or how to invest in a college fund. Instead the phrase "family planning" is a way for us to talk about how many people want to avoid or delay pregnancy at a given time, and that's where we get stuck. We get so focused on the "what"—namely the non-procreative sex that is taking place—that we don't spend enough time on the complexity of "why" such decisions are made.

Growing up in a post-*Griswold v. Connecticut*[1] world, I was inundated with contraceptive information and tools. From condom

---

1. In 1965, the Supreme Court ruled that a Connecticut law banning the use of contraceptives violated a person's right to privacy.

machines on the walls of public bathrooms to birth control ads in my magazines, I never had to think much about the availability of modern contraceptives, much less the impact that it had on my own life or society as a whole. At the same time, I was a churchgoer in a congregation that pushed me to take an abstinence pledge at the age of thirteen. I was given a gold band to wear on my left hand as a reminder of this pledge, with the instruction that I would give it to my future husband on our wedding night as a symbol of my virginity. The only mention of contraception I heard at church had to do with how condoms were essentially balloons through which the AIDS virus could easily pass.

In short, I knew from church that I was supposed to be chaste until I got married. I knew from society that I could get condoms and other contraceptives if and when I needed them. But I didn't know what, if anything, the two had to do with each other. Looking back, I believe that the church was primarily concerned with stifling my sexuality in adolescence, rather than preparing me for a lifetime of decision-making regarding my sexuality.

Once, while talking with a divinity school friend about the sexuality education I got at church, she told me that at her Catholic high school she was taught that unprotected premarital sex was considered less sinful than using a condom. She was told if you had the forethought to carry a condom, then the sex you were having had to have been planned.

One of the biggest omissions of our churches occurs when we fail to discuss sexuality in all of its fullness, to have the complex discussions with children, youth, and adults about what healthy sexuality at every life stage looks like. Too often churches aren't a resource for people in the pews when they do want to find a partner, or when they are discerning if and when to have children. And they have not always been a safe place for struggling and praying when those desires and other circumstances are in conflict.

Audre Lorde wrote, "Your silence will not protect you." As a church, we must face this truth. Our silence has failed not only to protect, but also to empower those sitting in our pews and outside of our walls. By remaining silent, we have sent a strong message that issues of sexuality are of little importance to the church and to God.

This is where we must change. We must move away from the tidy yet detached framework of "shall" and "shall not" and begin addressing the grayness of life's complexities. Rather than hiding behind propriety and discomfort, we must remove the barriers that keep us from authentically caring for all of God's people.

When I speak to churches across the country, I tell them about the realties women face around the globe, that in many parts of the world a pregnancy is a life-threatening condition. I share Alice's story about the women she must turn away and how many of them will experience pregnancies that their bodies cannot sustain physically, and their families cannot sustain economically. I watch as their faces sink, their heads bow, their hearts break.

But then I share that these deaths are not inevitable. Ensuring universal access to contraception is one of the central pieces of not only saving, but also changing, women's lives. Not once have I had a single person argue otherwise. As much as I'd like to lend that to my persuasiveness as a public speaker, I believe the real reason is that hearing these stories causes them to reflect on their own lives and experiences and to wrestle with the disparities between those who have and those who have not.

On the surface, the story of a rural woman in Kenya may seem distant from our own. But if we listen deeply and honestly, we begin to see the connections of our shared desire for health and well-being for ourselves and our families. In the gospel of John, Jesus tells his disciples that he came to bring abundant life. I believe that despite the injustices of our world, it is still God's desire that every mother, every child, and every family, no matter the circumstance, experience that abundant life. We are called by God to be partners in this work. We can no longer remain silent, hiding behind our discomfort and the safety of our church walls. It is time for us to answer the call to go out into the world and care for our neighbors as God cares for us.

A Woman Undone
by Grace Biskie

GRACE BISKIE is a passionate, big-dreaming, extroverted communicator. Grace holds a bachelor of arts in speech communications and is halfway through a master of divinity from Western Theological Seminary. She has served high school and college students in the nonprofit sector for over fifteen years. Grace has contributed online for Rachel Held Evans, Jim Wallis's God's Politics blog, A Deeper Story, and featured syndicated work on Blogher. She blogs regularly at her online home, www.gabbingwithgrace.com. Currently, Grace is working on her first book, *Detroit's Daughter*, a memoir about surviving her father, her brother, abuse, racism, Christians, boys, and poverty while growing up in Detroit. Grace is married to Dave and raising two ridiculously cute sons, Ransom and Rhys.

As a woman and an evangelical Christian minister there are many deeds one cannot admit to even being tempted by. I am no longer a Christian minister.

At thirty-four, married with two boys under five, life caved in. My eleven-year marriage was imploding. Like a cave without its cornerstone we'd lost all the things that mattered: trust, hope, and anything that could be construed as communication. Our failing marriage was just another aspect of my adult life caving in. It wasn't merely external circumstances threatening our fragile union, it was me. Clumsily feeling my way around dangerous situations like a drunkard carrying live dynamite, I was about to torch the whole damn thing and let it cave in on me and everyone else too. There would be no survivors.

There were triggers. There was this other man, first off. Not someone I loved or had even fallen for. Aaron *was* a friend, someone I'd grown up with who'd turned into my easiest escape route. The whole episode was maddening even to me. It made zero sense for me to consider throwing away my marriage, my ministry, and the entire *somewhat* stable foundation of my life for someone I understood to be a cheater, a liar, and a sex addict. But, ah, convenience. Never underestimate the lure of convenience in the midst of marital tragedy.

A month before Aaron came back into my life my husband and I celebrated Christmas at home with our two boys. There was something about the day itself that made me think there was enough left of our marriage to save. Perhaps it was the snow, the smell of sausage for breakfast, the sound of cheery Christmas jingles or the reality of Jesus's vulnerable entrance into this world. Or maybe it was our boys' excitement over shiny new things and my desire to give them a two-parent home and other healthy experiences I never had. On that day, I thought we could save it. Even if there wasn't much left to save, I was reminded there was enough worth saving it for.

Of our two boys, the baby was fourteen months and we'd spent the entire first year of his life inexplicably arguing over how messy the house was and how dinner was never at the same time every day. We couldn't resolve all the nuances of working in ministry together, working half the time out of our messy home and sharing the responsibility of fundraising six-figures annually. Also, our travel schedule was nuts, the level of chaos astonishing. I felt I was performing everything wrong. I wanted to disappear. In the absence of warmth and daylight sun, each night felt darker and colder than the previous one. Maybe it was the acute awareness of my bodily vulnerability or my postpartum depression or maybe just my regular old demons, but I felt tormented. But then, Christmas. With the hope of Jesus's birth came the hope of restoration for our marriage and maybe even, for kicks, restoration of my mental health.

That January, Aaron found me on Facebook. Within the week we'd talked, flirted, and texted multiple times per day. There he was, Mr. Convenient, ready to listen to endless bitching and pleased to throw in his two cents that my husband was a loser and that I should sleep with him instead.

I'd reached that frightening station in life when you know exactly what you should do but don't want to, and when you know exactly what you shouldn't want, but you want it anyway, and when you think you know exactly who you are, but you aren't sure anymore. It had become my unholy trifecta.

By God's grace, Aaron and I were 500 miles apart. The distance removed the temptation to even consider his requests for one hot night. But it was out there and the worse my marriage got the worse Aaron and I became embedded into one another. Finally, I faced it. It was an emotional affair. The idea itself was preposterous to Aaron, which made me question my own intuition alongside my rickety morality. I wanted my emotional affair to mean something, but it didn't. I wanted to be in love with Aaron but I wasn't. I wanted to see myself with Aaron, but I couldn't. It was lust gone wild, without the hot sex. My emotional affair was a disgrace to all emotional affairs. So in addition to not being able to keep my house clean or control my spending, I couldn't even pull together a normal emotional affair. I felt like the ultimate failure's failure.

The deeper I went in, the darker the temptations, as if the trigger for the cave demolition of our marriage set off the next and the next explosion. From Aaron to ridiculous spending to eventually wanting to abandon my ministry, my husband, and children and run off to Perth, I wanted to escape my life and not look back. Boom.

I *thought* I wanted all of that. I had a chance to see Aaron back in Detroit. We were both there, me in tatters and him in party mode. The first night, I wouldn't see him. The second night, he wouldn't see me. His rejection triggered deeper humiliation than I could process. I wanted to die. As a sexual abuse survivor, I'd lived the majority of my life using the one thing dear old Dad taught me: sexuality. I'd never been turned down for sex. I had no context to understand what that even meant. I felt squashed like an unnoticed, dead worker ant.

Amidst this level of turmoil and temptation I wondered where I would find grace as a Christian minister of the gospel and a master of divinity student. How could I even speak of it when my female colleagues were tempted by overindulging in chocolate and pictures of shirtless Ryan Reynolds? I was well out of my league. There was no context to understand my temptations. I couldn't see myself in other women serving as leaders in their Christian community. If they even had similar struggles, had they survived them? I was facing demons who engineered ludicrous ideas that dismembering my life was actually the better choice. Almost despite myself, I'd summoned them in for tea and crumpets. I believed I'd become the wicked witch of West Michigan. Even so, everyday I cried through the Psalms begging God to rescue me from myself. "Keep me" was my go-to prayer. This one truth I knew: *I had no ability to keep myself. If I were kept, it would be God who kept me.*

After strong, detailed plans of suicide wouldn't go away I said "uncle" and went to counseling. Chris was kind, gracious, empathetic. He was exactly what I needed. I trusted him instantly like a lifelong friend. When he mentioned that I was facing a female midlife crisis, I took it seriously. I'd seen it twice in person. I knew two women who, in their mid-forties, had affairs and gave their husbands the old heave-ho. Neither was a minister, neither felt morally responsible to thousands of trusting college students, so I didn't fully relate, but Chris's idea nagged me. If I were having some sort of midlife crisis, then maybe there was something, *anything*, normal about me after all. Maybe I *could* be rescued. Hope floated.

I told my husband the truth about spending too much, the emotional affair, the desperate desire to die, to leave him, to abandon our two precious boys, to escape to Perth. I couldn't get it out of my head that if I slept with Aaron he'd leave me. I thought I wanted concrete solidification that I was unworthy of being stayed with. I thought I wanted to blame my husband for launching me into a tailspin. Constant vacillating between teeny-tiny crumbs of hope and the persistent longing to be abandoned was exhausting.

But no, he wouldn't leave. He wanted me to pull myself up by my bootstraps and figure it out, live within his boundaries and on his schedule. He was understandably ridden with anxiety about my myriad of struggles. He couldn't figure out how to stop demanding change long enough to grasp the horrors I was facing. I needed him to be kind, or I needed him to go. He wanted a less troublesome, less bothersome version of me. I wanted a more gracious, less anal version of him. Neither was happening. Like any marriage on the brink, ours was complex. A man of God himself, he prayed and he loved through calculated silence. And he never left me, not in one single way.

A Christian-woman-on-the-bitter-edge is desperate for grace. What I needed to survive repulsive temptations was to be told that even though I felt too exhausted to want to stay with my children, I wasn't a bad mother until . . . I left. I needed my husband to tell me that even though I wanted to cheat on him, I wasn't a bad wife until . . . I did. I needed a lot of grace. For the most part, I got grace. It's how I survived myself.

I started honest conversations with my spiritual director. She seemed safe enough, being bound by confidentiality to protect my tomfoolery. She encouraged me to tell others. I told my supervisor, Fred. If I needed to be fired, I wanted to be fired. But what Fred did was sit across the table from me and ooze grace out of his nostrils. I told my closest friends, and they prayed, emailed, texted, challenged, confronted. Jean took every sobbing phone call for ten months straight. Jessica suggested we go on a weekend prayer retreat where she labored in prayer while I read Scripture and wrote out desperate pleas to the Lord, and where God clearly gave her visions of my freedom from Satan's death grip. God gave me a promise from Scripture—Ezekiel 36:26: "I will give you a new heart and put a new spirit in you; I will remove from you your heart of stone and give you a heart of flesh." I am making you new, God said. I clung to this promise like Velcro.

The more friends I told the more I realized my need for each one. While one helped me find small glimpses of hope in our nightmare marriage another would soothe me through the heartache of *even wanting* to leave the kids. I invited ministry partners to join a small group of people I'd send prayer requests to via email. They became my Aaronites, because as Aaron of the Old Testament held up the arms of a battle-weary Moses, they became my arm bearers. Coincidentally, my Aaronites saved me from my very own Aaron. I felt I had very little to lose in sharing more openly as I continued to make my bed in Sheol. I found the courage to invite others in because, at the time, I'd lost any modicum of respect for myself. What the hell did I care if *anyone else* respected me? That's what I love about God. He took my shitty intentions and turned them around to cultivate a community of people who rescued our children, our marriage, and my very life.

Some people judged me. And some concerned themselves with what I was going through, responding always in grace and kindness. Without this anticipation of grace, how do we expect ragamuffins to step forward and admit they are facing the absolute worst version of themselves? Without grace, there is little hope. Without hope we cave in and there are no survivors.

Sometimes we fight to keep the cave from falling in on us and sometimes, yeah, we think blowing the whole damn thing up ourselves is the best option. But it is God who holds the cave in his fingertips. My love for God looked like faith on some days and cowardice on others, but each frightening day I chose to trust in the one that had the power to protect me from myself. He answered our prayers. He kept me and we all survived.

I am new.

What do Cinderella, Lilies, and the Cross Have in Common?

by Carol Howard Merritt

CAROL HOWARD MERRITT is an author and speaker from Chattanooga. Before moving to Tennessee, she pastored Presbyterian congregations in Louisiana, Rhode Island, and Washington, DC. She has written *Reframing Hope* (Alban, 2010) and *Tribal Church* (Alban, 2007). She blogs at TribalChurch.org and hosts the God Complex Radio podcast with Derrick Weston.

As I drove over the bridge, my eyes followed the glistening water, snaking around the land, forming nooks where swans nested alongside the sailboat population.

I was in my twenties, serving my third year as a minister, and starting a new call in a completely different part of the world than I had previously worked. Like many young people entering religious life, I graduated from seminary, received my ordination, and started as a pastor in an economically awkward time. The cost of preparing for our calling had gotten more expensive, with education debt becoming an acceptable reality that no one realized, aside from the students who bore the costs.

As my husband and I picked out our tiny house, I had another shock. The cottage had been the garage of a larger home, converted into living space. Our family of three could barely fit into the home. It was nestled in the neighboring, less desirable town south of the church. Even with those factors, the cost of housing had ballooned far past what the church's previous pastor (who was retired) had to pay for a home. In fact, I started out in a debt hole that was substantially deeper than any minister who had served the congregation before me.

On the church's side, they had been slipping in attendance for decades. Their most faithful, older members, who seemed to have a sense of stewardship engrained in them, were passing away. They had to make necessary adjustments to the salary and figured that I wouldn't need a higher pay, since I was married and my husband would eventually have an income.

I was optimistic when I analyzed my family budget and decided to take the position. I expected that my husband would find a job quickly. There were many expenses around raising our child that I didn't know how to predict, but I was positive we could meet any challenge.

After a couple of years, the church's financial situation looked much brighter as the income steadily increased. More people attended the Sunday morning service and the members became aware of a spiritual vitality that led them to serve more in the community.

Yet my situation was getting worse. I received a modest cost of living increase, but it wasn't enough to cover my outstanding expenses. We had depleted our savings, my husband still couldn't find employment, the expenses for our child became more than we could manage, and I became desperate. "What should we do?" I asked my husband, as he cooked dinner and I held our daughter on my hip.

He shook his head in regret. "I don't know. I've applied for every position I'm qualified for and several that I'm not. Any job that I can get right now would not cover the cost of childcare." He placed the steaming dinner on our plates and added, "The church is doing okay, right? I think you're just going to have to ask for a raise."

I carefully collected my data, being sure not to make my request solely based on need, but on other factors as well, like comparable salaries and how much the offering income had increased since I had become their pastor. I was pleased when I assembled the information, because even though the church had been in decline before I arrived, our membership and annual church income had increased in the short time that I was there.

I invited a couple of key leaders of the church for coffee at our home. I placed the graphs on the kitchen counter before them and explained the situation. They seemed to be amenable to my appeal, so I brought the request to the larger board.

We met in a small conference room. I had moderated hundreds of meetings, but I couldn't help but feel nervous this time. As the negotiations were about to take place, I tried to exude the confidence of a high-powered CEO, but internally I felt vulnerable and scared. I tried not to let my hands shake, but I couldn't hide them. As I noticed my quivering fingers, I gave myself an internal pep talk: *You wouldn't be asking for the money if you didn't need it. It's okay. The church has grown since you have been there. People will understand.*

After I made the request, I left the room in order to allow the leadership to discuss it. After a belabored conversation, the leaders tabled the decision about whether I should get the raise for the next meeting that would take place in thirty days. During the ensuing time, I realized that my trepidation had not been in vain. I spent the next phase of my ministry dealing with backlash. A cacophony of comments began swirling around the community, and I heard them all secondhand.

"Her husband just needs to get a job," one man grumbled. "We shouldn't have to pay because he's unemployed. What's wrong with him anyways?"

"Carol's an egomaniac," a woman responded while rolling her eyes. "Did you see how she pointed to the growth in the congregation? Does she really think that it's all because of her?"

"I don't know why she expects a raise. I didn't get one at my job," someone else chimed in.

"She makes more than I do!" another woman protested.

"I saw her eating out with her family at a restaurant on Tuesday," a man shook his head. "We never had enough money to eat out at restaurants when our kids were little."

"Did she go in the ministry for the money?" a businessman asked with a chuckle, as they all shook their heads.

"I think she's just immature," an elderly widow replied.

Each day, I came home with new reports. I would sort them out with my husband as he sautéed. The air filled with the smell of onions and olive oil as I held our child and worried, "Is it true?

Am I immature, an egomaniac? How could they think that when I feel so insecure? I'm not sure how I can be an effective minister if this is who my congregation thinks I am."

I went to the doctor and found out that my body had become riddled with stress-induced illnesses. "Are you in a tense situation?" my doctor asked as we reviewed the results of my physical. When I nodded my head, she said, "Well, you're going to need to do something about that. Your body can only take so much."

As I took off the paper dress and put my warm clothes on again, I realized that the stress from my community's judgments began to outweigh the financial pressure. I tried to sort out my shame. Was I irresponsible with money? Was I immature? Was I some sort of diva? Or, did I simply need a raise? I made two promises to myself—that I would never ask them for anything again and I would find another church to pastor as soon as I could.

The words were so harsh and condemning that it seemed that there was more than just a matter of dollars and cents with which I was dealing. Their response and my humiliation seemed to be based on a deeper, gut-level reaction. I had brought up something that was taboo in my spiritual community.

The constant demands that my husband ought to have a job made me wonder if that would have been such a strong sentiment if it were a wife staying at home with her three-year-old. Did they have a problem with him being the primary caretaker of our child? When I doubled that with the charge of immaturity, it made me feel like the fact that I was a young woman meant that I shouldn't need or didn't deserve an increase in income. The charge of my inflated ego alongside the "Did she go into this profession for the money?" quips made me feel as if a religious leader should never ask for a raise. A toxic combination of three cultural and spiritual influences played into the situation: the myth of Cinderella, the parable of the lilies, and the theology of cross.

From the time little girls are in onesies, our culture feeds them a steady diet of Disney princesses. Even the die-hard feminist mom will have difficulty avoiding the myths in which we soak our children. Unless a little girl grows up in a bubble, she will hear that the troubled heroine gets saved by the handsome and wealthy prince.

Of course, now that we are a bit more enlightened, we know that a woman can save herself. But the myth has residual effects. Our culture often expects that within heterosexual couples, even the most successful women will still "marry up." In other words, if a woman is doing well, then her husband will make as much (if not more) than she will.

But what happens if the husband moves for his wife? His chances of finding employment without geographic flexibility might diminish his ability to make money or even find a job at all. The Cinderella story gets dismantled in reality, but not in the imaginations of those who hold to it.

When we think about gender alongside religion, the cultural myth becomes complicated with the addition of the lily parable. In the Christian tradition, we are told that Jesus looked out upon the lilies of the field and said that we ought to learn from them. When we feel anxious about how we're going to feed or clothe ourselves, we can survey those dainty flowers, knowing that God will provide for us just as God nurtures them. In light of this biblical truth, it can be unseemly for Christian leaders to talk about salaries. If we were truly living holy lives, God would care for us. And if God gives us food to eat and clothes to wear, then what do we have to complain about? Unfortunately, I found out that Sallie Mae, the student loan company to which I was indebted, didn't accept lilies for payment.

Finally, the theology of the cross makes money taboo. As Christians, our faith calls us to sacrifice. While other belief systems may appreciate a sense of balance or of paying what is due, Christian theology constantly beckons us to "lay down our lives" or "take up our cross." Throughout history, men and women who give themselves to Christian service have marked that commitment by turning over their private property, giving up their sex lives, or taking a vow of poverty. There is a sense that if we are following in the footsteps of Christ, we should be willing to give everything. Unfortunately, this passion can lead Christians to martyr themselves. Women ministers sacrifice salary, time, and energy until they are utterly depleted. We constantly have to whisper to our sisters working alongside us, "Don't forget to take care of yourself.

Take your day off. If you're empty and dry, you won't be any help to your community."

The problem with these cultural myths and spiritual beliefs is that they conspire against us to silence religious women from talking about what we need. They shame us so that we feel uncomfortable about negotiating our salaries and demanding equal pay for equal work. And, in the end, they allow injustice to flourish. We need to start reminding one another, "It is good and right to ask for fair and equal pay. Even if you do not need the money, do it for the women working with you and do it for the next generation."

Eventually, the congregation decided to give me a substantial increase in salary. Many members contributed in order to meet the necessary amount. Unfortunately, not everyone was pleased with this outcome. The comments and criticism got louder with the raise, so I continued my search for a new position. Within several months, I found a pastorate in a city where my husband could easily find employment and we could meet our financial obligations.

In my next position, I learned from my experience. As I negotiated housing, I clearly articulated what I needed. I worked with a therapist and spiritual director to overcome my fear and shame. I researched, read, and became more aware of the economic situation of women and younger generations. Realizing that my situation was not isolated, I began to write, speak, and advocate for economic issues for those under the age of forty. As I learned to break free from the cultural and spiritual myths that bound me, I was free to work on behalf of fair pay for myself and for others.

In the generations ahead, I pray that we will be able to break through our cultural and spiritual taboos in order to talk about salary inequities, and together work for fair pay.

Running into Glass Doors

by Atinuke O. Diver

ATINUKE O. DIVER is an attorney and writer. She blogs regularly at YesWereTogether.com, a humor blog about interracial relationships. Her work on race, culture, and relationships has been featured on BlogHer, Racialicious, The African Immigrant Journal, The Review Review, Love Isn't Enough, The Fresh Xpress, Wedding Nouveau, Beyond Black &White, and has been recognized as an Editor's Pick on OpenSalon.com. Born in Boston, Massachusetts to Nigerian immigrant parents, Tinu grew up in Prince George's County, Maryland. She earned degrees in English, law, and nonprofit leadership from the University of North Carolina at Chapel Hill, where the Creative Writing Program awarded her the Random House/Wanda Chappell Scholarship. Following law school, Tinu entered federal service as a Presidential Management Fellow and currently practices law at a transportation research center in the Kendall Square neighborhood of Cambridge, Massachusetts. Tinu serves as a board trustee of the Benjamin Banneker Public Charter School and as a board director of the Boston Center for Adult Education. She completed the 2012 Boston Marathon in record heat and lived to talk about it. Tinu and her husband Joshua reside in Boston and are members of Citylife Presbyterian Church in Boston.

I have a habit of running into glass doors. The first time, I was visiting family in Nigeria for a cousin's wedding. The morning of the engagement ceremony, the house was buzzing with people as we, the bride's family, prepared for the arrival of the groom and his family. To help facilitate the bustle, we left a sliding glass door open so people could move freely between the house and backyard where the festivities would take place. I became so used to the door staying open that I stopped checking whether the door was *actually* open. So when a cousin arrived later in the evening, I bolted down the stairs at full speed, running from the house to the backyard, excited to see her and—BAM!—I hit the door so hard that I actually bounced off of it, sporting a knot on my forehead for the next two days.

Since then, I have found myself running into glass doors of a different kind: namely, the church's ambivalence toward my professional life. Like the painful jolt experienced when an entryway becomes a barrier, I've found the church's reluctance to affirm my professional calling jarring and painful. Though I spend most of my days working in a setting not centered on my home, husband, children, or place of worship, the church speaks to me primarily about my marital status and reproductive system. The church challenges me to embrace a worldview with implications for every area of life. Yet rarely does the church acknowledge the realities of women in their pursuit of post-secondary education while single, married, with or without children; or as Rhodes Scholars, board trustees, CEOs, governors, or presidents. My church challenges me to bring my faith to work but remains silent as to how I bring my work to my faith.

On July 7, 1981 at approximately 10:47 a.m., President Ronald Reagan made good on a campaign promise by nominating Sandra Day O'Connor to be the first woman on the United States Supreme Court. But just two hours and forty-seven minutes earlier, thousands of miles away, a *slightly* more momentous occasion occurred, at least in my mind: my birth at Brigham and Women's Hospital in Boston, Massachusetts. The two events couldn't be more unrelated and yet so intertwined. As the first daughter born to my Nigerian immigrant parents, I embodied their hope for a progeny who would accomplish more and struggle less. And Justice O'Connor's ascension to the highest court in the land suggested that maybe, even for the daughter of immigrants, no opportunity was out of reach.

My mother's example taught me how a woman's work—both inside and outside of the home—wasn't solely a matter of theology, doctrine, or religious devotion. Sometimes it wasn't even a matter of choice, but survival. Mom worked to keep me from harm, to keep our home warm and our bellies fed. She worked to pray with me, lecture me, teach me, discipline me, and lead me in devotionals. And by witnessing how she cared for coworkers, students, and patients, I learned how to love people, even in the depth of their shortcomings and imperfections. Whether my mother was bringing comfort to a Senate chaplain taking his last breaths or a premature baby gasping for her first, I learned from her what it meant to be a faithful woman doing God's work.

But as I crossed the threshold of college student into the world of single, female, law student, I found the doors of the church open so long as I left my educational pursuits and professional ambition at the door. And when the questions I posed became less about last Sunday's sermon and more about how my understanding of justice would frame my legal practice, the church remained deafeningly silent, or responded like the campus minister who mentored me and said, "I don't know . . . ." And after several weeks of my grappling, doubting, and prodding, she relented. "You know, I don't think it makes sense for us to keep meeting. I mean—I really don't have anything to offer you."

As I sat in the passenger's side of her car and she explained why meeting with a first-year law student was no longer the best use of her time, I wondered if she was passing on a message from the church. Was the church telling me that speaking to the realities of women with a calling that included law school, a legal career, and leadership in the public sphere was incompatible with fully realized, biblical womanhood? Though this breakup wasn't as bad as the one at my eighth-grade dance in the middle school cafeteria, where my heart got trampled over to the soundtrack of Boyz II Men's *On Bended Knee*, it still took me a long while to get over.

For years I'd enjoyed worshipping in a church that included women whose range of life experiences and life stages couldn't be any wider. I connected to the church through a campus ministry and naturally thought it supported women professionals who worked outside of the home. After all, the church found it worthwhile to reach women on the college campus, women presumably preparing to work for at least some portion of life. But on the rare occasion that someone from church actually expressed an interest in my work as an attorney, it was only celebrated so far as it benefited the church and Christians rather than the public good. The conversation often went like this.

"Well I'm really interested in issues pertaining to public education."

"Well! PRAISE THE LORD! You know honey, we've just been a'praaaayin' for God to raise up some good, mighty, Christian warriors to bring prayer back to those heathen-den-of-abomination-public-schools!"

"Um . . . well, but see, actually—" I'd say.

"HALLELUJAH!"

Rather than struggling to encapsulate my answer into a Sunday morning, Christian sound bite, I wish I could've shared my story; how my own public education was anything but a den or abominable. If I needed to learn how to sew curtains for my dorm, or wanted to refill a Mary Kay order, or needed to borrow last month's issue of *Taste of Home*, I knew plenty of women from church whom I could call. But when it came to questions like: "Are there any women lawyers at our church? Are there *any* lawyers at our church?" the most common response (after a blank stare) was, "Uh, *weeeeell* . . ."

Discouraged but undeterred, I felt a tinge of hope when my church announced a "business professionals in the marketplace" event. I arrived to a room filled with about thirty men; I was one of two women in attendance. Unlike what the flier promised, the speaker was a pastor whose entire presentation could be summed up as: "Churches should be run like corporations!"

During the question and answer period I raised my hand.

"Hi, um, thanks for your presentation. But I was just wondering, I recently heard of this book called *Brothers, We Are Not Professionals*, by this guy named John Piper, and he argues against this exact approach. What do you think about that?"

I don't remember how much time the speaker took hemming and hawing before answering that he hadn't read the book, but I do remember the snickering and muffled chuckles from all the men in the room in response to my question. I don't know if they were laughing at me or at John Piper's claims. I was a woman entering a profession where my clients' livelihoods depended on my willingness to ask tough questions and challenge the assumptions. From their responses it seemed that I didn't get the memo that this type of deep thinking wasn't welcome in the church. Either way, I left the event looking forward to a workplace less hostile to my presence than the church.

In all these encounters I wish I could have been treated as an individual, not an archetype. I know it's easier to lump me in a pile of workaholic, aggressive, insensitive, man-hating, baby-avoiding lawyers who can't cook and have homes in shambles. It actually requires an investment of time and energy to know me as the laid back, impatient, always laughing, self-appointed Thanksgiving cook, who can make a balloon arch with her eyes closed. But I find comfort in knowing that where stereotypes, insecurity, and pride abound, grace abounds much more.

Swing and the Single Girl
by Meghan Florian

MEGHAN FLORIAN, MTS, is a writer, academic mentor, and tutor, and serves as communications coordinator for the Resource Center for Women and Ministry in the South (RCWMS), a nonprofit in Durham, North Carolina. She graduated from Hope College, received her master of theological studies from Duke Divinity School, and serves on the board of trustees of the RCWMS. She is a deacon at Chapel Hill Mennonite Fellowship where she also preaches from time to time. She is currently pursuing an MFA in creative writing at Queens University of Charlotte.

I've always been a terrible dancer, just as I have always wanted to be a good one. I showed up for the first week of an East Coast Swing dance class nervous but ready to pick up a new hobby. After checking in with the teacher, I surveyed my surroundings. The only men in the room, vastly outnumbered by women, were there with their significant others. I had expected that this would be the case but had hoped to be proven wrong.

Our teacher announced at the start of the class that it's traditional for men to lead and women to follow. However, we would be allowed to learn whichever part we wanted over the course of the next six weeks. A progressive dance studio. Perfect. Why not learn to lead? More often than not, in the absence of sufficient male partners, I end up dancing with women (or men who don't know how to dance) anyway. Knowing how to lead might actually help me to spend more time on the dance floor. And that, after all, is the point of taking a dance class: to dance.

So when he instructed those people who wanted to be followers to step to one side and the leaders to stay where they were, I stood still and watched all the women walk dutifully across the room. Except for me. The girl who wanted to lead.

Later in the class, when we rotated to new partners, the woman I was going to dance with next asked me, "Do you want to be the girl this time?" I wanted to yell, "I AM 'the girl!' I am the girl, LEADING!" but I bit my tongue. Dance class is not the place for a lecture on feminism.

As a twenty-eight-year-old feminist Mennonite theologian, dating is complicated. It's not like men flock to confident, freethinking women. They don't. Further, it gets harder and harder to even be friends with men as I get older—and they get married. This is even more of a problem for me than it might otherwise be because I am an intellectual in what is still, unfortunately, a male-dominated field. (This doesn't even begin to address the fact that I spend so much time trying to be taken seriously as an intellectual that my male colleagues often forget that I am, in fact, a not unattractive woman who might actually want to go on a date once in awhile instead of talking theology.)

People often ask me about my life as a single woman, especially in church contexts. Christian folks in particular place a lot of weight on marriage as a rite of passage to adulthood or as a holy institution. Singles ministries are popping up all over whilst well-meaning church ladies are passing out Christian dating books like Werther's candy. There is no escaping the inevitable questions and commentary on my life: "Ah, but aren't you just pretending to be content because you're jealous?" Or "You've just never really been in love." Or "Because you're a feminist you must feel like you have to hide your true feelings about these things." Or my personal favorite, "God will bring you the right person when you're ready," as if God is some kind of cosmic cupid. I've heard it all as people try to put me and single women everywhere under a microscope to try to figure out what's "wrong" with us.

The worst part of this whole cultural preoccupation with un-married women is the way we all get jumbled together into this one all-encompassing category: single. Three waves of feminism down the road, and one thing hasn't changed: as women, we are still defined by our marital status. What is so disconcerting about my presence in this world? And why is my lack of a spouse the defining factor of my identity for so many people around me?

I don't narrate my life as "the single life." It's the only life I know, and it has good days and bad days. Being single is not and never has been central to my life. I don't lie awake worrying about it. I don't cry when my friends get engaged and think, "When will my turn come?" I don't lust after diamond rings. (In fact, if I ever do get engaged, I don't want one. I have at least thought about it *that* much.) I don't believe in Prince Charming, soul mates, or "the one." I believe in companionship, love, and that marriage is hard work (and I hope it is worth it).

If we're lucky, at some point we find someone we want to share life with for the long haul. If we don't, we still get to share our lives with a lot of other wonderful people over the years. I live 800 miles away from my parents and siblings in a small apartment by myself. I may never have a spouse. But I have a family called the church, and I don't live my life alone. Last year, when I couldn't go home for Christmas, rather than a depressing day in a lonely apartment, I spent my afternoon sitting by a Christmas tree, eating homemade cookies, laughing and talking while my friends' children showed me their presents. The kids even fought over who would get to sit next to me in church that evening. I joked that I am their "spiritual auntie," and though I said it with a laugh, I really meant it. If churches spent more time being *family* to single people, instead of trying to fix them, single people and married people alike would see the love of God in new ways.

How different would my life be if I were married? I'd still get up and go to work every day as a writer and tutor. I'd still go to the farmer's market on the weekends, listen to *Back Porch Music* on NPR, be involved in my church as a deacon and Sunday school teacher, and enjoy craft beer with my friends when there's downtime. I'd still be a Kierkegaard scholar, a literature nerd, and a preacher, preoccupied with philosophy and critical theory and feminism.

My point isn't that marriage doesn't change things; my point is that my life is too full to spend much time worrying about whether or not I'll ever get married. I am too busy *living*.

This doesn't change the fact that people don't quite know what to "do" with me, a problem that is likely to get worse as I get older, if I remain single into my thirties and after. But I can suggest a few things: Invite me over for dinner with your family, share your children with me, and honor the life that God has given me as you help me serve the church with whatever shape that life takes in the future. Acknowledge that we all have much to give and receive. Realize that I might be happy with my life as a single person.

I remember a friend who once said to me, a couple of months into a serious relationship, that she missed being single. I think about the struggles some of my friends have had in their first years of marriage. I think of those who find themselves separated from their spouses before they even reach the age of thirty. I think about the men I have stayed with even though I was miserable with them. I think about the things I gave up to be with those men. I think about the things I have done, am doing, and will do, that do not depend on the presence of a spouse, and I feel content with my life.

It's true that I don't always have someone around to bring me a hot cup of tea when I'm up late trying to meet a deadline. But I have learned when I need to ask my friends for help, when I need them to show up at my door with Nyquil and homemade soup. And if no one is around, I simply go to bed early and hope to feel better in the morning. No one ever died from not having a spouse to nurse them to health when they came down with a cold (and most of the men I know aren't very good at that, anyway).

When I talk to my slowly dwindling circle of single friends about dating, I find these conversations center on the idea that now that we're out of school it's nearly "impossible" to meet someone. This feeling of desperation develops around the idea that if it doesn't happen soon it never will. I tell them, "There is nothing to be afraid of." It is hard to be honest about our experiences as single women. I am caught between contentment with my life as I now live it, and the possibility of sharing it with someone else in the future. I don't know if that will ever happen, and I have learned to live in such a way that I know life will be rich in the love of God and neighbor, either way. Not marrying is not settling for a backup plan, nor should marrying imply that my life as a single person was somehow inadequate.

People ask me about loneliness sometimes in these conversations about singleness. Some of the loneliest times in my life have been when I was in a relationship. I've learned that no individual person can complete you, that it's not fair to expect another person to fix your loneliness forever. Feeling lonely is part of being human. This is why true friendship, as well as romantic love, is such a gift—for a brief moment we reach beyond ourselves.

I experience love in small ways—a phone call or a postcard from a far away friend, small group with my church family, a goodbye hug from my favorite three-year-old babysitting charge, a connection with another human being over our shared passion for music, food, or a passage from a favorite book. I live alone in the sense that I don't have a spouse or even a roommate, but I am not living alone in the larger sense. There's a whole community of friends and family supporting me every day. If I were married I would still need them as much as ever.

I want love in my life as much as anyone. I need it. But like the character Marcus in *About a Boy*, who in trying to find a partner for his mother discovers a whole village of friends and neighbors, I know that two people are not enough—you have to have some backups.

The Beauty in Brokenness
by Nikole Lim

NIKOLE is the founder and executive director of Freely in Hope, a faith-based nonprofit organization dedicated to restoring justice, dignity, and hope by liberating women and their families from the bondages of poverty. Freely in Hope operates in Kenya, and provides educational scholarships, psychological counseling healthcare, and vocational courses for girls who are survivors of or vulnerable to sexual abuse. Nikole graduated with a degree in film production from Loyola Marymount University and resides in Los Angeles. She is an active member of The Salvation Army and works with inner-city youth. Her heart beats for young women whose voices are silenced by oppression, and desires to see every heart liberated and restored.

When my grandfather, Lieutenant Colonel Check Yee, was in ministry with the Salvation Army in China, he would often send me photos and stories of the people he served in the rural villages. Despite living in a broken society where food was scarce and the government had no concerns for its people, children were freely playing, women were chatting and laughing, and men were engaging over cups of tea.

I remember his photos were so vivid—they captured expressions of dignity and portrayed stories of hope. These stories, however, were also infused with issues my young mind could never comprehend. Oppression, imprisonment, and affliction were so foreign to my carefree childhood.

I was fascinated with these images that offered a glimpse into the intimate lives of the poor. They were filled with stories of overcoming hardship and persevering with dignity—even in their brokenness. I began to see that the stories of the poor were reflections of hope.

In the "first" world, where beauty is often synonymous with perfection, voices from the "third" world are rarely heard. Stories of war, famine, disease, and poverty are far too prevalent. Such stories have tempted me to deafen my ears with ignorance rather than to listen with compassion. Perhaps many of us choose not to hear these stories, afraid to identify with a broken reality in an attempt to conceal the brokenness in our own lives.

When I was twelve, I received a photograph from my grandfather of a little girl from a poor farming village in rural China. She was around the same age as I was. She was shy, timid, and quiet-looking with an unforgettably sad gaze. In China, girls are involuntarily born into oppression. With the strict rules on the number of children families can have, little boys are favored in order to bring dignity to the family, while little girls are shamefully labeled: unworthy of life. Baby girls are often aborted or abandoned in forests, especially in impoverished communities where families can't afford to pay the fines of having another child. If they're lucky enough to live, little girls are expected to adhere to the demands of others. Dignity is dependent on society's perception of their exterior lives. Their inner voices are silenced by cultural pressures to reach perfection that dominate their ability to dream. Because of the cultural pressure that often silences girls in China, it seemed that her confidence was broken—she hadn't yet realized the power of her voice. My grandfather titled this photo, "She reminds me of you."

It hasn't been until now, twelve years later, that I am faced with the haunting realization that this little girl could have been me.

And in some sense, I was like her.

I identified with her brokenness—feeling as if my voice was also silenced by self-afflicted lies of unworthiness that crept into my spirit. I was that seemingly shy, timid, and quiet little Chinese-American girl on the outside, but in reality I was boiling with a fiery attitude. I would avoid eye contact by rolling my eyes. When asked a question, I would shrug and not say a word. I would often stampede on hardwood floors and slam doors shut if I didn't get my way. I desperately tried to conceal my insecurities with a facade that said, "I hate you. Don't talk to me." Nothing in particular ever happened to me; I've never been abused, my parents were great, but internally I felt bitter and angry. I couldn't escape from myself, and I could never reveal the ways in which I considered myself broken.

Growing up as a girl in the church, I felt that there were cultural pressures to reach success, achieve perfection, and conceal the realities of inner pain. I felt that I had to mask my fears and never reveal this brokenness because that would be undignified. I couldn't embody the beauty, grace, and dignity exhibited in the women of my bloodline. My mother effortlessly displays dignity like I've rarely seen with others. Everything she says and does is full of assurance, confidence, and composure. Often feeling like I couldn't amount to her, I hid behind the image of who I thought she wanted me to be—afraid to come to terms with my own pain. This facade was secretly crying out for someone to simply stop to listen to my story—though I couldn't even listen to it myself.

My understanding of dignity was based on this perfected image of womanhood I thought I could never attain. Too many times had I opened my mouth, worn something boyish or responded with sass. My mother would dart her piercing eyes at me and say, "That's not ladylike." My quiet exterior hid how I was screaming on the inside.

And so I rebelled.

Feeling like I couldn't represent dignity as modeled by women around me, I resorted to telling stories through photography and film. It was my outlet—my way of voicing my opinions without having to be verbal about it. And so I hid behind the camera, sulking deeper.

When I was fourteen my mom became very ill. She had blacked out while out of town, and I remember when she came home a few days later she and my father were in their room behind closed doors. I could hear her sobbing uncontrollably and I knew that she had been diagnosed with cancer.

The thought of losing the person who epitomized dignity to me in the most quiet, yet most powerful of ways shattered my spirit.

That night, I remember going into my room and for the first time I cried out to God, asking him, "Where are you?" And in that moment of brokenness, I felt a sense of comfort when God responded, saying, "Because I loved you first, learn to love yourself and love others."

Through our family's trials, God was challenging me to recognize my pain and transform it into something of worth. He began to reveal purpose in our hardship so that I could learn to love more fully by recognizing the dignity in myself and in others.

During my mother's treatment I saw her in agonizing pain. Her usually calm and peaceful aura was stifled by the hormonal stress on her aching body. Yet her season of pain revealed the authenticity of her humanity. I watched her progress as she conquered this painful season with a transformed spirit filled with courage. She helped me understand that beautiful lives are made perfect through seemingly broken situations.

Through her story, I was learning to love myself despite my angry heart that held onto everything but the beautiful. I realized that my sense of dignity was based on what I thought I could never become, rather than leveraging the voice God gave dignity to.

Since then, I've been on a journey of unveiling voices of dignity—learning to build on God-given strengths to share stories that empower, restore, and transform. I've been learning how to speak—and not just learning to speak for myself, but learning to listen to others speak as well.

My experience behind the camera has taught me more about seeing and expressing dignity. I once thought that beauty, grace, and dignity were only attainable on the external appearance, but as I have delved deeper into my own story of transformation, I'm learning to see the beauty revealed through brokenness. I strongly believe that storytelling through imagery must disseminate truth with dignity. I've been a witness to countless images that portray the third world as a place of despair. For too long, images have been used to capitalize on individuals, families, and cultures.

From documenting a widow with leprosy in the jungles of Vietnam to seeing the plight of the homeless in the backyards of Los Angeles, I have been privileged to be a part of the lives of those who, in the midst of brokenness, can maintain their sense of dignity. Using photography and film as a platform for the stories of people living in situations of poverty has given me the opportunity to peer deeper into the human spirit. I've learned from their innermost struggles through darkness and despair, and I've seen their joy as they remember how they conquered their hardships. I've learned to identify with situations of brokenness by not dwelling on the imperfections in my own life but by recognizing that dignity is an inherent gift from God.

This lesson was made evident through the story of a phenomenal woman named Grace. Her name is already telling of her story and how she has risen above circumstances and, despite adversity, is impacting others.

I met her at Joyland Special School for children with physical disabilities in rural Kisumu, Kenya, where she works as a housemother. She lives in a large room with twenty girls she cares for. We sat down beside a hanging bed sheet that carelessly separated her room from the girls' room. There was nothing to hide here—just evident love for the girls, many of who can identify with Grace's story.

Growing up in a rural village, Grace's family didn't have enough money to send her to high school. At fourteen, she resorted to finding work to support the family. She left her small village in search of work in the city where she met a man who offered to hire her as a house girl. Her new employer brought her to a place where she could stay. She thought that it was a boarding place for children, but it was a motel.

He raped her.

Humiliated and afraid, she fled back to her home but was disowned by her family because of the stigma of rape in Kenya. Issues of rape and sexual abuse aren't talked about and the blame is often put on the girl. Grace was left alone and ashamed. She thought that her feelings of worthlessness made her destined to sell her body for profit. She was stuck in a cycle of hurt, abandonment, and neglect. She self-induced eleven abortions in her lifetime— overdosing on family planning pills, drinking chemicals, and even punching her womb.

At the age of forty-eight, she tells her story so effortlessly. I could tell that she's told it many times before—now freed from the guilt and shame that she once felt. Brought out of sexual exploitation, Grace encourages physically disabled children while teaching, caring for, and strengthening kids at Joyland. Grace found her new destiny. I was in awe of her relentless love for the children at the school; she calls all of them "her" children. She's shared her story with most of the girls at her school to affirm their beauty and worth—even when the world turns a blind eye to their pain and attempts to silence their voices. She is their source of a renewed sense of hope.

"Even someone like me can help orphans and widows."

Once a prostitute, overlooked and unheard by most, Grace has found dignity in a seemingly broken past. Her wounds tell the story of the obstacles she's overcome. Her transformation is an example of the strength and tenacity that I've learned from. Through her story, the life she leads and love she gives, she bestows the gift of dignity to those around her.

I captured her story on film and tried my best to knit her story together in a way that best represented who she is—beautiful, dignified, and full of grace.

Everything I aspire to be.

In some ways, I can identify with Grace. I identify with her fears, thoughts of inadequacy, and loss of self-worth. I identify with her dreams to achieve greatness, her aspirations to help others and desire to be made whole. I identify with her feelings of being bombarded with issues that seem to overwhelm but still being filled with hope to persevere and be victorious.

I identify with her fears of voicing her story but somehow finding the courage to unveil her brokenness as a thing of beauty.

I have heard so many stories of women worldwide who, like me, feel as if we were silenced by oppression as we erroneously trampled over our dignity to seek perfection. But as courageous women continue to share their stories, I'm given the opportunity to identify with their brokenness. As I begin to see myself in their stories, their audacity inspires me to reclaim my identity as a daughter of Christ. By rejecting the pressures to reach perfection,

I realized that I am then liberated to embrace my inherent worth.

Similarly, many church communities may unknowingly place an emphasis on becoming more attractive by perfecting their identity. But the pursuit of success may cause us to walk over the brokenhearted, the lonely, and the poor. By intentionally listening to the stories around us, we're given opportunities to develop relationships as an invitation of acceptance rather than judgment. The church should be a safe space for the broken to share their stories so that others can learn from their transformation.

In some strange way, learning to identify with the brokenness of others seems to help us repair our own brokenness. By listening to stories of incredible women, I'm slowly able to regain my own sense of dignity—my voice. Thinking that perhaps, if I am able to muster up enough courage to find my voice and provide a platform for voices of those who have already found theirs, dignity will be restored.

May we also identify with other voices of courage by embracing the beauty, grace, and dignity innate within our being—even in the midst of brokenness.

Celebration of Strength

by Christy Sim

CHRISTY SIM is working on her doctorate in global health and wholeness, with her main emphasis on theology and domestic violence, at St. Paul's School of Theology in Kansas City. She is a graduate of the master of divinity program at Nazarene Theological Seminary and spent time as an associate pastor and senior pastor before leaving an abusive home. Her recent paper presentations include "The Dehumanization of Abuse" at a conference on domestic violence in British Columbia in 2011. She launched a website, www.awakenimagination.org, for victims and survivors of domestic violence, which also serves as a resource for understanding violence for ministers, leaders, and advocates. At Friends University in Kansas she teaches imagining healing for violence, and poverty, ethics, and philosophy. She also works as an independent consultant for victims and survivors of violence, teaching courses on surviving violence for moms with young children, and helping women find access to resources.

We often hear religious folks say "Divorce is an abomination of the Lord!" or "God hates divorce!" Such phrases are usually pungent and painful, tainted with words that reflect mental images of weak people who are not "good" enough to work toward a healthy relationship. And if, by chance, we are placid enough to avoid harsh terms when speaking of God and divorce, we at least speak of it as being something that hurts God and must be avoided. Christians call it "straying from God's perfect plan" or something similar.

But what if we were free to rethink some of these ideas about divorce and still be Christian women? What if it were possible to be liberated from our previous notions so we could visualize what divorce might say about the strength of the women who choose it? Perhaps we could open our creativity and imagination to envision a new way of thinking and believing.

I stayed in a marriage far too long because I believed divorce was evil. He could throw things at me. He could tell my child I did not love him. He could dump my clothes on the porch and tell me I was not allowed in "his" house. He could take family pictures off the walls and hurl them down the hallway. He could tell me I was a failure and that he did not want to be a part of my failing career. He could accuse me of having affairs. He could jump out of a car while I was driving to show how deeply he loathed me. He could threaten to take up his coworkers' offers of sex. He could punch doors at my head level. He could do and say some of the most horrid things imaginable, but I could not allow myself to consider divorce.

I felt worthless and hollow. The very person who once adored me enough to vow honor and respect hated everything about me. In those days, I started to believe he was right. I was a failure—to my family, to God, to the church. I tried everything in my power to be better, to not fall short. But according to him, I did fall short, every time.

I refused to imagine divorce as an option for several reasons. Partly because I was convinced everything was my fault, but mostly because I believed this is what a good Christian woman did: stay married. I wanted my first marriage to be my only marriage. I too was a follower of this unspoken rule that divorce is an abomination and God hates divorce. I bought into the deception that I would be evil if I participated in that horrible sin.

However, after several years of deep suffering, the violence began to escalate, and it became more difficult to conceal my misery. Although I became an expert at hiding my home life from church members, eventually I could not keep secrets anymore. I was at a breaking point. Tears welled up in my eyes yet again. In desperation as I sat talking one day with an older, wiser friend in the church. I whispered descriptions of some of the things that were happening behind closed doors, like I had several times before to church leaders and pastors. But this time was different. Instead of encouraging me to get more counseling or try harder, this friend looked me in the eyes and said "Honey, if you leave, you are not giving up on your marriage. Your husband gave up and went back on his vows long ago when he started mistreating you."

In those moments things suddenly clicked for me. Truth entered my reality in spite of the lies that I was worthless. I recognized that death and violence were worse than divorce. Failed relationships were worse than divorce. Fighting one-sided to save a marriage was worse than divorce. In an instant, I began to be lifted out of a fog of blame and shame, and moved toward hope.

These are radical ideas in most churches today and certainly not a part of our proclaimed message. We act like playing with the potential for death is a better option than the horrible sin of divorce. We act like torturing ourselves in an unhappy marriage where we constantly feel worthless is better than separation. We act like we are not real people with real life situations. We often value the sanctity and sacredness of marriage over the person. But the truth of what matters can speak louder than these false messages of the Church. The people in the marriage relationship matter to God. When a woman finds the strength to admit it is not in her power to save a marriage, or it is not in her power to make her partner stop mistreating her, this should be celebrated!

It is an incredibly strong act for some couples to work toward saving their marriage, if both parties are willing. Marriage is sacred. However, we must realize it also takes an incredible amount of strength to keep putting one foot in front of the other to go through with a divorce. There were not enough tissues available to me the day I sat in the courtroom with two church ladies holding both my hands as I finalized my divorce and repeated over and over, "I have to let him go. I have to let him go," as if I had to convince myself. I remember the bailiff continued to check on me because giving up on my marriage was, by far, the most difficult thing I ever had to do, and it was obvious to everyone in the room I was not doing well. I could barely see through the pain; going back to him sometimes seemed easier. But somehow I persevered and found the fortitude to go through with ending the marriage.

Sometimes divorce is not simply straying from God's perfect plan or committing an abomination. Sometimes divorce is self-care. Separating from my husband helped me care for myself by realizing my value went beyond the failure he claimed I was to him, my son, and even my God. I was not without worth. Women who choose divorce for self-care, in the face of extreme violence or not, should be honored and not shunned. They are strong and they are beautiful. We must free our creativity and imagination from the bondage of viewing divorce simply as an evil act and envision a God who cares more about broken people than broken marriage covenants.

When I chose to enter into the marriage covenant, I did not commit to being dehumanized repeatedly by my partner. I did not obligate myself to a lifetime of being caught in cycles of power and control where I was consistently at the bottom. I did not give my life over to another person to be manipulated into hating myself. Instead I entered the marriage covenant with the promise to respect and care for my partner while receiving the same, through mutual compassion, in the midst of good and bad times. When this did not happen for me, divorce was the best option. It was a means of self-care.

It took me a long time to forgive myself and celebrate my own strength for leaving the person to whom I promised a lifetime commitment. Unfortunately, the church community, outside of those who walked alongside of me, did not facilitate my forgiveness of self. I will never forget the day a white-haired elder looked at me with a penetrating glare and insisted, if I wanted to continue to be a church leader, it was necessary that I take responsibility for my actions in seeking a divorce. He claimed there were always two people to blame in a failed relationship, and if I had any hope of ever serving the church again, I had better admit some guilt. But months later, after crying about this accusation endlessly, I realized taking such responsibility was the exact opposite of what I needed to do.

I spent nearly a decade trying to take responsibility for a situation outside of my control. I would be happy to take the blame!

I knew if I was to blame, I could fix it. If it was my fault, it was in my power to make it better. But when I chose divorce, I had to do the opposite of what the church leaders were asking—I had to give up responsibility, stop blaming myself, and find an inner courage to act toward separation while admitting I could not salvage this. It took guts. It took a lot of strength for me to let go of what the church expected of me to instead choose what I needed to do to care for myself.

The church community could have done several things to allow me, as a divorced woman, the opportunity for a fuller expression of my own life and faith. First, those in leadership could have empowered me to love myself enough not to stay trapped in a relationship where I was not treated well and was not thriving. Staying married to a man who treated me like a worthless object went against God's plan for my own health, safety, and well-being. The marriage covenant should strengthen a woman to become who God intends for her to be, and if the marriage fails to do this, we must empower the woman to choose divorce—and thus healing. For when we choose to act toward the empowerment of the person, we celebrate a woman's strength.

Second, I needed the church leadership to believe my story and reasons that I needed to divorce. I was not lying about my experience with violence or my own self-hatred and blame. I was not lying about needing to admit I could not repair my marriage. Talking about my situation was an incredibly vulnerable and embarrassing thing to do. If a woman has reached this point, she deserves the dignity and honor of being believed.

Third, I needed the church community to understand that leaving my marriage was not an easy decision that I came to without thought or deep consideration. I invested years before giving up, when, in all reality, I should have asked for divorce long ago.

And finally, I needed the church to allow opportunities for me to tell the whole story of who I am, including the story of my divorce. I needed to take ownership of my story, not skip over the "evil" mention of divorce. I needed instead to have the freedom to claim my divorce as part of what made me who I am today—beautiful and strong.

Divorce is not simply an abomination or a symbol of weakness. Perhaps we, as Christian women, can develop the imagination to dream beyond the formulas and prescriptions about what God thinks about divorce to care about the broken women who decide it is their best option. Perhaps we can celebrate the strength of the couples who work together to stay in marriages that foster human life not harm it, as my second husband and I do now. And we can celebrate the strength of those who must admit divorce is the best choice for self-care, for it is this celebration that is the key.

My Secret Buddhist Life
by Mary Allison Cates

MARY ALLISON CATES has worked primarily with college students since her ministry formally began in 2004. Giving credence to a whim, Mary Allison began a second vocation in the spring of 2012 as co-owner of Sew Memphis, a neighborhood fabric and sewing shop. She describes her vocation as the work of building community in many shapes and forms and helping to unveil the underlying messages of hope and liberation in sacred texts, others' stories, our own life narratives, and the act of creating. Mary Allison and her husband, Andy, share adventures in parenting two preschool-aged boys, who occasionally participate in her passions for quilting, cooking, painting, hiking, and practicing yoga. She holds a BA from Rhodes College and a master of divinity from Vanderbilt Divinity School.

I chose a tailored black dress for my interview and mulled over two years' worth of divinity school wisdom on pastoral care as I drove to the hospital. I parked in the visitor lot, slogged through spring Memphis heat waves radiating from black asphalt, strode through the automatic doors, and obtained a pass from the information desk. I found the clinical pastoral education office easily, only because my husband and I had done a trial run of this brightly-lit maze the night before. It was not until I was sitting in the tiny waiting room that my attention turned to the new, tiny nose stud on my face. Would a millimeter-sized cubic zirconium block my entrance to this hospital chaplaincy internship?

The decision to get my nose pierced was not an impulsive one. Now, more than ten years later, I laugh at the level of serious forethought that preceded my very sober, solo trip to the Trilogy Tattoo Parlor. As Paul, the locally renowned piercer, escorted me back to his sterile quarters and instructed me to "relax" in his vinyl treatment chair, he asked the question I had come to dread: "So, what do you do for a living?"

"I am a student," I quipped, evasively.

Paul pressed: "Oh yeah? What kind of student are you?"

"I am in school learning how to be a minister," I explained, and then I braced myself for Paul's reaction to this news.

I had grown increasingly frustrated with the variety of vexed expressions I received about my vocational path from strangers and friends. There were those who immediately felt judged, and there were those who judged *me* for being a woman seeking ordination. These reactions felt uncomfortable. But still, a small part of me died each time an agnostic or atheist launched into the familiar monologue about how little of Christian theology makes logical sense. I would listen to their pontifications about the inconsistencies in the Bible, the hypocritical nature of Christians, and the inexplicable horrors that exist in our world despite the supposed presence of an "all-powerful, all-loving" God. These conversations were excruciating to me because others seemed to think that I, as a candidate for ministry, had never opened my mind to this vast chasm of uncertainty.

But it was this chasm, and the possibility of divine encounters with others in the face of it, that lured me into the ministry. I wanted people to know that my vocation would not be filled with judgment. I hoped that by bejeweling my face I could jar others out of their theological and religious classification systems long enough to give me, and my honest struggles with faith and doubt, a chance.

I took Paul's simple response as a sign of success. "Well," he said with a chuckle, "you must not be an ordinary minister!"

My nose stud had the desired effect in some settings. Unfortunately, my interview for the hospital chaplaincy job was not one of them. I sat before the seasoned group of males and females, with my legs crossed properly at the ankles, ready to talk about my eagerness to be present with folks who were sick and grieving.

Instead, I fielded a litany of personal questions about my appearance that began with my choice of hair color (reddish), my shoe selection (clunkyish), my body type (skinnyish), and finally, the presence of the tiny sparkle on my nose.

"You don't look like a minister," they asserted.

"Thank you!" I countered.

"This is not a compliment," they admonished.

We haggled back and forth about the importance of looking the part, of gaining the immediate trust of patients and their families. I defensively accused them of being shallow and reminded them of how road-weary and unprofessional Jesus must have looked. And then, to my great surprise, they offered me the job.

At the request of my interviewers-turned-supervisors, I removed my nose stud each morning before work that summer and donned it every afternoon at five o'clock. My time at the hospital was full of hopeful reminders of God's healing presence in relationships. However, I continued to argue with the higher-ups about how much stock should be put in physical appearance. As a result, I learned something very important and maddening in those months: Ministry, even with its emphasis on matters of the heart, would never exempt my body from society's critical gaze. In fact, the authority ascribed to the position, combined with the amount of the time spent speaking in front of people, would only serve to heighten this kind of bodily scrutiny. I was becoming aware of a constellation of problems surrounding my body, or perhaps more accurately, the female minister's body, that would be present throughout my career.

With the end of summer came the end of my hospital job and the beginning of my year-long field education placement in the Presbyterian Church in which I was raised. I worked tirelessly on my first sermon, to be preached in the expansive gothic sanctuary to the very dear people who had helped my parents raise me. I agonized about the fact that I did not yet own a robe.

In my short time on staff, I had already found myself in several confusing conversations with male church members who would engage me in discussions of their weighty emotional issues and then, suddenly, name me as an object of their sexual attraction. Despite the assurances of my mentors and friends that I had done nothing to provoke these inappropriate remarks with my actions or appearance, I blamed myself each time. More specifically, I blamed my body—the same reddish, clunkyish, skinnyish, bejeweled body that took center stage in my hospital chaplaincy interview. The body that kept getting in the way of my ministry.

I borrowed a robe for my first sermon. I was overjoyed to be hidden inside of its black, voluminous folds. The sermon went well. But as my husband was walking to his car, a male church member approached him and said, "As your wife was preaching today, I couldn't keep myself from wondering . . . was she nude under that robe?"

Several months later, as I was engaged in conversation at the church's weekly soup kitchen, Herbie, a regular guest at the program, came colliding into my back side. He righted himself by strategically placing his hands on my rear end. I learned later that a group of men, also regulars, had dared Herbie to do this. Each week, the men would review the hilarity of the event with me. Each week, I would outwardly roll my eyes and scold them while I was inwardly blaming myself. I wondered, "Should I have worn a longer shirt or baggier jeans?"

I had learned as an adolescent to look critically upon my own body and to compare it to those of others. I had become almost comfortable with the sort of hyperbolic self-loathing that brought me to the conclusion, time and again, that my body was full of despicable flaws. That my body now seemed to attract the wrong kind of attention became yet another strike against it.

Before my journey to the ministry began, the church had been my refuge. I had learned to seek and find wholeness there. But my encounters in ministry were dismantling my wholeness, pitting one part of myself against another. I did not know what to do with the hospital committee's admonishments and the male churchgoers' lewd comments and actions. For comfort, I looked to Jesus, who must have experienced some of this complexity during his years spent on Earth inhabiting a body. However, what I often heard was the common Christian narrative that encourages believers to regard Jesus primarily as a now-disembodied spirit living inside our hearts.

But mostly, I didn't know what to do with my own body—how to dress it or tone it down. An older female minister friend told me that if I could just wait until I turned thirty, my body would not be so problematic. But I couldn't wait that long. Though I remained on track to become a minister, the yoga studio became my new refuge. It was the only place where my whole self seemed to fit in.

It was not a coincidence that the summer of my hospital chaplaincy was also the summer that I began practicing yoga. There was a jovial community of folks at my neighborhood studio who were as accomplished in the *asanas* as they were unorthodox and humorous.

I became fast friends with Mike and Steve, two men in their fifties, who were affectionately known as the "Bevis and Butthead" of yoga. Mike, who was Jewish, nicknamed me The Rabbi, and from then on, my real name was irrelevant. During my first class, Mike, Steve, and the instructor cheered as I struggled to make the unfamiliar shapes with my body. It felt so strange and freeing for my body to be at the center of something celebrated. I was proud of what it could innately do. But something else was happening, too. I was having a spiritual experience. My body was connecting me to God. There, in the neighborhood yoga studio, complete with Bevis and Butthead and all manner of buffoonery, my body was no longer a pesky display of self-expression to be squelched. Beginning with my first downward dog, my flesh and bones felt like a holy avenue to something sacred. And by the final relaxation at the end of the practice, I was able to actually *feel* divinity pulsing through me. I was literally fleshing out the words I had always heard in church but never really believed: I was made in the image of God.

I was hooked.

Young female bodies are objectified and worshipped, marketed and sold, airbrushed and idealized, forbidden and fanaticized. My mentor was right. My ministry is easier now that I no longer inhabit a young female body. I have carried, birthed, and fed two children with my body. In more and more settings, these visible signs of life and love seem to invite people to give me and my honest struggles with faith and doubt a chance. My ministry is also easier now that I work on college campuses. There is no more haggling over nose studs. But I still stand in front of the mirror sometimes, wearing garments that I adore, and hear the words of my hospital interviewers: "You do not look like a minister. This is not a compliment." And I change clothes.

My divinity school friend Eric once said of me, "If John Calvin and the Buddha were to have a baby, that baby would be Mary Allison." I love this notion that I am now a balance of Christian orthodoxy and eastern spiritual practice, that I am equal parts minister and yogi. But the truth is that the church and Christian orthodoxy haven't been my refuge since I started down the path of ministry. It feels shameful to admit this, given the wonderful church upbringing that my parents gave me. It feels hypocritical to admit this, given my profession. But I seem to have gotten more of Buddha's genes than Calvin's.

A Pastor in Hiding
by Marlena Graves

MARLENA is married to her best friend, Shawn Graves. He's a philosopher, and the love of her life. Together, they have two little girls: Iliana and Valentina. She received her master of divinity from Northeastern Seminary in Rochester, New York. She is a bylined writer for *Christianity Today's* Her.meneutics Blog, and her writing has also appeared in venues such as *Relevant*, *The Clergy Journal*, and the Conversations Blog. She is also a proud member of the Redbud Writers Guild. She has a book on spiritual formation forthcoming from Brazos Press. Eventually, she hopes to pursue a PhD in theological studies.

I am a pastor—a pastor in hiding. That is my confession.

As early as four years old, I had a deep, abiding sense of God's presence. It's not as though my parents were devout or intentional about teaching me God's ways. They weren't. Back then, my mother was a nominal Catholic, but spiritual. My father was a Protestant in name only. If I had to hazard a guess, I'd say some sort of Baptist. Occasionally, they spoke in reverential tones about God and the church. But the trials of life left them paying little attention to either.

My first encounter with Jesus was the medium-sized picture of him hanging in my parents' bedroom. My *abuelita* gave it to us. It was a picture of a solemn, porcelain-faced Jesus, bathed in light, pointing to his heart, a heart crowned with thorns. It was one of many versions of the Sacred Heart of Jesus. Every time I entered my parent's bedroom, I'd stare—captivated by the picture.

My other introduction came from the mother of my next-door neighbor and best friend, Kabari. We were both four when his mother hosted a five-day club in her garage. Every day for five days during that summer, I'd walk over, listen to Bible stories, and eat a snack. On the last day, she presented the gospel. It was 1982. I distinctly remember asking her, as I leaned against the chrome bumper of their late-seventies rust-colored Cadillac, "So if Jesus hadn't died for our sins, then the whole world, every single person, would go to hell?" "Yes," she said.

After we left California and Kabari and headed to rural Pennsylvania where my father grew up, my exposure to Jesus continued. I was ten years old when I told Jesus that I'd follow him. From then until I was fourteen years old, I'd read the Bible for two to three hours a day. After chores and homework, I'd hole myself up in my room to read of God, miracles, saints, and sinners. I became a little evangelist, telling my parents and anyone else who'd listen about Jesus. Even adults in my church, the country church I walked to because my parents wouldn't take me, asked me questions about the Bible. I was like twelve-year-old Jesus in the temple—teaching the adults about the ways of God. What I didn't know back then was how thoroughly Scripture-reading formed my soul and imagination. I lived and breathed the Bible. Saturated. I so desperately wanted to know how to live, wanted to know the nature of reality. Schoolmates often referred to me as "preacher." I was friends with everyone and my favorite thing to do was to care for souls, read the Bible, and tell others about God and his love for them.

At sixteen, I decided to go on a four-thousand-dollar mission trip to India. The problem was—we were poor. But I believed the trip was God's will, so I prayerfully flipped open the yellow pages and scribbled down the phone numbers of local churches. I called them up and told them about my trip and requested financial support. Twelve of the churches invited me to speak during their Sunday morning services. I usually had ten minutes to make my presentation.

After each service, parishioners lined the aisles to offer financial support and encourage me with comments like, "God has special plans for you" and "Your preaching is convicting." I discovered I loved to preach. Until then, I never thought I was much good at anything except being kind. Could it be that I actually had a talent? Thankfully, the churches believed in my mission and my abilities, and I earned enough money to go.

When it was time to make a decision about college, I narrowed my choices down to two: a reputable state university or a small, out-of-state, Christian liberal arts college. I chose the Christian school and gave up substantial scholarships. I figured faculty, staff, and students could teach me wise living. I met some of the most beautiful people on earth there, including my husband.

And it's where I first heard that under no circumstances could a woman be a pastor.

It happened in a class called God and Church. Our assignment was a spiritual gifts inventory. After completing it, we'd know our spiritual gifts. This knowledge was supposed to equip us to serve the church. My top four gifts were pastor, prophet, evangelist, and teacher. When the professor asked for volunteers to share their results, I listened and listened. Not one single female had shared that she was gifted pastorally. It made me uneasy; after a while, my hand shot up. The professor called on me. I said, "My top gift is pastor." He said, "Well then, you can teach children's Sunday school." I left deflated. Teaching young children isn't my forte. Besides, throughout school, I found I could intellectually hold my own with the men—especially when it came to theology. Whereas other girls shied away from talking theology with the guys, I jumped right in. If I thought they were off, I challenged them. I'd rather talk Bible and theology and Christian life over recipes, boys, and fashion any day. Yet because I believed the professor's pronouncement to be final and because I thought him an expert, I accepted my fate.

I could not be pastor.

His pronouncement ripped my soul apart. Until then, I had never lamented being a girl. But for the first time, I felt my gender was my scarlet letter. My gender was a lifelong prison sentence. I had always heard and believed that God didn't make mistakes. But now I wondered, "God, why did you make me a woman?" or sometimes I asked, "God why did you make me a woman with male gifts?" I was trapped. Cursed. The same Bible that was used to dehumanize African-Americans and to "biblically" justify slavery was now being used against me to "biblically" justify that I could not answer my calling because I was the wrong gender. I was a freak—a pariah.

Less than.

Uninvited.

After graduation, I married my best friend, Shawn, and we headed off to graduate school so he could earn his PhD in philosophy. I worked at a couple of agencies serving the Appalachian poor. But after two years, I started feeling lost. I envied Shawn; he had a set course for his life: graduate school, dissertation, and then university teaching. I, on the other hand, was off-course. Shawn's life seemed to proceed linearly, just like his internal workings. I, on the other hand, zigzagged. I initiated conversations, frequent conversations, about what I should do with my life. I'd routinely quiz Shawn with questions like, "What am I good at? What do you think I should do?" In my free time, I'd take lots of personality tests and career inventories, desperately hoping to discover my calling. Clergy and media personality were among those careers frequently recommended. Like clockwork, many of these talks occurred at our favorite Chinese restaurant. Eventually, things got to the point where, before I said anything, he'd remark, "Well, I know it's inevitable. We're going to talk about what you want to do with your life. So let's have at it." My existential angst quickly became cumbersome and exhausting for both of us.

Then one day, over spring rolls, Shawn asked, "Why don't you just go to seminary? You've always wanted to go."

"But what would I do with a seminary degree, just enrich myself? C'mon. We don't have money for that," I laughed incredulously.

Yet try as I might, I just couldn't shake the thought of going to seminary. So I did some research. I soon became enamored with the master of divinity degree program. Consequently, with Shawn's blessing, I applied, was accepted, and enrolled in the program the very next term.

There I learned how instrumental women leaders were in spreading the gospel. Priscilla and her husband, Aquila, both trained Paul and Apollos. Junia was called "apostle." Names in the Bible are never mentioned willy-nilly; these (and other) women were mentioned because they were prominent leaders within the church. A female professor and pastor taught my preaching course; when she was in seminary, she won the award for best preacher. In classes, I met other women who were excellent students, preachers, and pastors. I was deeply encouraged to be among women just like me. These female leaders throughout church history and in my classes had callings and spiritual gifts similar to mine. I wasn't a freak of nature after all! The truth set me free. Learning church history, theology, and biblical interpretation in seminary converted me to the belief that women so gifted could and should be pastors.

Forbidding women from being pastors or from serving in other leadership positions debilitates the Church. When women are barred from fully using their gifts in all offices, it's as if half of the body of Christ has been lopped off. And that is death. In order for the Church to flourish and for us to be good stewards of the gifts God has given us, we must utilize everyone's gifts. What is it about my being a woman that makes me unfit for the pastorate? What reason could God have for prohibiting me from church leadership positions simply because I'm a woman? It seems utterly arbitrary to draw the line at some purely biological characteristic, just as it would be to bar any person over six feet tall or with blue eyes from serving in the pastorate. But even if being female is not a purely biological fact, even if there is some female nature that is distinct from some male nature, many of the characteristics that are associated with being female are conducive to pastoring well.

For example, characteristics like compassion, mercy, nurturing, kindness, and loyalty are often regarded as feminine characteristics. In the Old Testament the prophet Joel declared, "And afterward, I will pour out my Spirit on all people. Your sons and daughters will prophesy, your old men will dream dreams, your young men will see visions. Even on my servants, both men and women, I will pour out my Spirit in those days" (Joel 2:28, 29). The Apostle Peter repeats this prophecy in Acts 2:17 on the day of Pentecost to demonstrate that Joel's prophecy had been fulfilled in and through Jesus Christ. Both men and women will now prophesy in the name of the Lord and for His glory. In his commentary on this passage Albert Barnes notes that the word *prophesy* means "in general, 'to speak under a divine influence,' whether in foretelling future events, in celebrating the praises of God, in instructing others in the duty of religion." This is what the prophets declared that both men and women would do!

One of my favorite stories in Scripture is of Aquila and Priscilla. Priscilla, along with her husband, was a church leader who worked alongside the Apostle Paul and instructed the powerful and learned Apollos in the ways of God. I'm struck by the fact that a woman taught theology—even back then. In order to have a healthy church, we need both men and women as pastors and leaders. Of that I am convinced. Yet still, I have to overcome some hurdles.

First, a historical hurdle: for most of global church history, women have been forbidden from holding church office. I believe this is so because for millennia, patriarchy has dominated our cultures, and thus we have read life and Scripture through a patriarchal lens. Even so, many Christians can't get past verses like 1 Timothy 2:12-14 (NIV), which states, "I do not permit a woman to teach or to assume authority over a man; she must be quiet. For Adam was formed first, then Eve. And Adam was not the one deceived; it was the woman who was deceived and became a sinner." I believe this apparent prohibition against female teachers and pastors is deeply cultural. One must understand the culture in which Paul wrote that statement in order to understand why he wrote it. The prohibition isn't normative for all times and places.

Secondly, I must overcome cultural hurdles. Most of the non-western world and church is still steeped in patriarchy. Many Christians in Africa, Asia, and South America do not believe Scripture permits women to be pastors or church leaders—unless they're leading women and children. Even in the United States there's cultural resistance. The majority of popular evangelical pastors forbid it. Those (mostly) mainline denominations that do ordain women are dismissed as liberal, peripheral, and captive to culture. There's some resistance even within denominations and local churches who support women's ordination. For example, when Shawn was nearly finished with graduate school, he served on a pastoral search committee in our former church—a church that strongly advocated for women pastors within the denomination, had women elders, and welcomed women pastoral interns. However, when well-qualified female candidates applied, they were summarily rejected because "the church is just not ready" and "many families will leave."

Soon after I graduated from seminary, Shawn completed his graduate classes. That summer he received an offer for a tenure-track position at our alma mater—the school where I was told I could teach children's Sunday school.

I didn't want to go.

Shawn was ready to turn down the job. However, I couldn't shake this nagging feeling that God wanted us there. I tried to argue God out of it—told him I'd be leaving a refreshing environment for a suffocating environment, one where my very being would be under suspicion and where I'd be forced into hiding. I simply didn't have the right plumbing to be a pastor or leader. Even so, no matter how hard I tried to talk myself out of it, I couldn't escape the conviction that, for some inexplicable reason, God wanted us there. Thus, God triumphed. And I went, carrying along my cross.

It has been six years and I am getting to the point where I am ready to either pursue an assistant pastorate and/or a doctoral degree in theology. However, even though there are many wonderful things about where we are, we are forbidden from joining churches that do not adhere to the school's doctrinal statement. That effectively eliminates most churches and denominations that ordain women.

But God has a sense of humor. Because while here, I've been on a preaching rotation at a church plant, asked regularly to do pulpit supply for a church in our former denomination, and have had the opportunity to continually offer pastoral care to students and congregations, all while currently being prohibited from pursuing an official pastoral position in a church. We cannot leave unless Shawn finds employment elsewhere. Unfortunately, tenure-track jobs in the academy are rare.

So until then, here I am—a pastor incognito, a pastor in hiding.

Questions for Discussion

1. What essay in *Talking Taboo* did you identify the most strongly with? Why?

2. Which essay did you wrestle with the most? Why? What do you think your wrestling teaches you about yourself?

3. What taboos did you feel were not covered in this book? What would your essay look like, if you were to confront your own taboo(s)?

4. What was your religious life like growing up? If you consider yourself a Christian, how do you think your Christian community (past and/or present) would react to some of the topics discussed in this book?

5. Before reading this book, how did you define sexism? Has reading this book changed your definition? If so, in what ways? Do you feel you have experienced sexism?

6. Multiple essays address the theme of women remaining silent in the face of overwhelming pressure. How does the silence of fellow Christians/fellow women contribute to creating or maintaining taboos? How do we ostracize women for being brave enough to speak out *against* this silence? How can we create spaces in which courage is rewarded?

7. Women's bodies are often the center of taboo topics. When has your body felt out of place or on display in your community? What does an embodied spirituality look like to you?

8. A number of essays address the concept of motherhood. Do you conceive of motherhood differently after reading this book? Do you conceive of God differently?

9. Many of us at one point or another have felt *shame* – shame for not being thin enough, chaste enough, sexy enough, masculine enough, feminine enough, etc. What is your not _____ enough? How do you overcome feelings of shame?

10. What did you read in this volume that gave you the most hope? How will share that hope with your community?

11. What questions are you left with after reading this volume? How will you continue to explore these questions in your community?

About the Editors

ERIN S. LANE, MTS is a communication strategist for faith-based authors and organizations. Her latest work with author Parker J. Palmer and the non-profit Center for Courage & Renewal combines her background as a book publicist with broader marketing consultation and program development for clergy and congregational leaders. She is also an active board member of the Resource Center for Women and Ministry in the South and is writing her next book about the hard work of belonging to communities of faith. Confirmed Catholic, raised Charismatic, and married to a Methodist, she blogs about the intersection of her faith and feminism at www.holyhellions.com.

ENUMA C. OKORO is a writer, communications consultant and an award-winning author of three books on the call and challenge to the spiritual life. With a professional background in Communications, Psychology and Theology, and her uniquely diverse global and cultural experience, Enuma's work embraces the dynamics of effective communication, the classic spiritual traditions, and the contemporary arts. She writes, speaks and consults on numerous issues and topics based off of four key areas: 1) Identity and Belonging in a diverse world; 2) Women and Culture; 3) Communities and the power of narrative; and 4) Spiritual formation, growth and holistic wellness. Her work has been featured on ABC's *Good Morning America*, The Washington Post, CNN, The Huffington Post, NPR, and *The Michael Eric Dyson Show*. She is a cradle Catholic with an ecumenical upbringing. Visit Enuma at www.enumaokoro.com.